# DOWN TO THE SUNLESS SEA

*A Troubled Samuel Taylor Coleridge in the Mediterranean*

For
R & S

# DOWN TO THE SUNLESS SEA

*A Troubled Samuel Taylor Coleridge in the Mediterranean*

**ANDREW** AND **SUZANNE EDWARDS**

sussex
ACADEMIC
PRESS
*Brighton • Chicago • Toronto*

Copyright © Andrew Edwards and Suzanne Edwards, 2023.

The right of Andrew Edwards and Suzanne Edwards to be identified as Authors of this work has been asserted in accordance with the Copyright, Designs and Patents Act 1988.

2 4 6 8 10 9 7 5 3 1

*First published in Great Britain in 2023 by*
SUSSEX ACADEMIC PRESS
PO Box 139, Eastbourne BN24 9BP

*Distributed in North America by*
SUSSEX ACADEMIC PRESS
The University of Chicago Press/Chicago Distribution Center
11030 South Langney Avenue
Chicago, Illinois 60628

All rights reserved. Except for the quotation of short passages for the purposes of criticism and review, no part of this publication may be reproduced, stored in a retrieval system, or transmitted, in any form or by any means, electronic, mechanical, photocopying, recording or otherwise, without the prior permission of the publisher.

*British Library Cataloguing in Publication Data*
A CIP catalogue record for this book is available from the British Library.

*Library of Congress Cataloging-in-Publication Data*
To be applied for.

Paperback ISBN 978-1-78976-125-2

Typeset & designed by Sussex Academic Press, Brighton & Eastbourne.

# Contents

*The Illustrations* vi

ONE
**Departure on the *Speedwell*** 1

TWO
**Strategising for Nelson in Malta** 29

THREE
**Sicily and the Prima Donna** 53

FOUR
**A Hand in Maltese Affairs** 85

FIVE
**The Grand Tourist Returns Home** 111

SIX
**Lectures and Legacy** 137

*Notes* 165
*Bibliography* 177
*Index* 183

# The Illustrations

**The Cover**
Samuel Taylor Coleridge (1772–1834), Harvard Art Museums/Fogg Museum, Loan from The Washington Allston Trust, Photo Copyright © President and Fellows of Harvard College, 6.1955. Sea image (Pixabay).

**CHAPTER ONE**
1. Main Street, Gibraltar, with the Griffiths Hotel, c. 1830 (Wikimedia Commons).
2. Site of the former Griffiths Hotel, Main Street, Gibraltar (Andrew Edwards).
3. Top of the rock, Gibraltar, overlooking Catalan Bay (Suzanne Edwards).
4. St Michael's Cave, Gibraltar (Suzanne Edwards).

**CHAPTER TWO**
5. The Grandmaster's Palace, Valletta, Malta, formerly used by the British Governor (Andrew Edwards).
6. San Anton Palace, Malta, formerly used by Alexander Ball as his summer residence (Andrew Edwards).

**CHAPTER THREE**
7. Karl Friedrich Schinkel's drawings inspired by G. F. Leckie's residence, Tremilia, Syracuse, Sicily (Wikimedia Commons).
8. The Castello dei Bonanno, Tremilia, Syracuse, Sicily, former residence of G. F. Leckie (Andrew Edwards).
9. The Arethusa Fountain, Syracuse, Sicily (Suzanne Edwards).

**CHAPTER FOUR**
10. San Anton Palace Gardens, Malta (Suzanne Edwards).
11. The Casino Maltese, Valletta, Malta, formerly The Treasury (Andrew Edwards).

CHAPTER FIVE
12　The Greco-Roman Theatre, Taormina, Sicily (Andrew Edwards).
13　The Lungarno, Pisa (Suzanne Edwards).

CHAPTER SIX
14　Manuscript draft of *The Ancient Mariner*, lines 201–12 (written in 1806), by Samuel Taylor Coleridge (The British Library: https://www.bl.uk/collection-items/a-variant-version-of-the-ancient-mariner-lines-201-12).
15　The former residence of the Gillman family, Highgate, London (Suzanne Edwards).
16　St Michael's Church, Highgate, London (Andrew Edwards).

CHAPTER ONE

# Departure on the *Speedwell*

> Day after day, day after day,
> We stuck, nor breath nor motion;
> As idle as a painted ship
> Upon a painted ocean.
> *The Rime of the Ancient Mariner*

Something needed to change. Marital disharmony, illness, an increasing reliance on opium and the attendant visitation of soul-disturbing dreams continued to plague Samuel Taylor Coleridge during the winter and spring of 1804. His solace was to be found by searching the horizon for an escape, a practice that had long been his coping mechanism and inspiration. Born in rural Devon and educated in London, Coleridge was prone to the temptations of an itinerant life, roaming from bucolic Somerset to the cities of Bristol and Cambridge, as well as the capital, by way of Shropshire and, famously, the Lake District.

When he first looked to wider horizons, he turned to Germany, the home of writers and philosophers he admired, namely Schiller, Kant and Bürger. Months spent studying at Göttingen University, made possible by the patronly largesse of the pottery magnates, Tom and Josiah Wedgwood, had allowed him the privilege of such study and travel. Despite the continuing support of the Wedgwood family, another winter spent in the snowy foothills of the Harz mountains no longer seemed a desirable prospect. He had already stated in letters and his notebook that enduring further winters in the cold dampness of the English Lakes would lead to an early grave. With this in mind, he naturally sought the warm embrace of the Mediterranean.

As with other British travellers during this era who were looking to visit the south of Europe, his choices were restricted by the Napoleonic

**1** Main Street, Gibraltar, with the Griffiths Hotel, c. 1830 (Wikimedia Commons).

**2** Site of the former Griffiths Hotel, Main Street, Gibraltar (Andrew Edwards).

**3** Top of the rock, Gibraltar, overlooking Catalan Bay (Suzanne Edwards).

**4** St Michael's Cave, Gibraltar (Suzanne Edwards).

Wars that had begun in 1803 when Britain declared war on France. Malta and Sicily became realistic options, both practically and in terms of the stimulus they could offer. By January and February of 1804, we find Coleridge making lists of Sicilian attractions in his notebook, complete with cryptic geographical asides. Such sites included Palermo's iconic Monte Pellegrino, Erice, the Benedictine Convent in Catania and the Latomie quarries in Syracuse.

In fact, Coleridge referred to Erice by its classical Greek name of Eryx, an unsurprising allusion given he had won Greek poetry prizes at both Christ's Hospital School and during his time as an undergraduate at Cambridge. Sicily is an island steeped in the Classical world and references to its myths and legends had already found their way into his poetry. 'The Mad Monk' features Mount Etna which is supposed to harbour the philosopher, Empedocles, who threw himself into the volcano's crater in search of immortality. Legend also tells us that, buried beneath the mountain, is Hephaestus, a Greek God famed for his blacksmithery. Coleridge's monk can be found in one of Etna's caves:

> I heard a voice from Etna's side;
>   Where, o'er a cavern's mouth
>   That fronted to the south,
> A chestnut spread its umbrage wide:
> A hermit, or a monk, the man might be;
> But him I could not see;
> And thus the music flow'd along,
> In melody most like to old Sicilian song . . . [1]

Sicily even makes an oblique appearance in one of the poet's most famous works, 'Kubla Khan': 'In Xanadu did Kubla Khan / A stately pleasure-dome decree: / Where Alph, the sacred river, ran / Through caverns measureless to man / Down to a sunless sea.'[2] Alph refers to Alpheus, the River God, who fell in love with the nymph, Arethusa, when she bathed in his waters. Suspicious of his intentions, she fled the scene, asking Artemis for her protection. In the face of a persistent Alpheus, she was transformed into a stream that ran under the Mediterranean from the Peloponnese to the island of Ortygia which forms part of the Sicilian city of Syracuse. Arethusa surfaced in what is now known as the Arethusa Fountain, a spring surrounded in papyrus a few short metres from the city's Ionian coastline. Undeterred, Alpheus flowed through the sea to Sicily where, at this very spot, his waters mingle eternally with hers.

Given Coleridge's attention to these myths and legends, it is easy to follow his wandering imagination which took him to Sicily along these ancient routes. Also prevalent at the time was a new wave of Gothic writing led by Ann Radcliffe whose books included *A Sicilian Romance* and *The Italian*, featuring fated passions with mysterious overtones and dark, brooding characters in melancholic locations. Coleridge, who also enjoyed German Gothic pot boilers, referred to the likes of Matthew 'Monk' Lewis and Radcliffe with a degree of teasing wit:

> Situations of torment, and images of naked horror, are easily conceived; and a writer in whose works they abound, deserves our gratitude almost equally with him who should drag us by way of sport through a military hospital, or force us to sit at the dissecting-table of a natural philosopher.[3]

He was able to see elements of merit in this genre but the themes would lead to ever-decreasing circles of plot originality and a satiation causing a weary sense of *déjà vu*. Some commentators have seen 'The Mad Monk' as an affectionate parody of Radcliffe, especially given the poem carried this effusive and didactic title when it first appeared in *The Morning Post*: 'The Voice from the Side of Etna; or The Mad Monk: An Ode in Mrs Radcliff's Manner'.

Many motifs must have been triggered in Coleridge's voracious brain upon mention of Sicily – from the Classic and Gothic to the Romantic. To these three 'isms' we can add the impressions of George Bellas Greenough, a friend and fellow student from his Göttingen days. Greenough kept a journal of his travels on the island and Coleridge was much taken with his colleague's 'doings and done-untos'[4] as he described them to the Wordsworths. Curiously, Greenough's travelogue is hard to track down in English, but it is available in Italian translation as *Diario di un viaggio in Sicilia, 1803* (*Diary of a Journey in Sicily, 1803*). It is from these original pages and conversations with Greenough that Coleridge jotted down the aforementioned recommendations in his notebook. He also made a mental note of the name G F Leckie, the English Consul in Syracuse whom, Greenough assured him, would be a genial contact. In addition, his friend expounded upon the Sicilians' desire to receive some form of British protection in such perilous times, although history tells us this was not a universally held view. Perhaps the most valuable tip that Greenough passed on to the always impecunious Coleridge was that the cost of living on the island was inexpensive.

Malta was a different proposition and largely came to be considered a destination for more practical reasons, namely it was already under British control and ships sailed directly to the island. Furthermore, thanks to Greenough, Coleridge knew that Syracuse was a mere six hours travelling time from Valletta by sea. Given these favourable factors, the poet pushed forward with his plans knowing that he had to set about finding passage on a ship going to Malta. His brother-in-law and fellow poet, Robert Southey, was friends with John Rickman, the clerk to the Speaker of the House of Commons and it was to Rickman that Coleridge turned for help in locating a suitable vessel. Samuel Taylor had come down from the Lake District leaving his wife, Sara, at the family home, Greta Hall, so he could be on hand if Rickman's enquiries bore fruit.

Coleridge had married Sara in 1795 amidst the on-off idealism of his plans to create a pantisocratic commune of like-minded literary souls where they would create great works inspired by living hand in glove with nature. Coleridge was never to create such a utopian gathering, despite periods of time spent living in close proximity to colleagues and friends, especially Wordsworth. There was always the question of money to fund such a lifestyle but, with the added responsibility of providing for his wife and three subsequent children, Pantisocracy had to take a back seat to the money-earning potential of journalism.

Sara was the more practical of the two and could be outspoken if provoked. In contrast, Coleridge constantly brimmed with ideas and dreams that would not always materialise into tangible reality. Projects were mooted, plans were started and, on occasion, he even took advance payment for books that were never finished and talks that were never delivered. There were early signs in the marriage that Sara's frustrations at living with Coleridge's unconventional mind would lead to disharmony; her husband finding excuse upon excuse not to return home. In a letter to Southey in 1803, he even admitted that it had been an 'evil day' when he married Sara, although he is at pains to point out that he wanted to shield this fact from her and act as her protector. He blames his own feckless lack of stability: 'I am no elm! – I am a crumbling wall, undermined at the foundation!'[5]

His foundations were undermined further by another Sara, the sister of Mary Hutchinson, one of Dorothy Wordsworth's good friends. When Coleridge visited their family residence at Sockburn-on-Tees for the second time, he fell irretrievably for Sara's charms; so much so that his reinvigorated poetry led to a series of verses christened the 'Asra' poems – a thinly veiled anagram of her name. Years after the event, he added a Latin postscript to one of his notebook entries which pinpointed the day, 24 November 1799, when Cupid fired his arrow. The contrast between the two Saras was marked, with Miss Hutchinson being his emotional rock in a marital storm. She was also intellectually curious and became a dedicated scriber of his poetry.

Coleridge struggled with his passion for Asra, both in terms of secular and religious morality. He could not countenance sexual infidelity, irrespective of the considerable cooling in his marriage. The years leading to his departure for Malta were plagued with sexual guilt and vivid dreams brought on by opium, taken in a laudanum tincture. One particular paragraph in his daily jottings describes the manifestation of a darkly-shadowed woman intent on digging out his right eye – perhaps the figure of a temptress plucking out the all-seeing eye of fate. The cure for his guilt and loss of control could only be found in more opium, leading to repeated bouts of momentary escapism and regret.

In 1801, Coleridge was suffering from what he called 'irregular gout'[6] which meant his leg joints were enflamed and excruciatingly painful. A local doctor prescribed exercises on a horse, which would take the weight from his limbs, and the calming effects of bathing in the sea. The poet needed no further persuasion to head for Bishop Middleton, near Durham, where Asra was staying with her brother, George. Coleridge and Asra subsequently rode down to see her other brother, Tom, on the Yorkshire coast where he could bathe as instructed. During the evenings, the pair were joined by her sister, Mary, and the three flirted freely. Physically, this is the closest Coleridge ever came to intimacy with the object of his desire, not to mention her sister, as they gently stroked his ailing body whilst he reclined between the two on the sofa. Outwardly, this may have been innocent – inwardly, it almost certainly was not.

By the early winter of 1803, we find Asra faithfully copying out

Wordsworth's *The Prelude*, which Coleridge intends to take with him and read in the Mediterranean. It is with a heavy heart and a farewell letter to Asra, which deeply depressed his mood, that he took leave of his beloved. Just as he described a few months earlier, he must have been feeling a degree of heartache at the distance between them – an all too common distance for such an unconsummated relationship. It was this frame of mind and inability to focus that had previously led to his poem 'Dejection: An Ode':

> My genial spirits fail;
> And what can these avail
> To lift the smothering weight from off my breast?
> It were a vain endeavour,
> Though I should gaze for ever
> On that green light that lingers in the west . . .[7]

Whilst in London, awaiting news of a passage to Malta, Coleridge's mood continued to vacillate. He wrote darkly to Wordsworth that he wished 'to retire into stoniness',[8] yet he was amply supported by Sir George and Lady Beaumont who gifted him £100 in travelling money and a bespoke escritoire. On a visit to his old friend, Charles Lamb, he once again met with William Godwin, the father of Mary Shelley, with whom he had previously enjoyed rigorous debate. On this occasion, fuelled by drink, Coleridge completely lost any sense of decorum and began to furiously hurl his strongly held views on religion and the war with France at a provoked and angry Godwin. The poet knew he had overstepped the mark as he quickly wrote an acquiescent letter of apology.

Coleridge knew his opium use was spiralling out of control and he had begun to see the trip to the Mediterranean as the only means of straightening out his life, and a way to heed the advice of his scientist friend, Humphrey Davy, who, in a letter full of praise, advised him not to 'in any way dissipate your noble nature'.[9] Leaving his well-meaning friends behind in the March of 1804, he finally received news that the merchant ship, the *Speedwell*, would be heading for Malta. Consequently, he hurried to Portsmouth in preparation for embarkation.

He initially took a room at the Crown Inn but was not happy with its less than hygienic environment and rumbustious atmosphere. The inn used to be situated at 33–36 High Street, which we discovered is now a rather unprepossessing Co-operative convenience store, redesigned in typical 1970s brown brickwork. Coleridge was fortunate enough to have been given an introduction to James Charles Mottley, who he would later describe as 'a dashing bookseller' and 'a booted, buck-skin-breeched Jockey'.[10] Mottley was a man of some influence in Portsmouth and instantly fell for Coleridge's famed gift as a conversationalist. The bookseller and correspondent for the local *Courier* offered him hospitality and was also able to take a somewhat apprehensive Coleridge on a tour of the dockyards. Mottley would go on to act as a conduit for correspondence, particularly that of the poet's wife, as he could send it on to Malta more quickly under the guise of government business.

Mottley's residence was in nearby St Thomas' Street, which still retains elements of Georgian architecture, particularly where it meets Lombard Street. Happily for Coleridge, his buckskin-breeched friend was also in communication with Sir Alexander Ball in Malta, which may account for his access to government postal services. Ball, the island's governor, would prove to be an invaluable contact once Coleridge reached his destination.

Between visits to the *Speedwell*, anxious studying of weather reports and convivial dinners with Mottley, Coleridge put his final correspondence in order – writing to his wife and sending a game to his children. He also entreated Lamb to transcribe interesting parts of his letters from the Mediterranean and send them on to Wordsworth, which is puzzling as he also intended to write directly to William and his sister from abroad. Nevertheless, Lamb was happy to oblige and wrote back in a similar tone to that of Humphrey Davy, imploring him to find peace: 'Make your European heart easy in Malta, all shall be performed.'[11]

After several false dawns, when the *Speedwell* expected to sail but a change of wind direction thwarted departure, the ship eventually left Portsmouth on 9th April, forming part of a convoy of thirty-five vessels carrying much-needed goods to those British and allied ports involved in conflict with Napoleon. Coleridge had many projects set out for the journey – he would continue his journal notes, write a review of Wordsworth's recent poetry, write some of his own verses and read Italian. At this juncture, he still intended Malta to be a stepping stone on the way to Sicily, but it is also true to say that English had yet to establish itself on the Maltese islands and any official communication would be in Italian, rather than the seldom written mother tongue or the English of their newly acquired rulers.

Initially, all these plans had to take a back seat when the waves began to swell. Yet to find his sea-legs, Coleridge took Captain Findlay's advice and retreated to his cabin bunk where he describes in his notebook how the furious sea bid him an angry farewell to British waters making restful slumber impossible. His cabin was made even less conducive to sleep by the presence of two fellow travellers who would be sharing his quarters for the duration – a lieutenant drawn to the bottle and a widow called Mrs Ireland, so fixated with food that Coleridge came to nickname her 'Mrs Carnosity'. As soon as he had found his sea legs, though, the poet was true to his own goals and rose early to study Italian until breakfast.

Coleridge was fortunate enough to have been gifted the aforementioned travelling escritoire, in addition to the grammar books and dictionary he used for language study. He was now also feeling well enough to go on deck where his poetic senses were mesmerised by the changing light as it bounced from the waves, altering their colour through the spectrum of blues and greens. Likewise, the sails would be at once a brilliant white and then, interchangeably, a host to the play of shadows. Initially, his reveries were untouched by the influence of opium or alcohol, as he maintained an abstemious regime at the beginning of the voyage. His concentration was such that his intense curiosity was able to delve deeply into form and function, resulting in page after page of his notebook being dedicated to the single focus of the ship's sails, both artistically and scientifically.

As the *Speedwell* made progress across the Bay of Biscay, the climate began to warm and, although the breeze was still a little chill, the crew felt the first subtle breath of balmier southern weather. Coleridge equally warmed to the magnetic pull of approaching land, specifically Spain's Cabo Ortegal peninsula on Galicia's north coast above Ferrol and La Coruña. The port of Ferrol, now infamously associated with Francisco Franco, the country's longstanding dictator, was then under British blockade, preventing a trapped French fleet from gaining access to open water. Coleridge was less inclined, however, at this point, to expound on naval manoeuvres or the magnificence of the shoreline's rocky inlets owing to another of this coast's well-documented squally storms. Not for nothing is this region known in Galician as the Costa da Morte (the Coast of Death). Shipwrecks abound and stone crosses dot the cliff-faces bearing testament to the ill-fated missions of seafarers through the centuries.

At the height of the storm, the ship was continuously punched by the relentless barrage of the swell causing Coleridge to comment that it would be 'a sweet image to precede a shipwreck'.[12] In an effort to prevent yet another stone cross, then as now, many lighthouses send their signal of hope to ships struggling in the same manner as the *Speedwell*; fortunately, after two days of peril, the convoy made calmer waters as it passed the mouth of the river Minho before sailing on to skirt the city of Porto. The poet took out his spyglass and was able to discern the outline of the city's more important buildings and its hilly backdrop. The *Speedwell* encountered many small fishing vessels as the river Douro met the sea. The scene brought to Coleridge's mind the Portugal so beloved of his brother-in-law, Southey.

Our own experience of Porto focusses much more on the Douro that adjoins it than the coast it appears to turn away from. Since the days of Henry the Navigator, supposedly born in the waterfront house known as the Casa do Infante, the city has revered this life-giving artery connecting the valleys of the hinterland and their vines with access to the open sea. Port wine, inextricably linked to the British merchants who first fortified it with brandy, is at the heart of the city's commercial identity. The wine lodges in Vila Nova de Gaia, ostensibly still a separate settlement, border the river, not the seafront. Coleridge would have been very aware of the city's reputation as an oenological hotspot given that the British 'discovery' of port dated back to the seventeenth century when the decision to fortify had less to do with taste than preservation.

Remarkably, the proximity to these bibulous glories was still not enough to tempt Coleridge back into bad habits. He was much concentrated upon continuing his journalesque letter to Southey in which he detailed the saddle-backed hills that many poets found less than aesthetic but which he considered a 'pleasant form'.[13] He would set aside the lengthy letter in the afternoon to snooze on the ship's deck in sight of the coastline at Figueira da Foz, approximately two hundred kilometres from Lisbon. By 17th April, the *Speedwell* had made its way to the Cabo da Roca which Coleridge refers to as the Rock of Lisbon, beyond which he fancies he can see the outline of Sintra with two towers that he assumes may be a palace or convent.

As far back as 1804, Sintra was famed for its collection of castles, palaces, monasteries and villas; consequently, it loomed large in the Romantic imagination. At the turn of the century, Southey had already spent time there, staying at his uncle's cottage where he considered the town and its surroundings to be 'the most blessed spot in the habitable globe'[14] and was content to 'eat grapes, and ride donkeys, and be very happy'.[15] Some years later, he would also include a description of the settlement in his poem, *Poet's Pilgrimage to Waterloo* recalling: 'In Cintra also have I dwelt erewhile, / That earthly Eden, and have seen at eve / The sea-mists, gathering round its mountain pile, / Whelm with their billows all below, but leave / One pinnacle sole-seen, whereon it stood / Like the Ark on Ararat, above the flood.'[16]

A more infamous denizen of Sintra was William Beckford, who scandalised Georgian society. Beckford, most revered and reviled for his gothic novel, *Vathek, an Arabian Tale*, had taken flight from Britain at the age of twenty-four when he was caught *in flagrante delicto* with the sixteen-year old William Courtenay who would go on to become the ninth Earl of Devon. Rather than face the judicial consequences, the wealthy landowner decided a continental escape was by far the best option. After eventually making his way to Portugal, he hired a house in what is now Sintra's Monserrate Botanical Garden, staying for six years between 1793 and 1799. The Lawrence Hotel also commemorates Beckford with a room in his name complete with a suitably ostentatious four-poster bed.

Five years after Coleridge made the hopeful sighting of Sintra from his deck, Lord Byron came to the town on his initial Grand Tour and decided he would like to see the building Beckford had called home – a detour he did not regret, describing it as 'the most desolate mansion in the most beautiful spot I ever beheld'.[17] Byron was very well-aware of William's reputation, referring in a stanza omitted from *Childe Harold* to Beckford's 'unhallowed thirst' and 'nameless crime'.[18] Little did Byron know that he would mirror Beckford's escape into exile when he left England in 1816 amidst rumours of homosexual activity and an incestuous relationship with his half-sister. In 1809, however, he was in full *Harold* mode, picturesquely poeticising the town's geographical location in the following manner: 'Lo! Cintra's glorious Eden intervenes / In variegated maze of mount and glen.'[19]

Despite many denials to the contrary, there is undoubtedly an autobiographical element to *Childe Harold,* not least of which is the trail the protagonist follows in the wake of the author. It has the flavour of a travelogue, albeit with a world-weary anti-hero. Coleridge once referred to Walter Scott in a letter as a 'Picturesque Tourist' who 'must be troubled with a mental Strangury, if he could not lift up his leg six times at six different Corners, and each time piss a Canto',[20] a quotation we have also seen applied to Byron. We do suspect, however, that had Coleridge's Captain Findlay docked at Cascais near Lisbon and given him some time ashore, Coleridge would have struggled to resist the urge to spray his own stanzas.

For the time being, he restricted himself to epistolary writing accompanied with doodles of the coastline for Southey to whom he noted that the voyage to Gibraltar would be unlikely to take more than ten days due to the favourable breezes. They duly rounded the Cabo de São Vicente in good time, subsequently passing the Portuguese – Spanish border along the Guadiana river as they cut across the Gulf of Cádiz where Coleridge was able to discern the outline of the city, another location that Byron was to crystallise into verse with these lines in *Childe Harold*: 'But Cadiz, rising on the distant coast, / Calls forth a sweeter, though ignoble praise. / Ah, Vice! how soft are thy voluptuous ways!'[21]

There is a degree of Moorish sensuality in Byron's words that he much associated with southern Spain, feeling the latent pulse of the Orient. The author of *Childe Harold* would go on to publish Turkish tales such as *The Giaour*, *The Bride of Abydos* and *The Corsair*, using language laden with a romanticised Orientalism, full of harems, passionate revenge and renegades on the high seas. Coleridge was more concerned with the real dangers of falling prey to Barbary pirates, given he could also see the North African coast as they approached Gibraltar. It was only the rapid progress of the *Speedwell* and its protective convoy that afforded them a safe passage. Coleridge had heard stories of becalmed vessels picked off at will by pirates darting out from the Moroccan and Algerian coastlines. He even compared acts of such temerity to a fox stealing a hen from under the nose of a tethered guard dog. With this long history of attack, Coleridge's fears were not without foundation. As far back as the sixteenth century, ships skirting North African waters were in danger of corsair attack.

In 1575, Miguel de Cervantes, the now famed author of *Don Quixote*, was on board the Spanish galley, the *Sol*, sailing west from Naples on his way home after recuperating from his injuries received during the

Battle of Lepanto. Bad weather pushed his ship back from the approach to Barcelona, isolating it from the rest of the fleet. On the horizon, three predatory vessels appeared, eventually hauling alongside the more cumbersome galley in preparation to board. Once the spoils had been divided, it was time to take the human booty which could gain a substantial ransom; thereby, to quote *Don Quixote,* depriving Cervantes of 'one of the most precious gifts Heaven hath bestowed upon man',[22] i.e. his freedom. It was to be five long years, peppered with escape attempts, before the charitable Trinitarians were able to pay his ransom, a figure that came attached with all manner of promissory notes.

Aside from such a real and present danger, though, in this modern age of resurgent isolationist nationalism, it is refreshing to hear Coleridge, from the silent pages of his notebook, refer to a lack of separation between the continents; he simply saw in 'the nameless silent forms of Nature two mountain banks, that make a noble river of the interfluent sea, existing and acting with distinctness and manifoldness indeed, but at once and as one – no *division*, no change, no antithesis'.[23]

The first Spanish town he was able to observe in any detail was Tarifa, the peninsula's southern-most point. As always with Coleridge, his focus turned more towards nature than any of the edifices constructed in the town. He was intrigued by the limestone sweep of the Betic Cordillera whose foothills now form part of the El Estrecho Natural Park. He was right to identify the limestone substrate which continues its karst formation beneath the waves. He claimed a resemblance between this scenery and Grasmere in the Lake District – having seen and appreciated both, we had to squint very hard to conjure the same comparison. Perhaps more curious was the perceived similarity between the cheek-by-jowl whitewashed abodes of Tarifa and the slate-grey conformity of Keswick. Even allowing for the stretch of centuries, it seems apparent that Coleridge was being driven by an emotional response rather than the physical reality.

The most southerly part of Gibraltar is known as Europa Point and would have been the first of the Rock's landmarks spotted by Coleridge from the deck as his ship entered the bay between Gibraltar and Algeciras. It now features an iconic red and white striped lighthouse which was built nearly forty years after the poet's visit. In 1804, however, it did possess a brewery which took its water from the nearby Nun's Well. Prince Edward, the Duke of Kent, had been posted to the colony in 1802 as Governor with the express instruction to ensure the discipline and sobriety of the garrison. Ninety-two taverns littered the Rock, dispensing alcohol to the unruly troops. He went as far as banning troop access to all but three, whilst also having the curiously inspired idea of cutting down on drunken behaviour by building a brewery. Predictably, the Duke was recalled to England just one year later.

It was alongside the Nun's Well that the *Speedwell* dropped anchor awaiting quarantine instructions. At the turn of the nineteenth century and a year prior to Coleridge's visit, yellow fever had ravaged across southern Spain, being especially prevalent in the cities of Cádiz and Málaga. It is, therefore, no wonder that the Gibraltarian authorities had decided to impose quarantine measures. Luckily for Coleridge, they had thus far managed to keep any incursion of the disease at bay. However, four months after he departed, a local named Santos arrived from Cádiz bringing the disease with him and it subsequently ripped through the local population, aided by the cramped conditions of Santos' housing.

Twelve years after this outbreak, Hugh Fraser, a medical inspector, was still lamenting the state of many Gibraltarian dwellings in a letter he published to the Earl of Chatham, then governor of the Rock, subtitled *Feverish Distempers of that garrison*: 'In the middle area of Boyd's buildings, confined and choked up by lumber, 18 persons were crowded together, some of them sleeping and cooking, in places called rooms, not larger than two ordinary sentry-boxes.'[24] It is no great shock to learn that the 1804 outbreak originated in Boyd's buildings, home to the unfortunate Santos.

The *Speedwell* was quickly given the all-clear and Coleridge disembarked on 20th April. His first impressions of the populace are characteristic of the attitudes prevalent at the time, but do him no service whatsoever. Despite his enlightened intellect, Protestant zeal led him to high-handedly label the Spaniards he saw as 'dirty dogs' which he only partially rescued by begrudgingly adding that 'with their cloaks, falling down very elegantly, and in groups often compose excellently'.[25] He went on to describe the Greek women he noticed as 'pretty Dowdies'[26] and a muleteer as having 'monkey teeth'.[27] Only an English woman he had previously spied from the deck of the ship escaped his clumsy barbs, although he just as stereotypically described her as having 'an angel face'.[28]

These lazy observations are not Coleridge's finest hour but were commonplace well into the twentieth century. The inhabitants of Gibraltar were disparagingly known as 'rock scorpions' and either ignored completely in the more militaristic accounts of the area, or were painted in broad brushstrokes as background colour. One of the most vile vignettes comes from the pen of George Waring who, in his 1843 *Letters from Malta and Sicily, addressed to a young naturalist*, made this blatantly racist comment about two Barbary Jews: '... who were so disgusting and so unlike human beings in their appearance, that at first sight I almost thought that a couple of the monkeys had come down from the top of the rock.'[29] Given the persistently negative manner in which the locals were viewed by the imperious colonists, it is a wonder they still feel attached to their British identity.

At least Coleridge celebrated Gibraltar as a 'town of all nations and all languages'[30] – a facet of the colony's uniqueness he welcomed as a rich stew rather than an undesirable trait. Coleridge was musing on these matters as he walked from the Europa Point dock to the Griffiths' Hotel. During our own visit to Gibraltar, the hotel's location cost us a little shoe-leather, given the establishment had ceased welcoming guests some time ago. It was thanks to an old print and a fortunate glance upwards at the right time that led us to the location. In fact, the Griffiths' was very central, located at the point where John Mackintosh Square joins Main Street. It is now just one more boutique establishment selling expensive gifts to the throngs of tourists. Its smartly painted bluish-grey façade is edged in white brickwork and faces the Gibraltarian Parliament.

In its day, the hotel was a social hub for travellers and a point of connection for those stationed on the Rock and those passing through. Owing to its status, we can see why Coleridge delivered his two letters of recommendation here on arrival – one to a Mr Frome and one to Major Adye, respectively the garrison chaplain and an esteemed author on military matters. The poet does not record his first topics of conversation at the Griffiths', but it would be surprising if he had not made some comment on the olfactory assault he had experienced on his way from the ship. In his notebook, he complained about the price his nose had paid for the delightful scenery experienced by his eyes. We have already touched on the cramped living conditions experienced by the Gibraltarians which undoubtedly led to the unhygienic odours pervading the streets. Added to the unsanitary conditions in such a small space were the roving gangs of sailors and servicemen, often worse for copious amounts of drink, despite the Duke of Kent's drastic tavern closures. An itinerant male population, alcohol and time on leave could only lead to one thing – a dramatic rise in prostitution.

By the time of Coleridge's arrival, a red light district of sorts had started to develop around Serruya's Lane which is now known as New Passage. We took a walk along this narrow street lined with modest town houses, their windows framed with identically designed shutters painted in different hues – an anxious attempt to proclaim some form of individuality. Although the street could never be called salubrious, it is now a quiet residential area with none of its former reputation. The Gibraltarian author, M G Sanchez, has written an account of Serruya's forgotten past in which he describes the nocturnal goings-on at addresses such as 35 Arengo's Lane. Many of the prostitutes were Spanish nationals who went to work in the brothels and commuted back and forth between the Rock and La Línea.

If not exactly encouraged, their trade was tacitly tolerated by the military authorities whose view was that the young, hot-blooded soldiers and sailors needed an outlet for their passions. This attitude obscures myriad stories of hardship endured by the Spanish and Gibraltarian women who populated the bordellos. The biggest issue faced by the prostitute and client alike was venereal disease; even in the early nineteenth century, the authorities were beginning to worry about the increasing wave of disease afflicting the military garrison. Their solution was not to address the behaviour of the soldiers but to target the unfortunate women and subject them to invasive examinations, which was not done with their interests at heart but as a purely protective measure to prevent the infection of the troops. The irony behind this move is well-exemplified by M G Sanchez who quotes the statistic that by the middle of the 1800s, 26.7 Prussian military personnel out of a thousand had venereal disease, rising to 43.8 amongst the French troops, 65.4 for the Austrians and an eye-watering 458.3 infected soldiers out of a thousand for the British army in India.[31] The situation was not much better in Gibraltar.

Owing to the fact that many of the prostitutes were Spanish, the authorities found it easy to institute a health permit without which the women could not gain access to the Rock. The medical examination was heartlessly thorough and carried out on a weekly basis. Similar inspections of the male member were cursory and far less regular; incredibly, it was thought that such procedures would damage the delicate pride of the supposedly fearless soldier. None of these measures were in place when Coleridge's olfactory senses were so rudely offended. As we know, the Crown had only just started to tackle the alcohol abuse and was not yet ready to inhibit other forms of hedonism. It is more than possible that Coleridge wandered along the cramped confines of Serruya on his way to and from the Griffiths' Hotel, especially given the fact that the area is close to the town centre and what was the heart of conventional society.

Coleridge's own attitude to prostitution and sex, in general, had changed over the years. Whilst at Cambridge, the poet's youthful exuberance manifested itself in the more scholarly pursuits of passionate political debate and literary competition, in addition to dabbling with excessive bouts of drinking and visits to the local brothels, as noted by Coleridge's excellent biographer, Richard Holmes. As Samuel Taylor matured and his philosophical thought aligned still further with Protestant doctrine, he eschewed acts of sexual libertinism. However, this was not easily achieved as his agonised relationship with Asra proves. In his *Confessions of an Inquiring Spirit*, published many years later, he was still struggling with his perceived imperfections: ' . . . and even with regard to Christianity itself, like certain plants, I creep towards the light, even though it draw me away from the more nourishing warmth.'[32]

Gibraltar, at this period in its history, was no place for the sensitive spirit intent on introspective self-development. Despite this aspect of his personality, Coleridge was no shrinking violet; however, the rumbustious garrison mentality, redolent of hard-living masculinity, must have been at odds with certain facets of his character. In his notebook, he is delighted to wander the alleys of this new location discovering geraniums trailing down the walls and prickly pears bursting forth in the most unlikely of places. He spots broom bushes the size of trees and new flora he admits he cannot identify. Coleridge confesses that he is most reluctant to return for a rowdy dinner at the Griffiths' where he knows he will be greeted by seventeen sea captains in various states of inebriation, along with food he dislikes and wine that burns his palate. To prove that it is not just the naval ratings and squaddies who indulged in the Rock's dissolute charms, Coleridge also tells us that he had to guide a tipsy Captain Findlay back to the

*Speedwell* where he poured him into his seat, only to later find that he had continued imbibing into the night with three visiting officers from recently docked merchant vessels.

It was not long before Coleridge started to explore further afield. The day after chaperoning Findlay back to his vessel, he climbed to the furthest point of what he refers to as the 'Mountain Ridge' where he encountered the last signal house on the Rock, overlooking the Mediterranean all the way across to the coast of Africa. This gave him pause for thought and he indulged in some jingoistic nostalgia for landscapes past, peopled by the stout yeomen of England – a misty-eyed reverie in which he favoured them over the Spaniards and Moors whom he pictured on either side of the Strait. In this section of his notebook, it seems to the modern reader that he takes with one hand but immediately gives with the other. From these chauvinistic musings of the Brit abroad, he soon moves to poetic descriptions of his 'Town of All Nations & all languages'[33] with its poplars, cypresses and aspens, prickly pears and marble rocks.

Continuing his walk and not knowing which road to take, he stumbled through the scrub crushing tansy flowers underfoot until he reached a precipice, its sheer face plunging down to what is now known as the Playa del Algarrobo, a rather unprepossessing gravelly beach. Its nearest neighbour to the north is Gibraltar's pocket-sized attempt at emulating a Spanish 'costa' resort going by the very prosaic title of Sandy Bay. Clearly, the Rock's military personnel who named this stretch of coastline were none too bothered with lyrical nomenclature, but it undoubtedly fulfils its purpose. Coleridge was unconcerned with the bathing possibilities, a fashion yet to fascinate the British traveller despite his gout-ridden expedition in Yorkshire. He turned his back on the view and, with a degree of effort, managed to find the road once again, heading towards St Michael's Cave. With the intervention of centuries, we had no such possibility of becoming lost as the fast-flowing stream of visitors carried us to the grotto.

Few places lend themselves as easily to the age-old game of association as Gibraltar. Say the name and a heartbeat later will come the response 'apes' or, for the less interested in natural history, 'monkeys'. We will leave the clichéd descriptions to the guide books but it is enough to say that the simians are as abundant and mischievous as visitors are led to believe. Unaware of the average primate's attitude to speleology, we thought St Michael's would be an ape-free zone. The naturally hushed tones of this extensive underground cavern were surprisingly broken by the excitable screeches and chatter of the playful apes as they chased each other amongst the spectacular formations, using the smoothed, drip-fed surfaces as a skating rink and slide.

Although Coleridge mentions these Barbary inhabitants, he had no similar encounters in St Michael's. We had to walk through a stage and seating area in the main cavernous hall before we reached the more intimate parts of the grotto. Coleridge was unencumbered by such human interference and was immediately struck by the sheer scale of the stalactites. It sent him into raptures of descriptive prose: 'The crown upon crown, a tower of crowns, the models of Trees in stone, here a row of tall slender Pine Trees . . . with nitches [sic] for Images not there/excepting that there were no Saints or Angels, it was perfect Gothic Extravagance.'[34] The first side-chamber he explored brought to mind the chasm and deep well described in *Osorio*, the play he had written in 1797, which was initially rejected by the Drury Lane Theatre and consequently not performed on stage. Coleridge had to wait until 1813 for a performance and critical acclaim under the new title *Remorse*. Without doubt, he would have recalled his Gibraltarian visit when the actors strode through the Granadan settings of dungeons, caves and forts.

> I could have sate whole hours beside that chasm,
> Push'd in huge stones and heard them strike and rattle
> Against its horrid sides: then hung my head
> Low down, and listened till the heavy fragments
> Sank with faint crash in that still groaning well,
> Which never thirsty pilgrim blest, which never
> A living thing came near—unless, perchance,
> Some blind-worm battens on the ropy mould
> Close at its edge.[35]

We too could have spent whole hours in the blessed cool, contemplating the intricate interplay of water and mineral that, over the centuries, had formed an artful blend of the scientific and the mystical. Coleridge would revisit St Michael's Cave, but for now, he was content to stroll back from the grotto in an uncommonly buoyant mood brought on by the heightening of his senses in a new location blessed with a climate that had enabled him to strip down to a lightweight shirt and nankeen trousers. His notebook gives further evidence of his upbeat frame of mind at this time as he breathlessly writes a list of all that has changed – from the flora, weather and landscape to the company he is keeping, which did not exclusively include hard-drinking sailors. This is apparent from the fact that he spent the evening after his return from the cave dining with the garrison chaplain, Frome, who provided a palatable meal without the onslaught of hard liquor and harsh wine. Coleridge was content to maintain his relatively newly acquired regime of beer and lemonade, which suited his delicate stomach, as opposed to the brandy and ginger water he had felt compelled to drink in more boisterous company.

He was misleadingly informed that the *Speedwell* would be sailing on 23rd April and, accordingly, decided that Sunday 22nd would be a day set aside for reading, writing up correspondence and jotting further observations in his notebook. The observations are also accompanied by ink sketches of the Rock's outline – simple line drawings cut with curvatures representing escarpments and dips in rock formation. Unfortunately, the letters that he penned on this day no longer exist but we know that one was sent to Asra, still uppermost in his mind, and to Charles Lamb. Research carried out by the academic, Donald Sultana, on Southey's correspondence with Coleridge, reveals that Lamb must have been told to notify the poet's wife that he had arrived safely in Gibraltar. Asra, it appears, is at the top of his correspondence list whereas his wife is informed, second-hand, merely of his safety.

If these thoughts of thwarted love provoked pangs of emotion to interrupt his otherwise cheerful state of mind, a bout of cramps further encroached on his wellbeing. One of his cabin companions, Mrs Ireland, was moved to remark upon his laboured breathing – a remark which, together with his gasping exhalations, caused him to lose the last vestiges of concentration on his reading material. He swore off further intake of the dreaded brandy and overly-sweet ginger, noting its effect on his stomach. Fortunately, the following day brought better fortune and he was able to pick up both reading material and correspondence to Southey before deciding to make a call on Major Adye, who would become his most favoured acquaintance in Gibraltar. The major's writing talents and the fact that he had attended school in Coleridge's home town of Ottery St Mary meant that they had much in common to discuss which, no doubt, made for lively conversation at dinner that evening.

Biographers are unsure as to whether Coleridge discussed the political feelings of Gibraltarians with Frome or with Adye. Given the poet's closer relationship with the latter, we feel it likely that the more worldly major would have informed him that the inhabitants were conflicted between a dislike of English behaviour and a terror of French government. Essentially, these attitudes can be distilled into a distaste for the individual comportment of the English and a fear of the collective behaviour of the French as a governing body. Returning to the local writer, M G Sanchez, we learn of the haughty manner exhibited by individual Britons towards the downtrodden 'rock scorpions'. He mentions Lady Emmeline Stuart-Wortley, from her book, *The Sweet South: Impressions of Spain*, in which she mercilessly patronises a travelling Gibraltarian silk salesman she encountered in Lyon – even resorting to *It Ain't Half Hot Mum* style skits on his pronunciation. No wonder, then, that Gibraltarians had an ambivalence towards the way they were treated by high-handed colonials with a superiority complex.

Adye had agreed to accompany Coleridge on a walking tour of the batteries, finishing back at Europa Point. Given the major's expertise, we learn that the pair discussed the military capabilities of the British garrison – specifically, the siege endured between 1779–83 from a Franco-Spanish force. They discussed the nature of threats from both land and sea, in addition to the famed impregnability of the Rock's fortifications. A hundred years later, the Spanish writer, Vicente Blasco Ibáñez was both bemused at his lack of resentment on visiting Gibraltar and surprised at the demise of its supposed invincibility:

> I must confess with a certain embarrassment, born of my weak patriotic feelings, that on entering Gibraltar and seeing the usurpers who were guarding it, I felt no indignation. If we were to be infuriated by every historic injustice throughout the centuries, we would spend our lives in a constant state of fury ... That unassailable Gibraltar we have all heard about since we were children has passed into legend. During the time when artillery had less reach and it had to lay siege to nearby squares, Gibraltar was impregnable, owing to the necessity of approaching it by sea or from the land side of La Línea that joins the Rock to the peninsula. (Translation: Edwards, A.)[36]

Blasco Ibáñez displays a remarkably even-handed and modern attitude in his lack of rage towards historic injustice, although one could argue, with the rise in twenty-first century populism, that we are once again resorting to the kind of opinions displayed by his fellow writer Pedro Antonio de Alarcón who, in 1891, wrote that he closed his eyes and lowered his head when his ship passed by the abhorred Rock of Gibraltar. Entrenched attitudes on both sides of the divide continue to plague the Rock's future, particularly as the United Kingdom government refuses to discuss even the sketchiest of plans to share any fragment of sovereignty with Spain and that Brexit will sweep away a freedom of movement desired by both the Gibraltarians and those Spaniards who live and work nearby.

Coleridge was not surprised by the admission that Gibraltarians wanted to remain under British protection but was startled to learn that this had little to do with any affection for individual Britons of their acquaintance. He notes that a preference for French manners could have led to French governance if peace between the two nations had continued. For the moment, though, Coleridge set aside such political thoughts with a note to study Anglo-French relations in more depth when he reached Malta, another important commercial and military outpost under British control, where he had also agreed to meet up again with Major Adye. Coleridge seemed somewhat oblivious to the more immediate claims of Spain to part of its own land mass.

For the time being, he was content to wonder, once again, at St Michael's rock formations and to further investigate the exotic flora, rock strata and even the curious mixture of merchants he had previously encountered at what he refers to as a type of exchange surrounded by aspen trees. The aspens still exist in Casemates Square, but the merchant warehouses have been taken over by artisan glass producers and local artists as well as coffee shops and bars. The diversity of the local population is still in evidence; when walking through the square, it is possible to spot Orthodox Jews mingling with Gibraltarian Catholics of Maltese, Spanish, Genoese and Portuguese descent, not to mention the coachloads of tourists bussed in from the Costa del Sol to find the familiar brand names they would be able to see on any British high street. We had crossed into Gibraltar from La Línea and the hybrid culture was disorientating rather than comforting. Having spent much time in Spain, we could not help but notice that the obviously Spanish landscape was at odds with the assertion of a curious Englishness parachuted into a Mediterranean context – a portal where traditional pubs sit next to tapas bars. The Gibraltarians move as easily between the two cultures as they do between the two languages, in some ways exemplifying an enviable European fluidity.

It would be fair to say, however, that Gibraltarian Spanish is rather removed from classic Castilian. In his book, *Gibraltar en el tiempo de los espías* (*Gibraltar During the Spy Era*), Juan José Téllez gives us a wonderful list of English eruptions amongst the stream of local dialect: 'a muchos les gusta el drinki' (many people like a drink), 'cierra la window, darling, que hace mucho cold' (close the window, darling, it is very cold) and 'mujeres in family way'[37] (pregnant women). Over the years, some of these Anglicisms have been completely Hispanicised, both in pronunciation and spelling; for example, *Melbil* meaning 'someone with an inflated sense of self-worth' from the English 'Lord Melville', or *focona* meaning 'the border with Spain' coming from the English 'four corners'. And it is not just English that infiltrates Llanito – the name for the local vernacular – but also the disparate languages brought by the Rock's many settlers; witness the number of inhabitants who carry the name Gianni from the Italian, Giovanni.

The essence of the area is best crystallised in these lines from Juan José Téllez who says that the Peñón, as the Spanish call it, has: 'a collective identity that comes from those who found a roof and a refuge in Gibraltar during the last three hundred years'. He elaborates, saying that they are 'people of the frontier, blood of the melting pot . . .'[38] To gain such insight would require time and study – Coleridge had neither the timetable nor the inclination to investigate further. Two days after his expected departure date, the *Speedwell* finally set sail on 25th April. Things would not go according to plan, with an inauspicious start heralding bad omens and the shape of things to come. Another vessel setting sail, whilst trying to avoid three other ships, nearly rammed the beam of Captain Findlay's craft.

The wind had also dropped and the rocking motion of the boat, together with the atrocious stench of bilge water, combined to make Coleridge ill and prone to sea-sickness which completely diminished his appetite. He tried to alleviate the boredom inherent on a becalmed ship by joining a trip on one of the *Speedwell*'s small boats in search of marine life, particularly turtles. He was also fortunate enough to witness a pod of dolphins and a shoal of tuna – a fish he would later hear about in Sicily where it was, and still is, prized in the markets of

Catania, Palermo, Syracuse and many other smaller towns. This tiny beacon of enjoyment was snuffed out when, some six days after leaving Gibraltar, he realised that virtually no progress had been made as he recognised the same stretch of water and coastline where they had searched for the aforementioned turtles.

Up until these listless days, becalmed on the rocking vessel, Coleridge had been successful in fulfilling his promise of avoiding laudanum; however, he now resorted to the daytime relief afforded by the drug. At night, though, he was beset by the all too familiar vivid nightmares that accompanied his intake. Even when the breeze picked up, it came from the wrong direction and the ship struggled near to the coast in full sight of the hues thrown by the sun on the distant peaks of the Sierra Nevada. He distracted his mind with thoughts of poetry inspired by this region, recalling his own *Osorio* together with descriptions and investigations from Southey's travels. In further preparation for destinations to come, he returned to studying Italian but lamented the saccharine poetry his grammar guide used to illustrate linguistic points. As anyone who has ever perused the pages of a phrase book will testify, he was also amused and confused by the vocabulary choices under the sectional headings; for example, under the section on accidents and diseases, the author had decided to include the Italian for 'fillip' whilst also listing 'kicks' and 'cuffs'[39] – both of which, it could be argued, would at least lead to an injury. Playfully, Coleridge combined them all in a mock conversation.

When the wind finally turned, our rather bored poet was so relieved, he penned a pseudo sea-shanty in praise of Captain Findlay who had foretold the change: 'When we made but ill speed with the Speedwell, / Neither Poet nor Sheep could feed well . . . / Bravo! Captain Findlay – / Foretold a fair wind / Of constant mind, / For he knew which way the Wind lay'.[40] There are other scraps of verse at this time which caricature his fellow passengers, including an amusing ditty poking fun at his bibulous cabin companion, Hastings. Sadly, the wind would not remain favourable all the way to Malta – hard rain, storms, mists and rolling waves plagued the convoy. The weather's descent ran in parallel with Coleridge's worsening health and mental state. Beyond the Balearic Islands, terrible agonies ensued as heavier use of laudanum completely blocked his bowels. He records a day when all he could manage was to sit over a bowl of hot water, his face convulsing and sweat running from every pore as he strained without result. By now, his bunk had been sectioned off with curtains to afford him a degree of privacy and to provide something of a windbreak for his unfortunate room mates who had to endure the emissions of the flatulent Coleridge.

His condition was deemed serious enough to fetch a surgeon from one of the other ships in the convoy who, upon assessing his patient, immediately left and returned, rather alarmingly, with a tube and syringe. If the indignity of lying prone, cordoned off, in a flatulent bunk was not enough of an embarrassment, Coleridge was now subjected to the downright humiliation of a rudimentary colonic in an attempt to flush out his impacted bowel. His pain was so great, however, that indignity gave way to desperation. He lay with a hot water bottle pressed against his stomach, waiting for the enema to ease his extreme discomfort. Unfortunately, the member of the crew allotted to help, had to witness a distressed Coleridge gouge out the offending hardened stool, the only method left to break the dam. The eventual release was a blessed relief but the shame of this experience was seared into his memory.

Once more, he foreswore the use of opium, helped in part by the dread of another enema, turning instead to a desultory reading of Wordworth's *The Prelude*, but he could not concentrate sufficiently to do it justice. He made a pact with his own conscience to go for a month 'unstimulated'[41] should he land safely in Malta. He longed for dry land and the comforts of friends and the familiar. The coastline of Sardinia receives nothing more than a brief mention in his notebook – gone is the enthusiasm with which he greeted the beaches and towns of Portugal. Donald Sultana tells us the emotion of the voyage led him to pray, not only for the Wordsworths and his longed-for Asra, but also for his wife. This is telling; in extremis, he finally brought his thoughts to bear on his long-suffering wife and mother of his children, admitting their marriage had declined into acrimony.

The wild dreams continued to plague his nights with visions of his unhappy childhood at Christ's Hospital School intertwined with the wrenching futility of his love for Asra. As the *Speedwell* approached Malta, his days were less agonised and he finally began to take interest in his surroundings and the thoughts they inspired with regard to literature. The 15th May saw his ship sail past Marettimo, one of the Egadi Islands situated off the west coast of Sicily. Humid, misty weather obscured his view of the shoreline and was a precursor to the following day's dramatic change, which brought the sirocco from Africa. This wind is a dreaded phenomenon in Sicily and much remarked upon by northern visitors. The Scottish traveller and author, Patrick Brydone, published his startled impressions as part of his book, *Travels in Sicily and Malta* (originally titled *A Tour Through Sicily and Malta In a Series of Letters to William Beckford, Esq*): 'I opened the door without having any suspicion of such a change; and indeed I never was more astonished in my life. – The first blast of it on my face felt like the burning stream from the mouth of an oven.'[42] Alexandre Dumas (père), later on in the century, was equally awed when he made reference to it in his novel about Sicilian banditry entitled *Pascal Bruno*: 'A drift of clouds to the northward announces the approach of the sirocco, the Khamsin of Arabia; a burning mist, rising from the Libyan sands, and wafted to Europe upon the south-east wind.'[43]

When the desert wind leaves the coast of North Africa, it leaves behind exceptionally dry, dusty conditions. The gust then meets damper air circulating in the Mediterranean basin, which, as it progresses across the sea gradually turns into cooler air that generates rainfall as it moves up the southern European landmass. Sicily feels both the hot breath of the Sahara and the soggy revenge of Europe's climatic defences, leading to the eponymous 'blood rain'. Under the sirocco's influence, Coleridge felt feverish, achy and complained of a sore throat. In 1830, a certain Dr Benza wrote his own impressions concerning the wind's impact on health:

> a general lassitude or torpor of the muscular system, attended by head-ache and heaviness and oppression of the nervous system, inducing an inaptitude to any exercise, either corporal or mental; everything that is touched is damp and clammy, particularly one's clothes, which feel as if they had been wrung out of water; appetite impaired; thirst increased; perspiration profuse . . .[44]

With these effects in mind, Coleridge vowed to note down any climatic changes that would influence his health, fearing a future onslaught. Luckily, this invasion from the 'Moorish wind-swarm',[45] as the poet, Lucio Piccolo would call it, was only to last less than two days.

On 17th May, Coleridge records significantly better weather and was delighted to gain his first view of Mount Etna, which would have reminded him of 'The Mad Monk' and all those Classical allusions he had studied over the years. These thoughts lifted his mercurial spirits, as did the arrival at Valletta just one day later. During the forty-day voyage, Coleridge had been charmed by his first experiences of the Mediterranean but had also endured one of the lowest and most humiliating points in his life. He was now more than ready to explore the future possibilities of his southern sojourn by which he had set such store. The harbour-front architecture of the Maltese capital, with its blistering white stone, moved the poet to recall Virgil's *Aeneid*, imagining he had found himself in a new Carthage. He was hoping to find his own Elysian fields, free from cultivation of the opium poppy which had threatened to swallow him in the maw of addiction.

CHAPTER TWO

# Strategising for Nelson in Malta

> A vain, speech-mouthing, speech-reporting Guild,
> One Benefit-Club for mutual flattery,
> We have drunk up, demure as at grace,
> Pollutions from the brimming cup of wealth . . .
> *Fears in Solitude*

The general layout of Valletta harbour remains little changed since Coleridge disembarked on that May morning, despite the inevitable expansion of its dockyards and wharves. His ship dropped anchor in the Great Harbour, which had already become strategically important to the British. It was well fortified and able to accommodate a large number of vessels. The peninsula forming the central arm of downtown Valletta also acts as the north-western border of the harbour. Rounding the arm, there is a second inlet known as Marsamxett Harbour which encompasses Manoel Island, so named after António Manoel de Vilhena, the Portuguese Grand Master of the Knights of St John. At the time of Coleridge's arrival, the island still had an active quarantine hospital known as the Lazzaretto. On this occasion, the poet was fortunate enough to avoid a stay within its walls and was able to head straight for his destination.

Mrs Ireland, his long-suffering cabin mate, offered him the chance to disembark on a boat owned by John Morrison, who we assume must have been the lover that she was anxiously awaiting. Her eager anticipation had been such that she could not resist telling all to Coleridge who, given their shared experiences on the voyage, had become rather more familiar with her than he had intended. After the journey to shore, however, he was left alone and to his own devices. With a lightness of step, he went in search of the Casa di San Poix. His main contact

**5** The Grandmaster's Palace, Valletta, Malta, formerly used by the British Governor (Andrew Edwards).

**6** San Anton Palace, Malta, formerly used by Alexander Ball as his summer residence (Andrew Edwards).

in Valletta was John Stoddart, the Chief Advocate of Malta who resided in the aforementioned house.

The Casa, located at the top of what is now Old Bakery Street, was also known as the Palazzo di San Poix. Its name derived from the fact that, until 1803, it was in the possession of the Bali de St Poix, but the French connection stretched further back in time as the building was originally constructed by the French Langue of the Knights of St John. The house occupied Number 3 Old Bakery Street, but the buildings once belonging to the Langue also included numbers 4 to 7. Stoddart was the lucky indirect recipient of Napoleon's policy to abolish the Langues on Malta. He took up the lease in 1803 and remained in the property until 1807. Our own search for the residence was dashed when talking to some interested locals on the street who informed us that the area had suffered heavy damage during the Second World War and the buildings constructed by the French had been destroyed.

Coleridge had almost as much trouble as we did in finding the Casa di San Poix. He spent two hours roaming the hilly streets of Valletta before finally reaching the property, only to discover that Stoddart and his wife were not at home. He was greeted by the advocate's sister and a gaggle of confused servants. Coleridge did not have the quickness of mind to send his letter of introduction in advance of his arrival; consequently, nobody knew the identify of this out of breath and slightly dishevelled Englishman. A further two hours passed whilst the sister and the servants bustled around, uncertain as to the proper protocol or the need to fetch Stoddart.

Old Bakery Street is a bisecting artery that runs along the hog's back of central Valletta. Lanes and alleyways spill left and right, inevitably flowing towards the waters on either side of the mini peninsula. When Coleridge eventually gained access to the inner sanctum of Number 3, he was effusively greeted by Stoddart and was able to closely examine his surroundings. The property was made of tanned yellow stone and was typified by the enclosed wooden casement balconies so common to Valletta. From the windows facing away from Old Bakery Street, Coleridge caught sight of Marsamxett harbour, along with the jumble of narrow stone steps and twisting passageways that were inundated with activity. Familiar with the fells of Cumbria and the coombs of the Quantocks, the infamously vertiginous streets of Valletta posed little problem to the poet, beyond a shortness of breath; not so, his fellow countryman and versifier, Lord Byron.

In 1809, some five years after Coleridge stepped ashore, Lord Byron followed rather more precariously in his footsteps, even staying at the Casa San Poix. Already in a foul mood thanks to the necessity of quarantine, Byron climbed the seemingly interminable Nix-Mangiari Steps that still lead from the fish market to the upper town. An infernal late summer heat impaired his progress as did the deformity in his right foot, a jarring reminder of the limp that he was always keen to deflect with acts of aquatic athletic prowess. The Steps, worn smooth with weathering and use, are still perilous to the unwary and are far from the only example of their kind in the city. They were a necessity as carriages would not have been able to safely negotiate the inclines from the ridge to the harbour. Byron was so annoyed by their presence that, on leaving Valletta, he took poetical revenge with this spiky rhyme: 'Adieu, ye cursed streets of stairs, how surely he who mounts you swears'.[1]

The day after settling into Casa San Poix, Coleridge tackled what he calls the Nix Mangiare Stairs and was less concerned with the precipitous descent than with the nomenclature. Recalling his German days at the University of Göttingen, he felt the word 'Nix' had a Teutonic ring. Valletta has a curiously hybridised network of location names due, in part, to the proximity of Sicily and the influence of Italian, but also to the various national Orders of the Knights of St John. This has been further compounded by the subsequent overarching influence of English. That said, the reasons for the supposed low German 'nix' are lost in the mists of time. There is nothing to suggest that the 'cursed' Nix-Mangiari has any Germanic connection and it is thought that the Maltese considered it English. The term is substantially bastardised Italian and literally means 'nothing to eat'. It stems from the shouts of the abundance of beggars to be found on the steps at the very time Coleridge arrived in Malta.

Making his way down the stone stairs, Coleridge was indeed assailed by beggars and he would have heard this plaintive cry from the hungry underclass, although he was at pains to stress their condition had improved greatly since the departure of the French. These cries would have blended with the cacophonous sounds of everyday life, including the exclamations from street vendors that so surprised the Englishman he was moved to note that they were 'broad and bulky noises, sudden and violent'.[2] He was also aware of the raucous music emanating from the taverns as they sought to attract the influx of newly-arrived British sailors. As we have seen in Gibraltar, this roving naval presence also attracted the oldest profession.

Under the rule of the Knights Hospitaller, in the fifteenth and sixteenth centuries, prostitution was rife, despite draconian measures to corral and prevent its practice. Having taken a vow of chastity, the Knights were keen to avoid detection and took the necessary measures to divert suspicion. There are notable instances of punishment as, from time to time, it was thought necessary to make an example of a particular subject in order to deter others. In 1608, no less a figure than Leonetto della Cordoba, an inquisitor, was summarily dismissed from his post. That same year, the artist and fugitive from justice, Caravaggio, found himself thrown into gaol after a drunken attack on the Knight, Fra Giovanni Rodomonte Roero, not long after Caravaggio, himself, had been raised to the Order. Under the surface of holy abstinence seethed the primitive emotions of lust and violence.

The situation did not improve with the arrival of the French. Under French rule, the Anglo-Bavarian Langue of the Order of Saint John housed in the Palazzo Carneiro, overlooking the entrance to Marsamxett Harbour, was converted into a hospital for venereal disease. Although the British would eventually disband this institution, they failed to stem the rise in prostitution. At the time of Coleridge's arrival, poverty, as illustrated by the prevalence of beggars on the Nix-Mangiari Steps, had forced many to turn to sex work. From the 1800s onwards, one particular street would be associated with this nightly transaction. Like Serruya's Lane in Gibraltar, it was Strada Stretta, or Strait Street, in Valletta that attracted the men from the boats and the opprobrium of the conservative establishment.

British sailors would eventually christen this narrow thoroughfare 'The Gut', alluding to both its status as the underbelly of Malta and its geographical bisection of Valletta. Doubtless, there would be nights to come during Coleridge's long stay in the city when his thoughts would have strayed to seeking the comfort of a lonely embrace; yet, as we will see in Sicily, he fought these temptations, even when they involved women for whom he had considerable affection. Walking The Gut today, we found scant evidence of its infamous past. Its worn, narrow, flagstone paving and high brooding walls retain a certain edgy atmosphere but the patrons of today visit restaurants and sushi bars to satisfy their needs. The occasional drinking establishment harks back to more bohemian days with brightly painted tables illustrating inebriated sailors chatting to scantily-dressed ladies. Ghostly signs still exist proclaiming locales long past into legend and one forlorn prostitute sits stencilled against a graffiti-clad door.

The governor in 1804 would have been all too aware that there were issues to be addressed but his priorities lay elsewhere. Alexander Ball, appointed a baronet and commissioner of the navy in 1801, would be a significant influence on Coleridge during his stay. Three years earlier, then a naval captain, he had been involved in the blockade of Malta, which led to the eventual surrender of the French troops who had assumed control. During the blockade, factions on the island were split between supporters of the French or British navies. Seemingly, the majority of the Maltese were in favour of British protection but there was reticence from foreign powers, including the Bourbons of Naples, who had accepted the sovereignty of the island after the Knights of St John.

During the siege in 1799, Maltese batteries were flying the British and Neapolitan flags as they fired upon the French. As autumn drew on, the French noticed the British flag had been lowered. Jean de Bosredon de Ransijat, a Commander and Grand Cross of the Order of St John, who was supporting the French, kept a siege diary in which he alluded to British double-dealings through this manoeuvre, surmising that the English had lowered their flag in order to deceive the Maltese, Neapolitans and Russians into thinking they had no desire to establish control of the island themselves.

Captain Ball claimed in a letter to the Maltese Congress, that the lowering of the flag was due to a wish not to provoke the jealousy of the Neapolitans and the increasingly involved Russians. He went on to say that the king would find it in his interest to give up any claim to Malta. This was not to be the case; Ransijat's accusation of 'perfidious Albion' came to pass for the French when Captain Martin and Major Pigot accepted the French surrender and Captain Ball entered Valletta with the Maltese delegation he had been aiding. In February 1801, Ball was sent from Malta to Gibraltar, only to return later in the same year as the Plenipotentiary Minister of His British Majesty for the Order of Saint John. To back up Ball's earlier claims, his job was to oversee the withdrawal of British forces.

Circumstances, however, were soon to change – with the Treaty of Amiens placing the island back under the Knights' control, the Maltese no longer felt secure. Although the Treaty required the removal of

British forces, the government in London decided war with Napoleonic France was too great a risk and that a garrison should be maintained. Alexander Ball now found himself *de facto* governor. This letter from Horatio Nelson, written just before it was known that would be Ball's appointed, illustrates the esteem the British believed the Maltese held for Nelson's friend: 'I pity the poor Maltese; they have sustained an irreparable loss in your friendly counsel and an able director in their public concerns; you were truly their father, and, I agree with you, they may not like stepfathers . . . . Believe me at all times and places, for ever your sincere, affectionate, and faithful friend.'[3]

Interestingly, Nelson's opinion of Ball had not always been so positive. The two had first met at St Omer in France where Alexander was seen strutting around in epaulets, much to Nelson's disgust, given he held a deep-seated dislike of such French fashion in naval uniforms. It appears Nelson thought him to be a 'great coxcomb' and their dislike was mutual. It would take fourteen years for them to become friends owing to Ball's actions during a significant storm at sea which saw Alexander come to his senior's aid. Coleridge, though, was never so taciturn in his initial opinions of Malta's British governor. From the outset, the poet saw qualities in the man that even some of his other great admirers would have struggled to detect.

In an article for *The Friend*, Coleridge's magazine project initiated four years after his return from Malta, he eulogises Ball in the following manner:

> He would listen, even to weak men, with a patience, which, in so careful an economist of time, always demanded my admiration, and not seldom excited my wonder. It was one of his maxims, that a man may suggest what he cannot give; adding, that a wild or silly plan had more than once, from the vivid sense and distinct perception of its folly, occasioned him to see what ought to be done in a new light, or with a clear insight.[4]

Coleridge first met Ball on 20th May 1804 when he went to the Governor's Palace with letters of recommendation and the hope of gaining some form of position in the island's administration. He was politely rebuffed by the governor whose policy was supposedly to place Maltese candidates in the majority of civil service posts. Once again, in *The Friend*, Coleridge ascribes this attitude to a certain frame of mind that ran contrary to the high-handed manners of many Englishmen abroad:

> There is no reason to suppose, that Sir Alexander Ball was at any time chargeable with that weakness so frequent in Englishmen, and so injurious to our interests abroad, of despising the inhabitants of other countries, of losing all their good qualities in their vices, of making no allowance for those vices, from their religious or political impediments, and still more of mistaking for vices a mere difference of manners and customs. But if ever he had any of this erroneous feeling, he completely freed himself from it by living among the Maltese during their arduous trials . . . [5]

Despite this initial polite, brief and noncommittal meeting, Coleridge had time to discover the glories of the Governor's Palace. Situated in Misraħ San Gorg or (St George's Square) at the heart of Valletta, the palace was formerly the Grand Master's residence and therefore once home to the head of the Order of St John. The outer building is little-changed since Coleridge's day; its honey-hued façade overlooks the downward sweep of the square, and opposes the Main Guard building, previously known by the Italian, Guardia della Piazza. At the height of summer, the sun's rays bounce mercilessly from the light stone, dazzling and searing the retinas of the newly arrived tourist.

A succession of Grand Masters made various embellishments, adding Baroque adornments, a clock tower and fresco sequences in the corridors. The Scot, Patrick Brydone, visited Valletta in 1770 when the Order of St John still held sway. He wrote copious letters and notes during his visit to Malta and Sicily and would go on to publish these in his best-selling account. He had this to say about the Grand Master's Palace: 'The palace is a noble though a plain structure, and the grand master (who studies conveniency more than magnificence) is more comfortably and commodiously lodged than any prince in Europe, the king of Sardinia perhaps only excepted. The great stair is the easiest and the best I ever saw.'[6]

The main staircase, like many of the corridors in the building, is frescoed, often depicting major events in the history of the Order of St John. Suits of armour guard the passageway and the lower walls are hung with portraits of previous incumbents of the highest office. Central to the ceiling is a faded red and white Maltese cross, surrounded by *trompe l'oeil* decoration masquerading as architectural detail. The frescoes on the upper walls tell their story of religion, battle and antiquity. Unlike Brydone, Coleridge was less than enamoured with some of the palace's frescoes, complaining of their lack of perspective – a trait he felt they had in common with the collection of Chinese paintings held by William Wordsworth's brother, John.

Two paintings, one by Spagnoletto and another supposedly by Michelangelo Merisi (Caravaggio), caught his attention more fully; so much so, he would refer to them years later when he wrote *On the constitution of the Church and State*. Donald Sultana feels that it was the *chiaroscuro* effects of the works that led him to compare these two *seicento* masters with the work of Rembrandt. It is interesting to note that there was some debate about the attribution of the Caravaggio as the palace does not currently house any works by the troubled Italian. The Cathedral of St John, however, displays the celebrated 'Beheading of St. John the Baptist' and his depiction of St. Jerome. The Grand Master's Palace does, though, contain works by the artist, Lionello Spada, who was unkindly nicknamed the 'ape of Caravaggio', due to his talent for *chiaroscuro* and his determination to mimic the naturalistic style of Michelangelo Merisi.

Light and shade are appropriate metaphors for a palace steeped in the history of an Order that was prepared to battle for its religious beliefs and place in the world. No wonder, then, that the Grand Master's former residence is also home to more than one spectral apparition. During the tenure of Alexander Ball, reports started to filter back to the governor that a female compatriot and guest had heard the sound of cats and dogs fighting in a nearby room. On entering, however, there were no animals to be seen and no means of escape. Joseph Attard in his interesting book, *The Ghosts of Malta*, tells us that the same woman contested that the spirit had, on another occasion, taken the form of a singular cat which disappeared in mid-leap through an open window. Another female visitor was certain that an other-worldly spirit was present in the room where she slept. Doubtless, a practical man of action, such as Ball, would have dismissed these nightly visitors as the phantoms of an overactive mind.

It was not long before Ball invited Coleridge to the palace and gardens at San Anton. The building was originally commissioned in the seventeenth century by Antoine de Paule, a knight of the Order of St John. Its size would seem somewhat excessive for the summer residence of just one knight, even if the subsequent enlargements are discounted, but perhaps not when we learn that de Paule decamped to the countryside with an entourage worthy of a king. Amongst his many servants were wig makers, food tasters, pantry boys, clock winders, a plethora of doctors and a baker who specialised in making bread for the sole purpose of feeding the dogs. The Frenchman eventually became a Grand Master, which saw the palace evolve into a regular residence for successive holders of this post.

After a period as a revolutionary Maltese headquarters during the French occupation, Ball initially took up residence in 1800, using San Anton as his favoured summer retreat. It was the British who added balustrades to provide a shaded walkway around the central courtyard. Today, it is the President of Malta who enjoys the privilege of having the palace as his home. Although the building is off limits, the gardens are open to the public, allowing the pilgrim and biographer to tread in the poet's awed footsteps. The lush vegetation, in marked contrast to the more arid open countryside, was a balm to Coleridge's spirits, especially when he was subsequently invited to stay at the palace for an extended period of time. For the time being, Coleridge was still in the process of finding his feet with both the island and its illustrious governor.

Political events were moving apace and there was much to discuss. Sir John Acton, Ferdinand IV's Prime Minister in Naples, was deposed on the order of the French, which prompted many in Malta to turn their thoughts to Sicily, with Alexander Ball seeing the key port of Messina as vital to British interests. He was actively entertaining thoughts of occupying the city, thus preventing French interference. These political manoeuvrings, laden with threats of violence, were designed to reorder the European chessboard, repositioning the central players in a calculated and advantageous manner.

Such scenarios were fertile ground for a mind as agile as Coleridge's. Ever since Gibraltar, he had been musing on the reception afforded the English abroad and it was the Sicily question that finally prompted him to argue his case. The garrulous enthusiasm of Coleridge found English haughtiness a rather alien concept, and he was confirmed in his negative opinions when observing the way in which the forces stationed on the island treated the Maltese. Furthermore, if the British were to become involved in Sicily, he was convinced that the morals of such political action would have to be deeply considered. Countries and their inhabitants were not pawns to be merely pushed around at the behest of over-weaning powers, blind to the moral consequences of their high-handed actions. In this, he thought he had found a perceived ally in Alexander Ball who, as we know, was respected by the Maltese.

In the midst of such political discussions on the evening of 28th May, whilst still staying at San Poix, Coleridge had his first significant bout of illness. Over dinner, he began to feel feverish and the bowel cramps returned with a vengeance. His host, Stoddart, was implored to provide him with laudanum which seems to be the first time he had succumbed to the drug in Malta. His notebooks also attest to the resurgence of Sara Hutchinson in his dreams and daily thoughts; always hovering in the background, she was now front and centre, exacerbating his feelings of solitude and loneliness. He comforted himself with a translation of Mateo Alemán's *Guzmán de Alfarache* and the writing of lines in imitation of his favourite German authors.

Perhaps surprisingly, given the feverish nature of his attack whilst dining with Stoddart, Coleridge was unperturbed by the increasing heat as summer approached. It was not the oppressive nature of the sun on an island with precious little natural shade that began to weary the poet, but rather the unrelenting tones of a brown parched landscape. It is no wonder, then, that Coleridge was uplifted when presented with the contrasting greens of San Anton's gardens. His visit on 4th July, though, was to present him with a wholly unexpected visitation.

It was a Wednesday morning and Coleridge had been invited to breakfast with Sir Alex, a favoured meeting time for the governor. Whilst they were deep in discussion, Coleridge raised his eyes and saw a woman who had a profoundly disconcerting effect on him; he recorded it in his notebook: '. . . saw a Lady with Hair, Complexion, and a certain Cast of Countenance that on the first glance of her troubled me inconceivably – after a while I perceived the likeness of S.H. & was near fainting'.[7] It was as if his dreams had conjured a manifestation to further torment his unmet desires. Whether Ball noticed his guest's sudden pallor and emotional turbulence is open to question, but if we are to believe Coleridge's description of events, it would have been hard to miss. We can imagine Sir Alex making a tactful enquiry as to whether the summer heat had already begun to take its toll.

It was around this time that Coleridge had his first offer of work from the governor. It was not an official stipend or even an ongoing commitment. Ball must have been aware of Coleridge's literary prowess as a poet, but it was his previous experience as a newspaper columnist and polemicist that would have drawn the administrator's attention. The governor had been working on a document concerning French activity in the Mediterranean which he intended as a report for policy-makers in London. He used Coleridge's skills to polish the piece, who then went beyond light proofing when Ball also tasked him with the completion of a paper on Algiers with particular reference to commerce, politics and connections to the French. Redaction, research and compilation were a welcome distraction for Coleridge and played to his strengths.

Ball was happy enough with Coleridge's work to make him a temporary offer. Edmund Chapman, one of the governor's secretaries, had been sent on a corn-buying exercise and would be away for some weeks. Consequently, Ball was in need of someone to take his place. Although Coleridge was reluctant to take on Chapman's full duties, he nonetheless eventually agreed to take the man's place on the assurance that his obligations would be minimal and that he could still undertake his planned trip to Sicily. The position meant Coleridge could finally move out of the Casa San Poix and into the Governor's Palace where his accommodation was in one of the towers with views over the harbour and Città Vecchia. The poet was immensely grateful for these 'cool & commanding Rooms'[8] and to be gainfully occupied; a boon to his emotional and financial stability.

There is little doubt that the now regular exchanges with Alexander Ball influenced Coleridge's own political thought on Mediterranean matters. Despite the humanitarian views he had displayed with regard to intervention in Sicily, Coleridge was content, in effect, to be a mouthpiece for Empire. Ball was a champion of Malta as a key to British imperial policy and he saw the island as the base from which the French could be prevented from interfering in routes to Egypt and India. In modern terms, Coleridge was a propagandist, backing Ball's views with his own spin on British commercial interests that would be enhanced by the retention of the Maltese islands.

Political apostasy is a common charge made against the poet and it is difficult to refute at this particular moment in his life. There is no doubt in the mind of Daniela Corona, who wrote 'S.T. Coleridge's Colonial Gaze', that he had somewhat sold his soul to the imperialist cause when pandering to the rhetoric of government in an era that saw peoples as pawns in a game of profit and loss. It is difficult to gauge the extent to which Ball saw mere profit in his cultivation of Maltese opinion, but it would be harsh indeed to charge Coleridge with a lack of consideration for the people his government were intent on colonising.

The poet also had a hidden agenda when writing for the governor; the acting Under-Secretary had no intention of keeping the reports to himself and every intention of releasing his own redacted versions to the press, specifically to Daniel Stuart who was editor of the *Courier* back in England. In terms of his civil service position, this would seem ethically questionable, especially as Coleridge would have been expecting payment for the information. The modern world of spin and counter-spin would undoubtedly term this practice as 'leaking', yet at no point does he wrestle with his own conscience when rushing to complete his 'packet' of letters to be shipped home at the first opportunity. Rather, he saw his role of columnist as compatible with the agenda being pushed by Ball. Only once does he mention a concern that the published pieces should avoid the same phrasing as the reports.

The governor was now providing him with some very useful contacts including Vittorio Barzoni, the editor of the local paper, *The Argus*, and Selim Effendi, the Mamelukes' agent in Malta. Donald Sultana makes reference to Coleridge's growing ability in Italian, the *lingua franca*, through grammar exercises and a polyglot version of Pascal's *Les Provinciales*. At turns, he mentions his reluctance to speak it in society, then his supposed confidence in conversing with Effendi in that language had the Mamelukes' man been a speaker. These rather contradictory statements bring into question Coleridge's actual proficiency in Italian but we do know, through Edoardo Zuccato's research in the work, *Coleridge in Italy*, that the poet had taken pains in the spring of 1804 to make notes on Italian metre, which Zuccato pinpoints as the seven syllable verse form common to opera arias. It seems that Coleridge ignored the syllable count and confused the stress patterns of Italian, placing accents in all the wrong places thus revealing his lack of mastery.

Thomas De Quincey, author of *Confessions of an English Opium-Eater* and, for a period of time at least, a friend of Coleridge's, was far more scathing of the poet's prowess with foreign languages. In the pen-portrait he wrote for *The Treasury of Modern Biography*, he had this to say about Coleridge's meeting with the poet, Friedrich Gottlieb Klopstock, during his sojourn in Germany:

Neither Coleridge nor Wordsworth, on the other hand, spoke German with any fluency. French, therefore, was the only medium of free communication, that being pretty equally familiar to Wordsworth and to Klopstock. But Coleridge found so much difficulty even in *reading* French that, wherever (as in the case of Leibnitz's "Theodicée") there was a choice between an original written in French and a translation, though it might be a very faulty one, in German, he always preferred the latter. Hence it happened that Wordsworth, on behalf of the English party, was the sole supporter of the dialogue.[9]

It is true to say that Coleridge may have been better advised to speak in Ancient Greek or Latin, over which he had ample command. Despite De Quincey's slightly barbed comments, Coleridge continued his German studies until he felt capable of translating Schiller, although his accent was littered with Devonian inflections and must have startled even the politest of his German hosts. At no point did the poet become sufficiently versed in Italian to attempt a translation of any authors for publication. However, as we shall see in a subsequent chapter, official notices outlined by Coleridge as *Segreteria del Governo* were written in Italian. The degree to which he penned these himself is open to question.

One of Coleridge's most revealing notebook entries on language comes from his stay in the Mediterranean. He starts by comparing the advantages of one language over another with regard to specific vocabulary – English excelling in practical words of a manufacturing nature, French in scientific terminology of trade and diplomacy – whereas:

> German exclusive of its world of mining, metallurgic, & mineralogical technical & scientific words has an incomparable army of metaphysical and psychological Phrases, & both by its structure & greek-rivalling facility of composition is of all others the best adapted to logic & intellectual analysis, that the Italian is the sweetest, the Spanish the most majestic in its sounds, (capable indeed of as much sweetness as is desirable, adding falernian strength, and thus calling forth all worthy powers of articulation [,] it may be considered as the perfection of Sound – at all events, very very far more above the Latin, than it is below the Greek[)] . . .[10]

Italian is relegated here to that cliché of sweetness that Byron referred to as 'that soft bastard Latin, / Which melts like kisses from a female mouth . . . '[11] Sultana provides us with the amusing visual vignette of Coleridge listening intently to an old aristocrat conversing in Italian with, most likely, Barzoni of *The Argus*. The doddery grandee, whose actual identity is unknown, was described by Samuel Taylor as a 'Pomeranian noble of ½ century back at Malta'[12]. Sultana postulates that the noble was a throwback to the Knights of St John, one of a mere handful who had been allowed to remain on the island. We have visions of a wizened, periwigged old gentleman, his black garments, having seen better times, now faded and dusty from the heat.

Coleridge still had time to indulge his linguistic investigations as the acting role he had taken was as light as had been promised. Despite this, he felt increasingly integrated with the governor's household and, consequently, when the summer heat dictated a more permanent move to the palace at San Anton, Coleridge was invited along with the entourage. Whilst he dabbled in writing about British involvement in Egypt, he had the opportunity to explore the palace gardens more fully. Back in 1770, Patrick Brydone had been rather scathing of the grounds:

> From this we went to see the Bosquetta, where the grand master has his country palace; by the accounts we had of it at Valletta, we expected to find a forest stored with deer and every kind of game, as they talked much of the great hunts that were made every year in these woods. We were not a little surprised to find only a few scattered trees and about half a dozen deer; but as this is the only thing like a wood in the island, it is esteemed a great curiosity.[13]

He was equally dismissive of the palace itself, it being 'as little worth seeing as the forest; though indeed the prospect from the top of it is very fine. The furniture is three or four hundred years old, and in the most Gothic taste that can be imagined; but indeed the grand master seldom or never resides here.'[14] Not so Ball, who favoured the location and allowed the grounds to flourish. There was an exoticism to the flora that relaxed Coleridge's mind but also opened him up to periods of reflection and melancholy. He wandered through the gardens regularly, distracted by the flowers, shrubs and trees, as well as the movements and colours of the animals, especially the vibrant lizards darting into the undergrowth. He lamented the lack of a copy of Linnaeus, the Swedish originator of botanical nomenclature, which he could have used as a reference guide for the broad-ranging flora. In fact, Linnaeus would subsequently have an impact on a poem he would write inspired by San Anton, as we shall see after Coleridge returns to Malta from his trip to Sicily.

Ball's attention to the gardens had seen them become more formalised, but it was thanks to Grand Master de Paule that a diversity of tree species were introduced as he instituted the tradition of asking visiting dignitaries to plant a sapling. Carefully tended over the years, these young trees have been allowed to mature, providing unusual amounts of shade for an island so predominantly devoid of tree cover. In the modern era, almost every tree is accompanied with a descriptive plaque detailing the botanical name and common area of origin. Coleridge was able to distinguish, amongst others, these more common species – pomegranates, oleanders, pepper trees, citrus, dates and the ubiquitous prickly pear.

Today, the visitor enters the garden through a gate guarded by two stone lions and is soon confronted with a marble fountain backed by a concave, patterned, limestone wall. The eye is drawn to the central feature of two cherubs, struggling to hold aloft a mythical bird with outstretched wings. Paths continue onward through intimate archways softened with creeping ivy and vines. Weathered urns, low sun-bleached walls and clipped hedges compartmentalise the gardens into outdoor rooms, some of which contain stone benches curved towards the cooling flow of water from further statuary; perfect places to rest in the shade and let the mind wander. Continuing in the tradition of contributions made by visiting officials, there is even a copper pagoda donated in 1970 by Takaoka Copperware and the Japanese Cherry Blossom Association. It is framed by the abundance of oleander which would have been recognisable to Coleridge, even if the pagoda seems a figment from the dreamscape of Kubla Khan.

The sheer abundance of tree species, some of which predate Coleridge by nearly one hundred years, becomes clearer the deeper into the garden you venture – alii figs from Central Asia vie with silk floss trees from South America; kurrajongs from Australia grow opposite pony tail palms from Central America; jacarandas from the same region develop in harmony with native stone pines and the ubiquitous date palm. The under-planting in summer provides a soft tapestry of colour thrown at the feet of those towering, protective masters. Coleridge would not have recognised much of the garden's current formality but, most assuredly, its variety. In these sensory environs, he began his long-awaited letter to the charitable Beaumonts, whilst continuing to lament the absence of Sara Hutchinson: 'Yesterday & today I seem to live / O Sara! – yes, I could be happy here with you!'[15]

We know that Dorothy Wordsworth had written to Lady Beaumont on 25th July complaining that they too had not heard from Coleridge since Gibraltar. It must have been a debt of gratitude combined with a guilty conscience and the time he now had at his disposal that prompted him to finally put pen to paper. It was during this period that his friend from the Rock, Major Adye, arrived in Malta. Conveniently for Coleridge, the major was breaking his journey before sailing on to Messina in Sicily and the poet was happy to arrange a berth on the ship with his friend. He also promised, in his first letter to the Beaumonts, that he would write a journal for them, detailing all his subsequent travels. Adye agreed to take these papers home with him when he was scheduled to leave Sicily; these documents would also include a letter to Wordsworth about William's ongoing struggles with his magnum opus, *The Prelude*.

Further afield from the garden, Coleridge was making notes on the peculiarities of the Maltese landscape and he was intrigued to hear of the wheel rut phenomenon, which he annotates in the following manner: 'marks of carriage wheels on the extreme edge of the sea coast opposite Gozo'.[16] Always keen to observe the unusual or quirky, he must have been drawn by this strange archaeological feature. Located near Siggiewi, or as Coleridge would have known it, Città Ferdinand, the prehistoric site of Misraħ Għar il-Kbir has a criss-crossing network of what appear to be cart tracks carved in the stone bedrock. In fact, Misraħ is one of several sites that show these mysterious markings.

The latest official research claims these ruts are due to wooden wheels eroding a limestone surface easily prone to wear through prolonged action. Repeated journeys over the same landscape wore away both the soil and then subsequently the rock itself. Logic would dictate that these kind of formations need a relatively restricted geographical space where travel would be necessary between certain commonly used points – Malta certainly fulfils this description. A swift internet search will, however, furnish the viewer with many wilder theories on the construction of these tracks, particularly as some appear to lead straight to cliff edges or directly into the water. Everything from Atlantis to Axis Mundi, the mythological concept of the world's navel or *omphalos*, has been postulated. The wildest hypothesis of all attempts to explain their creation through the appearance of ancient extraterrestrials, in a similar manner to those theories attributed to the Nazca Lines in Peru or the Pyramids in Egypt.

In Coleridge's day, proto-archaeology would have attributed their existence to a previous Maltese civilization without having the necessary tools and scientific know-how to investigate further. Given their fascinating layout and considerable distribution, it is puzzling that Coleridge was not drawn to deeper theorising about their origins. We have been unable to uncover any profounder ruminations he made on the subject. If he did visit them in detail or have discussions with regard to their formation, he made no in-depth notes or else these have been lost.

As ever, Coleridge's enquiring mind darted fluidly from subject to subject and his leisurely hours at San Anton, surrounded by natural wonders, prompted speculation on the nature of being; his interest in Spinoza's Pantheism reawakened, despite the fact that it clashed with the poet's religious beliefs. Spinoza's melding of God, man and nature seemed to conflict with Coleridge's idea of one creator and notions of personal liberty. His foray into the world of political administration would also have been an influence on the tracks his mind would follow – how nature, religion and politics interact to produce varied consequences. In many ways, Coleridge was completely unsuited to the role of a civil servant with its routine, bureaucracy and order. It was just as well that, in these early days, Ball allowed him a large degree of freedom; Samuel Taylor felt constrained if denied his enthusiasm for intellectual enquiry.

In 1816, he brought together his ideas on behaviour in government when he wrote *The Statesman's Manual*. The text draws on his belief in spiritual thought as a necessary tool of governance. His role in Malta, the observations of his reports and ideas in his notebooks, must have contributed in a haphazard manner to the *Manual*. In this segment, Coleridge places metaphysics at the heart of revolution:

> To the immense majority of men, even in civilised countries, speculative philosophy has ever been, and must ever remain, a

*terra incognita*. Yet it is not the less true, that all the epoch-forming revolutions of the Christian world, the revolutions of religion and with them the civil, social, and domestic habits of the nations concerned, have coincided with the rise and fall of metaphysical systems.[17]

He goes on to proclaim, in the thoughts below, that enthusiasm of action is key to losing oneself in a higher purpose. These are idealistic notions that would have jarred with Ball's no-nonsense, military practicality, although he may have enjoyed debating them over drinks.

> Nothing great was ever achieved without enthusiasm. For what is enthusiasm but the oblivion and swallowing-up of self in an object dearer than self, or in an idea more vivid? . . . in the genuine enthusiasm of morals, religion and patriotism, this enlargement and elevation of the soul above its mere self attest the presence, and accompany the intuition, of ultimate principles alone. These alone can interest the undegraded human spirit deeply and enduringly because these alone belong to its essence, and will remain with it permanently.[18]

*The Statesman's Manual* is rather confused and rambling. It is a prime target for accusations of political apostasy given its conservatism – a conservatism that grew during his Malta years. It was heavily criticised, not least by his former friend, William Hazlitt, who thought Coleridge had succumbed to sophism: 'Truth is to him a ceaseless round of contradictions: he lives in the belief of a perpetual lie, and in affecting to think what he pretends to say'.[19] With the benefit of hindsight, in these words and those of the essay itself, we detect hints that there were subjects upon which Alexander Ball and Coleridge would never agree, which must have been apparent even at this early stage. Additionally, the report writing for Ball was already creating the very contradictions in thought and action that Hazlitt would complain of in his criticism of the *Manual*.

There was one topic, however, on which Coleridge would not be swayed. Catholicism was his intellectual and spiritual blind spot. On first visiting the Governor's Palace in Valletta, he was shocked to see a painted cross in the Anglican chapel and wanted to know if it pre-dated the British or was a concession to what he referred to as 'Maltese superstitions'.[20] Back in Gibraltar, he had felt that the Spanish dishonoured Christianity, a clear reference to their Catholicism and, potentially, a veiled allusion to the *leyenda negra* (the black legend), in other words, the nation's association with the evil deeds of the Inquisition so embellished by Protestant countries.

Unlike several other Romantic poets, Coleridge had a firm and demonstrable faith. Not for him, the extravagant atheism of Percy Bysshe Shelley or the nonchalant acceptance of God without the adherence to religious principles of Lord Byron. Coleridge was the son of an Anglican vicar from rural Devon and religious enquiry was often uppermost in his mind. When lecturing in Bristol during the firebrand years of the mid 1790s when, despite evidence to the contrary, he was labelled a 'damn'd Jacobin'[21], he still chose topics of an intensely religious nature, berating atheist radicals whilst espousing the benefits of his brand of essential Christianity to the poor underclasses so neglected in that era.

Coleridge's beliefs eschew the need for ritualistic practice, preferring instead a direct, almost evangelical, relationship with God. Whilst in Malta, he picked up a copy of Antonino Diana's *Resolutiones Morales*. Diana was a Catholic moral theologian and a consultor for the Holy Office of the Kingdom of Sicily. He is chiefly known as a casuist, someone who refers to particular cases as a means of resolving moral dilemmas by demonstrating a theoretical rule. His book is a compilation of such cases and their resulting resolutions. Interestingly, modern theologians criticise him for his laxity as did the seventeenth century French philosopher, Blaise Pascal. Coleridge was equally disdainful, particularly in his opposition to Diana's espousal of the 'one visible church'[22] and liking for 'ceremonial observances',[23] as Donald Sultana points out.

In the immediate years following his return to England, Coleridge's introspective thoughts, prompted by his stay in Malta, ranged across the full gamut of the theological spectrum. He reread the New Testament and advocated the exploration of one's own soul which, as Richard Holmes indicates in *Coleridge: Darker Reflections*, was not seen by the poet as an automatous entity but a consciousness that responds through Nature's hierarchy. It is a conscience that does not operate in isolation but is affected by other humans to the extent that the human race can be viewed as a single spiritual entity. This mysticism is viewed by Holmes as a heightening of Coleridge's earlier idea of 'the One Life', which leads us back to his 1794 poem 'Religious Musings', a work that encapsulates much of the poet's early thought:

> There is one Mind, one omnipresent Mind,
> Omnific. His most holy name is Love.
> Truth of subliming import! with the which
> Who feeds and saturates his constant soul,
> He from his small particular orbit flies
> With blest outstarting! From himself he flies,
> Stands in the sun, and with no partial gaze
> Views all creation; and he loves it all,
> And blesses it, and calls it very good!
> This is indeed to dwell with the Most High!
> Cherubs and rapture-trembling Seraphim
> Can press no nearer to the Almighty's throne.[24]

As was often the case for Coleridge, these metaphysical musings would be interrupted by the practicalities of daily life, made all the more dutiful by his temporary position in the government whilst in Malta. He was aided in his role by a pick and mix selection of characters who had found their way into the Maltese civil service by accident or design. Ball's Private Secretary was a vicar, the Reverend Francis Laing. The Scotsman, Laing, was the son of an architect who had led a rather peripatetic university life that saw him study at Edinburgh, Glasgow and, eventually, Oxford before taking Holy Orders and travelling to Malta as chaplain to the troops.

In one of those curious, 'found in the attic' moments, Laing's time on the island resurfaced in 2015 when a letter was discovered at the National Trust property, Dudmaston Hall in Quatt, near Bridgnorth. The letter was hidden in a book on Nelson held at the property's library and has been confirmed as being in the Admiral's hand. It seems that whilst scribing for Bell, the vicar, who was the great-great grandfather of the last owner of Dudmaston, had been pocketing some correspondence as a keepsake. Other letters have also come to light, but they were dictated by Nelson with merely a short comment added by the Admiral as a postscript. Sadly, this tiny treasure trove does not feature any correspondence written by Coleridge.

The Public Secretary and Treasurer was Alexander Macaulay, the first official to hold this post which had been ring-fenced by Lord

Hobart. Prior to Ball, Macaulay had not been universally liked or respected. The overlap of the administrative and financial arms of government was formalised when Ball combined the Secretary's position with that of the Treasurer. However, this created a gorgon-headed monster of a job that must have been considerably taxing for the already unwell and aged Macaulay. Waiting to jump into his shoes was the younger and more dynamic, Edmund Chapman, who we know had been sent to the Crimea allowing Coleridge to temporarily fill his post. Chapman was favoured by Ball and there has been speculation that this may have had something to do with the fact that Chapman's brother worked in the War Office back in London, which was much involved in the island's affairs.

Completing the eclectic mix of officials was Giuseppe Nicolo Zammit or Zamittello, known as the Maltese Secretary. Zamittello would have much to do with Coleridge when the poet returned from his trip to Sicily, and is generally considered to be the real workhorse behind the administration's output. Fluent in Italian, the language used for official pronouncements, Zammittello put his signature to many documents. In 1805, in exchange for land needed by the British government, Casa Pensa was given to the then auditor, and became known as the Palazzo Zamittello. The property had once been the Italian Langue for the Knights of Malta and is now a luxury hotel to be found in Valletta's Republic Street. Zamittello was, himself, a Knight Commander of the Order of St Michael and St George, and a judge. You will search in vain to find tangible monuments to the other secretaries during this period of direct British rule but the native son, Giuseppe Nicolo, is remembered with a statue in Upper Barakka Gardens. His daughter, Maria Theresa, married into the upper echelons of Mittel-European aristocracy.

Given this cabinet of curiosities, it is now clear how Coleridge was able to dabble as Under-Secretary and still be given the opportunity to play the tourist in Sicily. In the weeks leading up to August 1804, his duties were lessening, and his attention began to turn to his impending trip. On 9th August, he was handed the princely sum of £50 by Macaulay which represented two months' salary. If the MeasuringWorth.com website is to be believed, this 1804 amount is approximately equivalent to £4,500 today – not a bad return for writing a few reports and leaking some information to the British press. Furthermore, Ball insisted Coleridge remain on the payroll whilst he was in Sicily and Chapman was still in the Crimea. On the following day, suitably moneyed and ready for a change, Coleridge joined Adye and set sail for Syracuse.

CHAPTER THREE

# Sicily and the Prima Donna

> Boldlier swept, the long sequacious notes
> Over delicious surges sink and rise,
> Such a floating witchery of sound
> As twilight Elfins make . . .
> *The Eolian Harp*

In 1804, Sicily was in a perilous situation and under threat from Napoleonic invasion. A few years earlier, in 1798, after the British victory at the Battle of the Nile, the monarchy of Naples and Sicily had decided to join the Second Coalition as part of the war on revolutionary France. However, this gave France ample excuse to invade Naples, the seat of the kingdom's government. The royal family fled to Sicily when General Championnet took command of the city and proclaimed the Parthenopean Republic. From Sicily, the royals schemed with Nelson to supply arms to ensure the demise of the republic, which was brought about by Cardinal Fabrizio Ruffo's army and the significant backing of the English fleet.

Nelson deeply distrusted Ruffo, though, and, as John Julius Norwich points out in his history of Sicily, this is not surprising given that the Catholic Cardinal-Deacon would have been the mirror opposite of the Admiral's right-wing Protestantism. Ruffo, who had once championed agricultural labourers struggling on feudal lands, was accused of leniency with regard to the Parthenopean rebels. Nelson overruled Ruffo's decisions and insisted on the unconditional surrender of all the insurgents. Over a thousand had been saved by Ruffo from mob vengeance and were expecting to be allowed to return home with a guarantee of safe conduct. The end result was not so compassionate; when the rebels emerged from their sanctuary, they were immediately clapped in irons and a good proportion were executed. To this day, it

**7** Karl Friedrich Schinkel's drawings inspired by G. F. Leckie's residence, Tremilia, Syracuse, Sicily (Wikimedia Commons).

**8** The Castello dei Bonanno, Tremilia, Syracuse, Sicily, former residence of G. F. Leckie (Andrew Edwards).

**9** The Arethusa Fountain, Syracuse, Sicily (Suzanne Edwards).

is not known if it was Nelson who directly gave this order or whether he was influenced by William Hamilton, the British envoy to the kingdom, and his wife Emma, with whom Nelson was already having a passionate relationship.

Ferdinand IV of Naples or III of Sicily, depending on which title he chose to use, did not return to mainland Italy until 1802. When he did so, Naples would have a new English envoy, Hugh Elliot, who had travelled with Nelson as far as Gibraltar on his passage out to the city. Norwich tells us that, during this voyage, the Admiral was plying Elliot with much information, including disastrous appraisals of what could happen to Sicily. Just as Alexander Ball saw Malta as crucial to British interests, Nelson saw Sicily as absolutely central to the survival of the monarchy headed by Ferdinand. In Nelson's opinion, the kingdom could survive the loss of its heartland in Naples but not the loss of Sicily. Needless to say, the Admiral's preoccupation with the survival of Ferdinand's rule represented his concern for British interests and his belief in the right of kings.

Into this political maelstrom sailed Coleridge, clutching a letter of introduction written by Ball to G F Leckie who was the British honorary consul at Syracuse. At this point in time, Coleridge was riding a wave of good fortune, both in terms of health, company and personal wellbeing. The last weeks in Malta had been invigorating with early swims, long walks and much table-talk. He was now fulfilling his long awaited dream of visiting Sicily with money in his pocket and the prospect of solid contacts on the island. When the ship docked, Coleridge was greeted by the sight of Syracuse with all its Classical Greek associations, which must have been uppermost in the poet's mind. At the turn of the nineteenth century, the city was wearing a Baroque face which had started to appear in the seventeenth century but had been accelerated by rebuilding after a disastrous earthquake. Jeremy Dummett's fascinating history of the area's development, *Syracuse: City of Legends*, states that the Baroque utterly changed the look of the settlement, particularly Ortygia, the tenuously connected spit of land which houses many of Syracuse's jewels. He goes on to explain that the architecture, although subsumed into the prevailing fabric, was so arresting it could not help but alter the face the city presented to the world.

Many are struck by Syracuse's combination of the Classical and Baroque. The Spanish author, Alejandro Luque, who recreated Jorge

Luis Borges' journey through Sicily, had this to say of Ortygia's central piazza:

> We retrace our footsteps through the little oval of alleyways until we stop in the Piazza del Duomo, a tremendous arc open to relaxed families, flirting adolescents and passing visitors. Excepting the Piazza del Campo in Siena, I don't know a public space as perfect as this one. The sense of spaciousness, of *air* given by one of its entrances, is unique to the genre. Even its nighttime illumination, which for many would be insufficient, creates a beautiful game of backlit silhouettes among the strollers.[1]

One of the buildings lining this piazza is the cathedral (duomo) itself. It is unusual in that the façade, started in 1728, was built around the pillars of a Greek temple. Its gleaming white stone would have been fresh and clean to the eyes of Coleridge. Sadly, his first impressions of the city are lost to posterity, either because he was too engaged in new sensation to put pen to paper or the pages in question have been lost. He may also have had to quarantine for a period of time. He will return to Syracuse in due course, but for now, we can only pick up his trail in Catania at the foot of Mount Etna.

Catania is Sicily's second largest city and synonymous with the volcano that dominates its landscape. Although the gift of volcanic ash has given the city's hinterland an incredibly fertile soil, the pre-eminence of Etna also carries a deadly threat. In 1669, the mountain's most violent eruption in recorded history saw lava burst from fissures and flow towards the city, burying everything in its path. For fifteen days, the city walls held out against the molten onslaught but were eventually breeched leading to the decimation of buildings. Coleridge would have been able to see evidence of the remaining lava deposits in places such as the Castello Ursino which, to this day, still retains a broken layer of petrified rock at the foot of its battlements.

Towns such as Mascalucia, San Pietro and Nicolosi, further up the mountain's slopes, were either partially or completely subsumed. If Etna provided the deadly molten lava to destroy these settlements, it also provided the materials to quickly redevelop them. The rock does, however, lend a sombre hue to the façades of the buildings in the ring of towns and villages on the volcano's slopes. By the time of Coleridge's visit, Nicolosi had been completely reconstructed. We know he passed through here on his ascent of Etna as he mentions the monastery of San Nicolò l'Arena in his notebook: 'Monastery with its six pines and its shivering birches.'[2] The Nicolosi location is further reinforced by his Anglicised reference to Monte Rossi: 'This the strait line/to my right 1. scattered Trees on the bare-lava ascent of M. Ross.'[3]

Coleridge had done his research on this location by reading two works that dealt with Etna, namely, Henry Swinburne's account of climbing the volcano in his 1780 work *Travels in the Two Sicilies* and Francesco Ferrara's *Storia Generale dell'Etna*, published in 1793. In reading Ferrara's work, we came across the following description:

> Monte Rossi, not far from the village of Nicolosi, is a mountain that encloses two equally big craters which gives the impression of being two mountains that have taken their name from the red colour of the material forming the inside and edges of the craters. The form is almost conical: the base is about two miles around ... The highest part ends in two opposing points, united by two half-moon shapes. Monte Rossi was formed twelve days after the start of the famous 1669 eruption.[4] (All Ferrara quotes translated by the authors)

In fact, Coleridge also mentions the hue of the twin cones noting their 'color of the rich dark brown Heath hills of the North'.[5] The Italian name does, of course, suggest that Monte Rossi has a reddish-brown tone.

Sadly, Coleridge's account of the higher regions of Etna has been lost, as we shall later see. His words stop at the descriptions of 'The golden Bracelets & Necklaces of the Chestnut Tree',[6] 'the bare Lava'[7] and 'the Sun on Etna'.[8] He actually claimed to have ascended the mountain twice but some have cast doubt on this assertion. James Dykes Campbell, in *Samuel Taylor Coleridge: A Narrative of the Events of his Life* (1894), even goes so far as to say that 'it is improbable that he went much higher than the village of Nicolosi'.[9] In the absence of Coleridge's own words, we must recreate his assumed trek to the summit through the eyes of the author accounts he read and others who made the same journey.

Ferrara describes how Etna is divided into three distinct regions:

After the First Region, Etna rises a little more rapidly – much more on the eastern side – and that area, up to a little over half the height of the mountain, forms the *Second Region*; the *Third Region* is the highest part of the cone. Throughout the entire extension, from the foot to the summit, conical mountains of varying heights fork out here and there.[10]

Monte Rossi is one of Ferrara's conical extrusions and the village of Nicolosi is firmly in the first region. When discussing this zone in detail, Ferrara leaves behind his scientific leanings and turns to more purple prose:

> One can't form an idea of the fertility and beauty of the First Region; it is beyond imagination . . . One breathes sweet and healthy air everywhere; adapted to all types of agricultural production, the earth gives everything in profusion. The grower, hitherto frustrated in his desires, will always see nature spreading its beautiful riches over the countryside.[11]

Swinburne takes us on to the second zone of forestation:

> We now begin to leave the cultivated, and to enter into the woody region; at first straggling trees and patches of shrubs marked the skirts of a forest, and tillage-land grew gradually more and more scarce; soon after large wastes opened on each side with scattered thickets, and here and there a piece of vineyard, which some industrious peasant has ventured to plant higher up than the rest.[12]

The Englishman found that the summit looked like less of a tapering cone the closer he came to it, and more of an 'immense ridge'.[13] At the foot of the ridge, he saw 'gloomy vallies (*sic*) of prodigious depth, separated from each other by snowy mountains, before which most beautiful woods form a mighty girdle round the frozen region'.[14] It is clear from both these authors that Etna is a mobile landscape, prone to constant metamorphosis. Ferrara tells us that 'before 1759, Etna's crater was almost in the middle of the upper part of the cone', but that 'when the summit became twin-peaked, it shifted more to the east of the accumulations that were made in the western part'.[15]

One of Ferraras's comments that must have appealed to Coleridge, when reading the text, was a recommendation to philosophers, specifically, that they try and reach the summits of the highest peaks because 'in such a lofty and peaceful place, the soul seems to participate in the purity of these ethereal regions: it acquires a breath of calm'[16] which the author claims will make one's existence more precious. Given Coleridge's delight in the heights of the Lake District and his musings on the ascent of the Brocken in the Harz mountains, it is of great regret that we cannot see these 'ethereal' heights through his eyes or that we are unable to capture his inquisitive mind alighting upon the vegetation and mineral wealth, particularly as Ferrara's description of the mountain's sulphur is other-worldly: 'This can be seen in the dust similar to that used by artists, the so-called *fior di solfo* (flower of sulphur), often containing small crystallised filaments of the same substance, which covers the surface of some lava and scoria formed inside the crater cavity.'[17]

Etna, though, is not all sublimity and geological wonder; its landscape is also the celebrated home to myth and legend, some of which is, indeed, fantastical. Another author, Patrick Brydone, whose own ascent of the mountain has been called into question, relates one of the most amusing tales concerning Etna's mythical status. He was also in the region of Nicolosi and had been lava hunting, searching for curious mineral deposits. He had fashioned himself a magnetic needle and a small electrometer in order to detect the 'electrical state of the air',[18] which he quickly hid when joined by some locals lest he should be taken for a conjuror as had previously occurred on a trip to the Apennines. The Sicilians were not fooled by this or by his joking claims that his countrymen could transform stone into gold.

One of the party started to question Brydone in more detail with regard to his motives for visiting Etna, suspecting a treasure-hunting expedition, but was reassured by the explanation that the mountain scenery was enough of a draw. As they all started to relax a little, the locals wanted to know exactly where this curious northerner called home. On learning that he was an 'inglese' (which, in itself, is not strictly true as Brydone was Scottish), the most vocal of the party asked him if the English believed in God, to which Brydone cheerfully nodded. The response to this was an unexpected '"mi pare che non credono troppo"',[19] implying that he thought their belief was not that strong. Deeper questioning led to the discovery that the locals could never understand the obsessional motivations behind English visits to Etna, except that the more senior members of the community told of an English queen who 'had burnt in the mountain for many years past; and that they supposed these visits were made from some devotion or respect to her memory'.[20]

Amused by such a discovery, Brydone's wry riposte was that 'the Inglese had but, too little respect for their queens when they were alive, but that they never troubled themselves about them after they were dead'.[21] Wracking his brains, he could conceive of no possible queen who could have been the inspiration for such an outrageous legend until, that is, they gave him the name 'Anna'. Even then, it took the further explanation that she had turned a king from a God-fearing Christian into a heretic by marrying him, before the penny dropped. The woman condemned to burn in the hell-fire pits of Etna was none other than Anne Boleyn, the second wife of Henry VIII, and the reason why Henry abjured his Catholicism. Brydone, still unfazed by the extraordinary story, observed that the husband deserved this fate far more than his wife did. Nevertheless, the locals warned the Scotsman against venturing further, as being one of Henry's erstwhile subjects and such a heathen, he could suffer the same fate.

Coleridge also had ad-hoc encounters with the locals on the mountain but found no-one, that we know of, who could make him or herself understood in standard Italian, unlike Brydone's mythologiser. We have a small vignette of him and Adye stopping to lunch on meat cooked over a fire washed down with the local wine whilst endeavouring to make themselves understood to some pretty, young village women. Coleridge relates how the women refused to believe that the pair of foreigners could not understand their voluble Sicilian and continued to barrage them with questions. It occurred to him that, if only he could immerse himself in this chatter for a short time, the rusticl anguage would come easily as would, we suspect, the opportunity to enjoy a flirtatious response.

The only personal evidence we have for Coleridge's ascent to the highest regions comes from a letter he wrote some ten years after the events described here. As biographer, Richard Holmes, elaborates, it was during a time when he was deeply troubled by religious doubt brought on, in no small measure, by his opium consumption. He recollects when 'I stood on the summit of Etna, and darted my gaze down the crater; the immediate vicinity was discernible, till lower down obscurity gradually terminated in total darkness'.[22] He compares the pursuit of biblical truths to the blackness of night owing to his own flawed faculties. In this sense, Coleridge's remembered experience of Etna's depths reflects the locals' vision of the mountain as a castigation for the perils of questioning one's faith. His notebooks, however, quote a more joyous vision of Etna's reinvigorating properties via an inscription found at the monastery in Nicolosi which rose from the ashes: 'Ætnei montis impetus jacuit / Pulchrior e ruinâ surrexit / Iterum terræ motu collis. / Nobiliorem induit venustatem / Eo adversæ Fortunæ Condumento . . . '[23] ('It was laid low by the eruption of Mount Etna, but rose more lovely from its ruins. Again, through an earthquake, the hill put on a nobler grace, in such a garment of cruel fate . . . ' (translation: James Diggle).

From this contemplation of death, renewal and Etna's 'nobler grace', the Coleridge trail runs cold until he reappears in late August, outside the gates of Syracuse. It is here that he has come to seek the company of Gould Francis Leckie, the English representative and honorary consul at Syracuse. We know that Ball had written to Leckie in a text dated 24th August, extolling the virtues of Coleridge and suggesting he be employed to write another political paper:

> You have admirably described the leading features of my friend Coleridge, whose company will be a delightful feast to your mind. We must prevail on him to draw up a political paper on the revenue and resources of Sicily, with the few advantages which His Sicilian Majesty derives from it, and the danger he is in of having it seized from him by the French. We should then propose to his Majesty to transfer his right of that island to Great Britain upon condition that she shall pay him annually the amount of the present revenue.[24]

Several things are apparent from this text; firstly, that Leckie must already have met Coleridge prior to his trip to Etna; secondly, that the military man, Ball, and the merchant, Leckie, agreed upon Coleridge's loquacity, merits and ability to speak on many subjects and, thirdly, that Ball was continuing to push his Mediterranean island agenda by intending to use Coleridge as his instrument of political incision. As we shall subsequently see, Ball and Leckie had similar political outlooks with regard to Mediterranean strategy. Leckie saw the French as the great disruptors of the balance of power within Europe and his solution, as noted by Gould Francis' biographer, Diletta D'Andrea, was, in his own words, the following: 'We must therefore sometimes conquer, and if we are excluded for a time from the continent of Europe, form for ourselves an insular empire, complete in its parts, and sufficient to itself.'[25]

Leckie had taken up residence in an area of Syracuse called Tremilia in a property now known as the Castello dei Bonanno, built on the site of a dwelling supposedly once belonging to the Ancient Greek statesman, Timoleon. It took considerable research and kilometres on the ground to discover the history and specific location of Leckie's former property. Through a series of Italian and German sources, we now know that the villa in question can be found along the strada provinciale 77, approximately four kilometres from the Neapolis Archaeological Park. Confusion arises over the spelling of Tremilia which we have seen with a double 'm', double 'l' and a 'gl' (Tremiglia). By 27th August, Coleridge had been invited to lodge with Leckie and his attractive wife at the villa. In fact, Gould Francis drew an outline of the countryside visible from the property in Coleridge's notebook. It shows lower-lying land, rising to a vegetated escarpment under which nestles the actual building complex. In this respect, not much has changed – flat farmland surrounds the current edifice which is backed by trees and scrub that cover the hillside.

The first reference to the land and buildings comes from an 1104 Latin text with the following noted: 'Concedo Syracusanae Ecclesiae Matri . . . monasterium S. Petri de Trimilia cum omnibus pertinentiis suis, et terrarium terminis.'[26] The land was donated by Count Tancredi to the Syracusan Bishop Rugero for a Benedictine monastery known as San Pietro. As Marco Monterosso tells us in his work, *Massæ, massari e masserie siracusane*, the monastery was built on the foundations of a previous religious building constructed in the sixth century. Once the church had taken over the land, it was intent on increasing its holdings over the years and was responsible for the seventeenth-century introduction of sugar cane production.

Viewing the estate in 1803, Leckie was struck by the fecundity of the land and the beauty of the surroundings. He felt sure he could increase yields by using English methods of production and decided to approach the *conservatore generale d'azienda*, Donato Tommasi, to ask for a long-term lease of the land. Eight months of contacts and negotiations ensued leading to terms which saw Leckie agree to construct a mill, a new church and pay over some of his annual profit. The most interesting clause, as outlined by Monterosso, was the stipulation that Gould Francis should renounce, whether in private or public, any of his Protestant religious practices. If Leckie had mentioned this aspect of his lease of Tremilia to Coleridge, it surely would have provoked intense discussion, given Coleridge's feelings on the rites and practices of the Catholic church.

One of the best portraits of the property and the surroundings we have at the time of Coleridge's stay comes from the pen and ink of Karl Friedrich Schinkel, the German architect. Schinkel was a Prussian renowned for his work as a city planner and a designer of neoclassical and neogothic buildings; he was also an accomplished painter. The Mediterranean undoubtedly had an influence on his work, in particular the Castello dei Bonanno, as we know from the text on his career, *Aspekte seines Werkes*, edited by Susan M. Peik. One of the book's contributors, Emanuele Fidone, considers Schinkel's completed treatise and drawing of the castello as fundamental to his 'aesthetic formation'.[27] The architect saw Leckie's villa in 1804, but there is no evidence that his visit crossed over with that of Coleridge given that Schinkel sent a letter from Syracuse to a Berlin book editor, dated May 1804, in which he proposes the publishing of drawings already made of Leckie's buildings and land. The dates, however, are so close that we can confidently say that Schinkel's view of the villa would have mirrored Coleridge's own experience.

The German's travel diary correctly locates the property on the slopes of Epipoli and he further notes the 'pleasing position of the villa of an Englishman at the foot of the mountain; grotto, water basins, ruins of a bishop's castle above'.[28] The use of the term 'mountain' is rather exaggerated as it is, at best, an escarpment, but Schinkel's romantic etchings wonderfully capture the newer building inhabited by Leckie at the foot of a forested slope, with additional touches of his own architectural poetic licence. The pillars and colonnades of the ruins blend sympathetically into both the landscape and the more modern villa. Evidence of Leckie's agricultural experiments are visible in the foreground of one of Schinkel's drawings where a cattle-drawn cart, filled with hay, is being off-loaded by workmen while goats sit idly in the sun next to the agaves. These elements add a pastoral element to the classical aspect and their inspiration is in keeping with Schinkel's newfound philosophy of incorporating nature into his construction projects.

Included in the German's proto-treatise are detailed architectural vignettes of intricately sculpted Corinthian capitals topping segmented column drums, an arched semi-circular fountain, a detailed floor plan and topographical sketches, providing an idealised version of the villa. *Aspekte seines Werkes* also includes sketches and views from Epipoli looking towards Syracuse, Etna and Augusta from the hand of other visitors; they bear many similarities to Leckie's outlines in Coleridge's notebook and the poet's own descriptions written later in October of the view towards Syracuse: 'I was in part of Epipolis, and a glorious View indeed. Before me a track of stony common & fields, Acradina, Ortygia, the open sea & the Ships, & the circular Harbour its embracer . . .'[29] Coleridge also referred to Timoleon's villa being in the field above Leckie's house and it is true to say that Greek remains are evident, including an aqueduct. The attribution to Timoleon was most prevalent in the seventeenth century and therefore still current during the visits of both Schinkel and Coleridge. Fidone points out that no evidence has been found to reinforce the Timoleon theory, except to say that significant development took place on the site during the Classical period.

From 1803 onwards, and therefore during Coleridge's stay, we know the inhabitable property consisted of a coach house, the main dwelling (converted from the former monastery church), some houses for the estate workers, a grotto chapel and a hermitage. The structure surviving into the twenty-first century is, unfortunately, in partial ruin and many of the elements listed above are no longer visible to the casual observer, although if you take the path to the left of the main structure and achieve a side view of the property, looking seaward, much of that portrayed in an ink drawing by Gigault de la Sale (*Aspekte seines Werkes*) is still very evident. The architectural façade of the main building we see today is not due to Leckie's redevelopment, but to the aristocratic Baron Giuseppe Bonanno who bought the estate when Gould Francis relinquished his lease in 1811, hence the name quoted by Marco Monterosso and others. Bonanno extended the building towards the flat plain and added gothic arched windows and machicolations to the parapet – a neogothic pretence at imitating the defensive archery positions of the Middle Ages.

As we know, one of the features attracting Leckie was the potential of the agricultural land, which today is still heavily planted on the flat ground leading to the property. Despite the fact that the ecclesiastical authorities had managed to grow sugar cane, Leckie was sure the land was under-producing and that more modern methods would yield a greater crop. From the outset of his lease, he concentrated on applying his theories which, in many ways, chimed with his aforementioned political views. D'Andrea also quotes his opinion that 'the revenues of that island will then probably pay the expense of its maintenance and defence'.[30] The word 'then' is crucial here as it implies British interference leading to an increase in incomes and profits. With Ball and Leckie both on the same page, the conversations at the villa between Coleridge and the Leckies would have had a familiar ring to them, with the added bonus of the charms of Gould Francis' wife, and, at quieter times, an extensive library where he consulted both Brydone and Swinburne.

Coleridge would already have been familiar with some of Brydone's more strident opinions through Greenough's account of the island which he had read in England before setting sail. We have noted previously that George Bellas Greenough and Samuel Taylor were old friends from their Göttingen University days. Greenough approached Sicily from multiple perspectives – cultural, political, anthropological and, by no means least, given his academic specialism, geological. Coleridge would have trusted his opinions and been amused by his commentary. Greenough had the following to say about Brydone's feelings with regard to Sicilian aristocracy:

> They have always behaved well towards us – there can be nothing more ridiculous and unfair than Brydone's description in which he accuses this class of people, whose role it is to protect travellers from thieves and murderers, of being thieves and murderers themselves. We have always found them to be honest and helpful, correct in their behaviour, open and frank, and eager to be of help whenever possible.[31]

(This, and subsequent excerpts, are translated back into English by the authors from the only current publication of Greenough's Sicilian diary, *Diario di un viaggio in Sicilia, 1803*.)

When Greenough turned his thoughts to the land and those employed to work upon it, his opinions presaged the views Coleridge would now discover in Leckie's household. As someone who was well-informed of cutting-edge techniques for working the land to extract agricultural and mineral wealth, it is unsurprising that Greenough was shocked by conditions he saw amongst the Sicilian peasantry and he was not shy of apportioning the blame:

> ... it is distressing to see the number of the poor, close to starving; their government, their religion, the climate, all join forces to make these people idle in a land where every step would amply repay the industrious and where laziness is more pernicious than it could ever be in northern climes ... the eminent citizens are content with that produced by their land stewards, well aware that they are too powerful to be arrested for debts. Not only do they refuse to personally inspect their land, but also seem to brag about never even knowing their own property.[32]

Harsh words, indeed, but a well-founded and common criticism of the absentee landlord, latifundista estates found in Sicily at this time. The world, portrayed here by Greenough, is captured in its last dying moments by Giuseppe Tomasi di Lampedusa in his renowned novel, *The Leopard (Il Gattopardo)*. At least Prince Salina has the decency to visit his land once a year, although the family visit Donnafugata as a refuge from the late summer extremes of Palermo, rather than through any interest in the estate's productivity; Lampedusa even refers to Salina's feelings of feudal proprietorship.

If Greenough is scathing of the nobles' lack of concern for their land, he reserves his harshest criticism for the church and members of the judicial profession: 'The friars and nuns, on the other hand, and the lawyers are like dead members of the body politic, who corrupt and destroy the living.'[33] Coleridge was able to observe, first-hand, the plethora of churchmen in Syracuse and we are sure it is no coincidence he makes a comparison with the number of poor people: 'In one street I met 5 or 6 Clergymen/and on no particular Day/They are more numerous than even the beggars'.[34] In another aside, he makes the claim that the clergy were the only ones with rounded stomachs in Syracuse; clearly, at this point, he had not come across many aristocrats. His opinions on agriculture were undoubtedly influenced by Leckie and his brother-in-law, Denison, with whom he toured the Epipoli estate and surrounding areas.

Coleridge was used to the soft fecundity of the fields in Somerset and Devon rather than the under-utilised, pebble-strewn furrows of Sicily. He was also scathing of the area he referred to as 'that poisonous marsh' near Syracuse, lamenting the fact that it could easily be drained. In actuality, it was known for the papyrus plant, which grew with such vigour around the Ciane river, that Syracuse could, and still can, boast of Europe's largest natural colony of the plant. One of the most visible clusters of papyrus can be found in the Arethusa fountain on Ortygia. Coleridge does make reference to its water (a spring rather than fountain) but only in context to its use as an outdoor laundry by the poor women of Syracuse. Under his description of the flat stones worn by years of hard scrubbing, he writes rather ironically in Greek 'Hail, Arethusa!'[35]

This rather throwaway line, laden with disappointment, is his only comment on the legend that found its way into 'Kubla Khan', specifically 'Where Alph, the sacred river, ran / Through caverns measureless to man'.[36] We have previously referred to Alph, the shortened form of Alpheus, the river god, who fell in love with the water nymph, Arethusa. Ortygia is the site where their waters mingle. Coleridge does attempt a sketch of the vicinity, portraying a triangular outlet for the water, which today is more of a semi-circle. Gone is his 'square court walled by the rampart',[37] replaced by a curved wall and railings from which to view the reinvigorated spring and its profusion of much-pampered papyrus. The only reference that Coleridge seems to have made to the plant can be found in a notebook entry concerning a river trip with Denison where he is hemmed in by the 'lofty Syrinx'.[38] It is a fair assumption that the poet is referring here to papyrus by way of Greek myth. Syrinx was another of Artemis' nymphs who fell foul of one more in the long line of Classical stalkers; instead of Alpheus, Syrinx was pursued by the god, Pan, and, to escape, was transformed into hollow water reeds which made a melancholy sound when moved by the breath of the god. It is from this myth we derive pan pipes and the hollow-tubed syringe as a medical instrument. To Coleridge's mind, the tall slim stems of the papyrus resembled these reeds of legend.

The plant, in its more practical guise as an early vehicle for literature, seemed not to be of particular concern to Coleridge who was more apprehensive about the marshy areas in which it grew, given their propensity for generating disease. He later admitted to suffering a fever in Sicily, although as Donald Sultana points out, he described it as a 'nervous'[39] fever. We do not know if he medicated with laudanum, but we do know that he was both shocked and fascinated to learn that Sicily cultivated the opium poppy. There is much irony in this discovery considering he had chosen to go to the Mediterranean, in part, to flee from the clutches of addiction, prompted by the very substance he was now viewing.

Rather than hurriedly walk on, he inspected the crop in detail, noting cultivation methods, spacing, the watering regime and time of year when harvesting took place. He even made some incisions in the poppy heads and took away some grains. In his article 'The First Documented Case of Drug Addiction in Malta – Samuel Taylor Coleridge', Dr Paul Cassar asserts that Coleridge also discovered Indian hemp growing in Sicily but that he seemed to have foresworn the use of intoxicants whilst on the island, although this would not have included alcohol. The only evidence we have for him not partaking is that he makes no mention of it, but we can, however, discern that Coleridge continued, at least initially, to ride the wave of well-being he had first experienced whilst at San Anton in Malta.

Whether accompanied by Leckie, Denison or alone, Coleridge began to explore his surroundings more fully. He took trips to Augusta, to the north of Syracuse, and Noto to the south, although there is a frustrating lack of detail, particularly with regard to Noto which is one of the jewels of Baroque Sicily and now a part of the Val di Noto UNESCO World Heritage Site. Levelled in the 1693 earthquake, it was rebuilt over the following decades some ten kilometres from the original site. This audacious plan was overseen by the landowner, Giovanni Battista Landolina, with much input from the Syracusan architect, Rosario Gagliardi.

The soft tufa stone used for the buildings lends a warm hue to the town, especially during the early evening light, but its benign aura hides the potential demise of many façades as the tufa is incredibly prone to weathering. The gloriously sculpted balconies supporting ornate balustrades show signs of significant deterioration as air pollution and the rigors of nature eat away at the structures. As with many aspects pertaining to his time in Sicily, we cannot be sure that Coleridge did not expound more fully on Noto in documents that have subsequently gone missing, but perhaps we should not be surprised if there is little mention, given he was less than enthusiastic about the Baroque style observed in Syracuse itself.

Closer to Tremilia, he explored the Classical ruins of Neapolis and the Forum. For someone who read Latin and Greek, he showed scant interest in the buildings built by the Ancients. He visited the sites but it was always a geological feature or a quirk of nature that drew his attention, rather than the romantic imaginings inspired by the remnants and gleaned from the Classics that so excited other writers and diarists. Only once does he wax lyrical about the spit of land 'where Alcibiades & Nicias landed'[40] for the siege of Syracuse. As for the Forum, located in front of what is now Piazzale Guglielmo Marconi, he was more concerned with the locust trees, brambles and lizards than he was about the columns and capitals. In truth, we can understand this sentiment as the Forum is one of the least well-preserved areas of Classical antiquity in the city. It may be a little less wild than in Coleridge's time, but the decapitated columns still rise upwards from a tangle of wild berries, long grasses and oleander shrubs which, along with the railings, prevented us from striding between the pillars to measure the distances as the poet was able to do in 1804.

From here, he walked uphill along a path which now forms Corso Gelone towards Neapolis (the New City of antiquity) and the Latomie quarries. In fact, he made more than one visit to this area of Syracuse. In his notebook, he describes rooks flying overhead and, to his right, a blue 'wedge' of sea. Development in modern Syracuse has obliterated the view from the Corso but, to Coleridge, it seemed as though the city was a raft, yet to disgorge its passengers on the mainland. He makes cursory mention at this point of caves and caverns, but given these formations were spotted by him whilst descending to the bay, they do not appear to refer to the quarries at Neapolis. In later notebook entries, he makes specific reference to the named caves within the Latomie, specifically the Ear of Dionysius and the Grotta dei Cordari (The Rope-makers' Cave). He sketches a line drawing of the Ear, so called because legend has it that Dionysius used the cave to house prisoners and, thanks to the acoustic properties of its formation, was able to eavesdrop on their conversations from the cliff above. The name was coined by the painter, Caravaggio, who may well have also invented the story.

Once again, disinterested in the Classical allusions, Coleridge focused on the geometric layout and sound properties that the construction created. This was not the case for many fellow travellers who were drawn to this phenomenon, amongst whom was Swinburne who adds a footnote in his book attributing the nomenclature to

Caravaggio; although, it has to be said, even he is sceptical of the Dionysian connection as he explains the quarry was a place of confinement prior to the tyrant's reign. Brydone does not question the legend but mentions the cave as a monument to the ruler's 'ingenuity and magnificence'[41] as well as his brutality. He claims that the small hole at the top was where Dionysius concealed himself in order to listen in to the treacherous talk of his detainees and it is undoubtedly true that the walls are scarred with marks made by slave labour. One of the most accurate descriptions contemporary with Coleridge comes from the pen of the American, Washington Irving, who published *Notes and Journal of Travel in Europe, 1804–1805*:

> The Ear is a vast serpentine cavern, something in the form of the letter g reversed; its greatest width is at the bottom, from whence it narrows with an inflection to the top, something like the external shape of an ass's ear. Its height is about eighty or ninety feet, and its length about one hundred and twenty. It is the same height and dimensions from the entrance to the extremity where it ends abruptly.[42]

Of course, like any tourist who sets foot within the confines of the Ear, Coleridge could not resist the temptation to play with the echoes made by various sounds, from the human voice to the tearing of paper.

A few metres from the entrance to the Ear is the Grotta dei Cordari where, ever-observant of natural occurrences, Coleridge noticed the continual dripping of water from the cavern roof he describes as 'pink coloured' with the floor being 'shallowly flooded, and in dimpling Circles from the Drops'.[43] It is precisely this presence of water that made the cave ideal for the art of rope-making. Coleridge calls it the 'Rope walk Cavern',[44] which suggests a degree of artificial excavation that can be seen when looking at the geometrically sculpted entrance, not to mention the stone pillars and blocks left within the structure. We will not be the first to suggest that Coleridge's references to Neapolis are somewhat perfunctory and lack the vigour and excitement he saves for sites of natural splendour which provoked greater internal emotion. Given the poetic landscape of 'Kubla Khan' with its 'caverns measureless to man' and 'deep romantic chasm',[45] there must have been, however, an element of recognition and reinforcement in the poet's imagination as he wandered through the Latomie.

Coleridge was happier walking the Epipoli ridge through Neapolis and down to the Bay of Magnisi (which he incorrectly refers to as Manghisi), than he was exploring the crowded streets of Ortygia and its environs where, more than once, he referred to the filthy conditions; there was the less than salubrious setting of the meat stalls at the city gates and the grimy conditions he experienced near the opera house. He encountered Sicilians who were able to indulge in discussion about the opera and the weather but he lamented that, in the 'doctissima civitas of Cicero',[46] he could find no-one 'native' to talk of further subjects calling them 'ignorant beyond belief'.[47] This is an unforgiving assertion and some of the reason behind it is belied by another comment he makes on language. He complains of the islanders' bad Italian, also bemoaning his difficulty in learning a new language. He seems not to have realised that, from the peasant to the aristocrat, the people of Syracuse would have been conversing in Sicilian, not merely a dialect of Italian but, essentially, a separate language. Sicilian has a rich literary tradition, including an early poetical school and renowned poets contemporary with Coleridge, for example, Giovanni Meli. Therefore, there was a world of conversation and literary stimulus to be had that was denied Coleridge due to his inability to communicate in the vernacular.

Undoubtedly, Gould Francis Leckie shared a similar view of Sicily's aristocratic class and would have influenced Coleridge's own opinions. There is much British hauteur in these sentiments but historians recognise the core truth that there was a general dereliction of responsibility amongst the island's landed gentry during the twilight of the Bourbon monarchy. A few years after Coleridge's visit, Leckie went to the lengths of penning his own essay on Britain's influence which he called *An Historical Survey of the Foreign Affairs of Great Britain*. The book is very much of its era and shrouded in a degree of colonial rhetoric but there are moments of startlingly modern clarity:

> . . . in affairs of state, when we find that a plan undertaken has failed, and that the failure was occasioned not by the fortune of war, but by inattention to circumstances highly necessary to be considered, we naturally are led to appreciate the political abilities of the ministers under whom it originated; and it thence becomes a duty to dissipate the myths of falsehood with which adulation delights to envelop the historic page.[48]

He is equally piquant on the attitude amongst European nations towards international law: 'The law of nations and the sanctity of treaties are everywhere violated with impunity, and without shame.'[49]

The first three tracts are dated 'Syracuse, 1806' and he bangs the drum for the British Empire being the 'only opponent'[50] to aggression and conquest, which has a certain irony considering he was a proponent of intervention in Sicilian affairs. This mind-set, mirrored to a degree in Coleridge's own outlook, is rather blind to the arrogance of empire, seeing only the good in Albion's influence on the world stage. In his work *Written on the Water*, Samuel Baker argues that Coleridge's Mediterranean sojourn shows an 'imperialist evangelism' yet one tinged with 'reflections'[51] on his own opinions which incorporate both the Whig and Tory outlook in his political thinking. Baker makes the point that Coleridge seems to have lacked the foresight to appreciate the degree to which insular empire building would involve him in matters political, made even more complex by imperialists of Ball and Leckie's stamp.

Leckie would have discussed with Coleridge his philosophy with regard to British expansionism which he termed an 'insular strategy'. Leckie saw Mediterranean islands such as Sicily and Malta as key to British interests and a block to French domination. Diletta D'Andrea, who has written extensively on Leckie in Sicily, notes that he was in contact with the more proactive elements of the Sicilian ruling class, such as Abate Balsamo and Prince Belmonte, who favoured progressive policies; a testament to the fact that not all members of the aristocracy were rooted in the past. D'Andrea highlights the central plank of Leckie's philosophy, that the French were disruptors of the balance of power and that, consequently, Britain had to conquer an empire of islands. He makes no bones about the fact that this was far from a selfless act: 'By the conquest of these, she opens new fields of commerce, colonisation and riches to her own subjects.'[52] D'Andrea further illustrates his modus operandi which astutely recognised the power of arms was not, in itself, sufficient and that articulate persuasion and propaganda through journalistic endeavour were essential.

Given this stance which saw much power in the press, Leckie would have appreciated Coleridge's eloquent efforts in drafting reports for Ball and intended to use him for similar purposes. Coleridge referred to Gould Francis as 'a Sicilian subject and a man under especial obligations to the king of Naples'.[53] This was part of the reason why

Leckie could not, in 1804, openly voice his more risky political ideas; therefore, mouth-pieces were required to formulate policy concepts that he, himself, felt wary of enunciating. Coleridge, in the eyes of this Machiavellian puppet-master, was a useful conduit through which his message could reach a wider audience. Early on in his Sicilian notebook, Coleridge makes the assertion that the Italians would like to be English, by which he implies a desire for British protection against French invasion, specifically with reference to Sicily. He first read these views in Greenough's account, but attests to having heard these opinions from the mouths of intelligent orators. In the next entry, he gives an example of poor men and women having to resort to buckets and pails, trudging a distance to retrieve water because their absentee landlord was too short of cash and too disinterested to bother repairing the aqueduct. These initial ideas were only reinforced through long conversations with Leckie over dinner at the villa.

Once free of the constraints Coleridge describes, we can see through Leckie's subsequent writing how his opinions became more trenchant. His ideas of British influence in Sicily came to a degree of fruition when Lord Bentinck was sent to the island in 1811 by the British Foreign Secretary, Lord Wellesley. This led to the 1812 Sicilian Constitution which was based on a British model. No longer resident in Sicily, in the same year, Leckie published a tract entitled *Essay on the Practice of the British Government*, which was greeted by howls of protest from the more liberal and progressive sections of the commentariat. In the text, Leckie proposes a reactionary curbing of parliamentary reform, unless it went hand in hand with an increase in royal power:

> Let the violent advocates for Parliamentary reform and universal suffrage urge what they please, they will be cruelly disappointed, if they expect ever to convene an assembly of men perfectly wise and virtuous . . . Parliamentary reform is at best but a dangerous experiment, unless, at the same time, the royal prerogative be strengthened.[54]

The *Edinburgh Review* was scathing in attacking Leckie for both his opinions and prose style. Francis Jeffrey, in his review of the tract, claims that the *Essay* was 'the most direct attack which we have ever seen in English, upon the free constitution of England; – or rather upon political liberty in general'.[55] Jeffrey felt sure that Leckie was directing his ire at the 'inconveniences resulting from parliaments or representative legislatures...'[56] At the same time as Britain was helping to set up a constitution in Sicily, partially enacting the influence Leckie had advocated, the self-same man was attacking those who wanted to reform British constitutional arrangements at home. These ironies and contradictions were not unnoticed by Lord Byron's friend and fellow poet, Thomas Moore, who created a fictional poetic letter parodying correspondence between Colonel M'Mahon and Leckie:

> He thinks with you, the imagination
> Of *partnership* in legislation
> Could only enter in the noddles
> Of dull and ledger-keeping twaddles,
> Whose heads on *firms* are running so,
> They even must have a King & Co.,
> And hence most eloquently show forth
> On *checks* and *balances* and so forth.
>
> But now, he trusts, we're coming near a
> Far more royal, loyal era;
> When England's monarch need but say,
> "Whip me those scoundrels, Castlereagh!"
> Or, "Hang me up those Papists, Eldon,"
> And 't will be done – ay, faith, and well done.[57]

Byron, himself, had his own run-ins with Gould Francis. Moore recounts the story of Leckie's friend, Colonel Greville, taking exception to certain passages in the poem 'English Bards and Scotch Reviewers'. It was down to Leckie to deliver a missive to Byron, summoning the poet to a duel. Fortunately for all concerned, the matter was settled amicably. In another pointed barb, one of Byron's most famous poems, *Childe Harold*, contained a footnote adversely alluding to Leckie's political pamphlet, a comment that piqued the anger of its author who communicated his annoyance via letter to his Lordship. On this occasion, Byron had the grace to call upon Leckie, presenting him with a bound copy of the poem which specifically omitted the offending text.

These anecdotes and Leckie's own works provide ample evidence of his increasingly reactionary stance. Coleridge's willingness to co-operate in Leckie's propagandist schemes, albeit years prior to the events mentioned above, lend further weight to the accusations of political shape-shifting levelled at the poet. There are, however, hints of dissent in his notebooks — at one point, he reminds himself to watch his own tongue with regard to the merits of others and complains, 'will you never learn to appropriate your conversation to your company'.[58] There is also a further passage that criticises the narrow scope of Leckie's views, by which he is not just criticising political opinions but matters spiritual and philosophical as well. Coleridge championed the moral in public life but, as Donald Sultana illustrates, such issues were considered of little import in Leckie's political world view. At no point, though, do we ever get the impression that the two men indulged in heated argument, rather that they enjoyed their verbal sparring, with Leckie refusing to acquiesce to Coleridge's more forceful arguments.

Conversation at table was enlivened by the presence of Leckie's wife, whom Coleridge could not fail to notice as, indeed, was the case with many of the young officers who had cause to visit Tremilia during those years. A later passage in his notebook appears to refer back to her with an accusatory remark about coquettishness and her penchant for assuming that any man who glanced her way had nothing but lascivious intentions. These attitudes show Coleridge pulled in two directions — a very natural attraction to a striking woman, and, at the same time, a dislike of her reactions, leading to comments that frame the female as the disruptor of his equilibrium. His equilibrium was to be disturbed more violently still by Cecilia Bertozzi, the Prima Donna.

Cecilia, sometimes referred to as Anna-Cecilia Bertozzoli, was to become the leading lady of the Palermo opera company in 1809. Back in 1804, she was part of a touring group that had included Syracuse in its itinerary for the autumn season. Bertozzi first appears in Coleridge's notebook amongst a list of performers just above the tenor, Francesco Cariche. Underneath the list, he jots some phrases from the libretti of Guglielmi and Nasolini. These names appear in George Hogarth's *Memoirs of the Opera in Italy, France, Germany, and England* published later in 1851. He asserts that Guglielmi was of the Neapolitan school and achieved much fame on the continent, but was less-known in England. Nasolini also enjoyed his time in the sun but by the middle of the century, his works were fading. It is not known if the first opera attended by Coleridge was by either of these composers, but it is safe to assume that some of their works were performed by the company as they were still part of the canon at the time of Coleridge's stay.

Despite several attempts at researching Bertozzi's life and work, we were only able to uncover scant detail regarding her career. We know through Alessandro Loreto's *Musica e musicisti a Siracusa nel XIX secolo* that Cecilia was performing in the city the previous year, where she was listed as the 'prima buffa'[59] in *La Pescatrice*, a comic opera in three acts by Niccolò Piccinni. Bertozzi also makes an appearance in Christopher McKee's biography of the American naval commander, Edward Preble. In 1804, Preble set up a base in Syracuse and started to enjoy all that the city had to offer. McKee states that the opera house attracted the best singers in Sicily and that they benefitted from the largesse of the American sailors. The officers would throw coins on to the stage in appreciation of the performance; one officer in particular, in the months following Coleridge's visit, was enthralled by La Bertozzi and, as McKee says, maintained her well, financially. Said officer was Lieutenant John H Dent of the American ship, *Scourge*, and the above suggests a relationship that went beyond mere adulation, blurring the lines between romance, passion, sex and dependence.

These broken boundaries, splitting asunder the propriety found in English provincial life, were beyond anything that Coleridge could countenance; accordingly, he was tortured by his sexual attraction to Cecilia. It became apparent very early on in their friendship that the Prima Donna was equally attracted to him and happy to pursue a physical relationship without agonising over the consequences. Coleridge's notebook shows him theorising on the '"meeting soul" in music',[60] intellectualising the intensity of his operatic experiences – perhaps a way of deflecting his physical longings. However, it is during the small hours of the dark Mediterranean night that he seemed overcome with guilt at his true feelings, acknowledging to himself that his real desire was to consummate the relationship with Cecilia. To further complicate matters, Coleridge had seen a likeness in Bertozzi that reminded him of a younger Asra. To sleep with Cecilia would mean being unfaithful, not only to his wife but, principally, to Asra. On 11th October, he lay in bed at Leckie's villa unable to sleep, scribbling the following line: ' . . . (*here the voice of Conscience whispered to me, concerning myself & my intent of visiting la P. D. tomorrow*)'.[61]

Coleridge continued to visit Cecilia and the opera, punctuating his notebook with plot and titles such as the *Villane cantatrici*. We can imagine the nervous anticipation of each rendezvous as he made his way to the entrance of the theatre. The first sight today of the opera house is usually from Via Roma to the side of the cathedral and was the direction in which we approached the building, catching an initial glimpse of the scallop-shelled inset archway on the side of the structure. Gone are Coleridge's swaying poplar trees and the 'green lane'[62] he describes, replaced by traffic in an area planned before the invention of the automobile and, along the pedestrian routes, the throng of expectant tourists. Coleridge was later to claim that he was saved from succumbing to temptation by a vision of Asra's face whilst at Cecilia's bedside, painting her as 'the too fascinating siren',[63] under whose spell even Odysseus would have yielded.

To appreciate the situation from Cecilia's perspective, we turn to Maria Enrica D'Agostini and her work *Il paese altro*, which actually deals with the influence of the East on German culture, a society we know Coleridge appreciated. The central influence of the Orient is a metaphor for La Bertozzi's effect on the poet and D'Agostini makes the point that Cecilia, tired of Coleridge's 'intellectual idyll',[64] unambiguously took the initiative. We have, if somewhat stereotypically, the Englishman's cool, sexually-repressed Protestant theorising, in opposition to Bertozzi's Catholic seizing of the moment. It is little wonder, then, that the prima donna was subsequently happy to accept the more corporeal attentions of Lieutenant Dent.

Analysing Coleridge's behaviour at this moment of lust and guilt is a complex proposition and one that has to be filtered through a personal and societal lens. He is most definitely not of the Romantic school of free love which would be advocated by Percy Bysshe Shelley, who even suggested that Mary, his soon to be wife, indulge in a relationship with his friend, Thomas Jefferson Hogg. It is also wholly inconceivable that, had Byron been by Bertozzi's bedside, he would have refused her attentions. Coleridge appears to have seen Cecilia's uncomplicated offer as an endless maze of moral complication that could only lead to a corrosive regret. This is, in no small part, due to his religious beliefs. There is a revealing passage in his notebook that talks of Catholicism's reduction to the simplistic poles of pain and pleasure, concluding that even the good think, not of Heaven, but of Purgatory. His thoughts, conversely, would twist and turn, visions of Asra alternating with those of Cecilia, seemingly taking the roles of the angel and devil in his own nature. In this Miltonic clash of forces, Asra was the conquering power.

Coleridge, the pastor's son, saw this as a victory for his better nature. Was there, however, buried beneath this over-intellectualised analysis of feeling, the merest hint of frustration at a missed opportunity? Or were there fears of a more biological nature; had his years of opium abuse dulled his physical response?

Anthony John Harding sheds further light on the poet's motivations in his work *Coleridge and the Idea of Love*. He explains that Coleridge saw the love shared by brother and sister, devoid of any sexual connotation, as of great value owing to its purity, and that he held highly Christianity's doctrine that morality take precedence over physical desire, subordinating it to the conscience and will. Harding makes the claim that Coleridge's experiences in the Mediterranean, especially through his dreams, led to the realisation that he could separate love from sexuality, promoting the former without recourse to the latter. These conclusions would come on later reflection. In the moment, Coleridge felt a heady attraction for the talented, exotic Bertozzi in the sensuality of the Syracusan heat; Asra provided the icier water of platonic love to extinguish his desire. Interestingly, Coleridge's wife does not appear to enter the equation and she was clearly not the force required to reset his moral compass.

By way of distraction, Coleridge jotted his musings on the nature of opera itself. He had clearly read Metastasio, the librettist and poet, even quoting one of his letters, written in Italian, in his notebook. The passage mirrors Coleridge's own thoughts on the medium: 'And in fact one cannot talk to an audience and be clearly understood, without raising, extending and sustaining the voice notably further than in everyday speech . . .'[65] Metastasio goes on to say that these important alterations in voice require a degree of art. It was once again thanks to Leckie's well-stocked library that Coleridge had access to the Italian's letters. He also avidly read *Viaggio in Dalmazia* by the abbot, Alberto Fortis.

Unsurprisingly, being a Venetian, Fortis had chosen to write of his travels in Dalmatia, many of whose coastal towns still, to this day, bear the footprint of Venice. Coleridge had no intention of following in the abbot's footsteps, but he appreciated the clarity of his Italian and was attracted to the folkloric elements in the text. Fortis uses the term 'Morlachia'[66] to describe the hinterland of the area with specific reference to the Morlach people who could be either Catholic or Eastern Orthodox. Some scholars have postulated their connection to the

Vlachs, although for many centuries the Venetians saw them as anyone subject to the Ottoman's yoke. Fortis was drawn to the mournful epic ballads they sang, telling of their days under Turkish rule. It was this sprawling grandiose poetry that attracted Coleridge.

Whilst in moments of repose, he would also spend time preparing details for a political paper he intended to write on Sicily. This document has never come to light, although we can hazard a guess that it would have drawn substantially on the opinions and research of Leckie. It is a fair assumption that Coleridge gave the report to his friend, Adye, along with letters and, possibly, more detailed travel notes of his stay in Sicily. Adye collected the packet when he returned to Syracuse and then made his way to Gibraltar. It was there that, unfortunately, Adye succumbed to yellow fever with all his possessions being burnt to prevent the spread of infection. Coleridge had not taken the precaution of making copies and we can only glean hints of their potential content through his notebooks and writings in subsequent years.

It is also possible that the papers could have made reference to American ambitions in the Mediterranean theatre. At Leckie's villa, Coleridge was introduced to more than one American officer, including Commodore Preble and Captain Stephen Decatur who would also attain the rank of Commodore. Robert Allison, in his biography of Decatur, seems to suggest that Coleridge first met the captain in Malta, although Donald Sultana is convinced that they first rubbed shoulders at one of Leckie's evening gatherings. Decatur was principally a man of action who delighted the poet with nautical tales of adventure. Sultana describes him as little interested in lengthy debate and argument, although we can detect a flavour of his table-talk filtered through a Coleridgean lens, given that Samuel Taylor quoted him from memory in his essay, *On the Law of Nations*:

> Without local attachment, without national honour, we shall resemble a swarm of insects that settle on the fruits of the earth to corrupt and consume them, rather than men who love and cleave to the land of their forefathers. After a shapeless anarchy, and a series of civil wars, we shall at last be formed into many countries; unless the vices engendered in the process should demand further punishment, and we should previously fall beneath the despotism of some military adventurer, like a lion, consumed by an inward disease . . .[67]

This implies that Coleridge felt Decatur held the belief that America was growing rapidly and, at such a pace, it was in danger of imploding as success would come without the necessary struggle. This intricate analysis of his country's political and international development seems to fly in the face of his much quoted after-dinner toast, 'Our country! In her intercourse with foreign nations may she always be in the right, but our country right or wrong!'[68] This famous, perhaps infamous, quote has been challenged through the years, even being contested in the lyrics of the song 'For America' by the former Eagle, Jackson Browne.

There are many issues pinpointed in Coleridge's notebooks that indicate the simmering cauldron of tensions at this time in Sicily. Thrown into the pot, we have a Syracusan populace reliant on distant cities like Palermo and Messina for essentials; a distracted and disinterested aristocracy chasing hedonistic pursuits reminiscent of the Ancien Régime; a British presence pressing its own self-interested agenda; the addition of *arriviste* North American forces, and circling like sharks around the edge of this simmering stew, the French waiting to attack. At this very moment of delicate relationships, and just as Coleridge was planning to move on to Messina, a French privateer captured two British merchant vessels, hoping to obtain a ransom by dragging them to Syracuse harbour.

A map produced in 1784 by the Spaniard, José Moreno, shows that little has changed with regard to the basic shape of the port. Ortygia island throws a protective arm across the harbour mouth. Moreno refers to the bridge connecting the island to the mainland as the Puerta de tierra (Land Gate). Today, there are two bridges – the Ponte Santa Lucia and the Ponte Umbertino – either side of which small boats are moored. Just to the south east of the former of the two bridges is the modern yachting marina that looks out onto the commercial port where larger vessels dock. This area is well within the shielding curve of the bay and, according to Moreno's plan, was overlooked by castle ramparts. It was from these very fortifications that Coleridge saw General St Cyr's French ship lead his English captives into the harbour.

On 4th November, three days after the initial capture of the vessels, Alexander Ball in Malta had got wind of the debacle and had sent a navy cutter, *L'Hirondelle,* from Malta to Syracuse in order to intercede with the city's governor on behalf of the British. St Cyr did exactly the same on behalf of the French. There was a diplomatic and military stand-off with rhetoric and guns aimed at each other. Coleridge became involved when a deputation arrived at Leckie's villa requesting translation services on behalf of *L'Hirondelle's* captain, Skinner. Leckie, the American, Decatur, and Coleridge duly proceeded with a degree of haste back to the port to find a potentially explosive situation and a chaos of raucous opposing voices and insults.

Leckie, much more versed in Italian and experienced in the ways of Sicily, took the initiative. Although, as Donald Sultana indicates, Coleridge was relieved to understand the governor's clear Italian and was also able to make himself understood. It was Leckie who took down Skinner's demands and provided a written translation of them to the authorities. Coleridge decided that the best thing he could contribute was a calm and clear account of events that could be passed on to Ball in Malta. Richard Holmes highlights the crux of the matter as resting on the legitimacy of the French privateer's papers – could the ship rightly claim the spoils of war or was it simply a pirate vessel sailing under a flag of convenience? Despite Leckie's early realisation that the French would probably be proved in the right, especially after the papers were translated for the governor, Coleridge spent 6th November trading points of law with the port authorities whom he was convinced favoured the French.

The man charged by the Syracusan governor with assessing the situation duly returned a verdict in favour of the French and Captain Skinner was immediately put on the back foot. To aid the unfortunate mariner's account of events, Coleridge hastily agreed to leave for Malta on his ship so that he could present his own report which aimed to mitigate any loss of face and put forward the British case. In boarding *L'Hirondelle*, Coleridge turned his back on the transport that was waiting to take him to Messina. He lamented leaving the island and clearly still had plans to reach the city on the straits at some point in the future.

He left behind the siren of Syracuse but took with him a degree of psychological baggage and some poetic capital. Daniela Corona who, as we know, writes of the colonial influence on Coleridge, sees the resurgence of his thought about the poem 'Christabel' as suggestive of the reptiles and serpents spotted in the Syracusan landscape – a sultry parallel with the West Indies. For Corona, though, Sicily is orientalised and alienated by association with these elements of the Mediterranean world's nature and weather. It is true that Coleridge's government work was skewed towards Britain's colonial ambition, but his poetic imagery always drank from the well-spring of nature and for him to now turn away from a diverse landscape with all its sublime and thorny aspects would have been asking too much. The Mediterranean has been exerting its allure on northern Europeans for centuries and will continue to do so. It is a cliché to say that it is a voluptuary – a repository of sensualist imagery – but one that writers have fought against succumbing to easily. The author and journalist, Luigi Barzini, wrote convincingly on the sybaritic effect that crossing the Alps had on the Germans.

As Coleridge rounded Capo Passero at the tip of Sicily, *en route* for Valletta, he had many thoughts to reflect upon. He had escaped the land of the poppy and hemp largely unscathed by recourse to opium. The lively company of Leckie and the sheer enthusiasm for exploring a new location had occupied his mind and provided him with a degree of stimulus. There were low moments in his notebook where description and philosophy lapsed into melancholy and self-reproach; however, in better health than anticipated, he returned to Malta with renewed vigour and an appetite for further exploration of both Sicily and the Italian peninsula.

CHAPTER FOUR

# A Hand in Maltese Affairs

> Resembles life what once was deemed of light,
> Too ample in itself for human sight?
> *What is Life?*

On approaching Valletta on 8th November, *L'Hirondelle* made for the quarantine harbour at Manoel Island. Coleridge was now facing the prospect of a period of enforced confinement owing to the outbreak of yellow fever in Gibraltar which had made the Maltese authorities extremely wary of incoming vessels. Desmond Gregory in his book, *Malta, Britain, and the European Powers, 1793 – 1815*, informs us that Malta already had an efficient quarantine system prior to British rule and that it was one of the reasons why ships from the Levant used it as a common port of call throughout the eighteenth century. During periods of epidemic, no passengers or crew were allowed to disembark the vessels and any cargo brought ashore had to be disinfected. Gregory points out that the penalties for abusing this system were extremely harsh – anyone leaving a ship that had arrived from an infected area received the death penalty and anyone neglecting to inform the harbour administrators of rule infringements would be sent to the galleys for life.

From 1800, a certain William Eaton was given the position of Superintendent of Quarantine and told to follow the rules put in place by the Order of St John. One of the more fascinating aspects of the quarantine system, highlighted by Gregory, was the abuse of these laws for political ends when the British held uncertain power between 1801 and 1803. Ships carrying supporters of either the Order or the French were prevented from disembarking under the pretence of disease prevention when little in the way of contagion existed. This enabled the British to take matters even further and confiscate correspondence for supposed

**10** San Anton Palace Gardens, Malta (Suzanne Edwards).

**11** The Casino Maltese, Valletta, Malta, formerly The Treasury (Andrew Edwards).

disinfection when the real purpose was to copy any intelligence discovered; therefore, Eaton also doubled as a spymaster.

During the yellow fever outbreak of 1804, a lapse in quarantine saw a ship from Gibraltar offload goods and crew. The Royal Navy were notoriously contemptuous of these regulations. News of this breach reached the Italian coast and vessels from Malta were consequently placed under draconian measures. Alexander Ball realised the economic impact of this failure to follow the rules and created a Board of Health to oversee the situation. Coleridge, caught in the middle of this clampdown, found himself restricted to a cabin on board *L'Hirondelle* and unable to present his report in person to Ball – the very reason he had walked away from the carriage to Messina and rushed back to Valletta. The written report was passed to the governor without any of the verbal mitigations that Coleridge had intended to deliver. The quarantine also put pay to any notions of immediate onward travel to the north-eastern tip of Sicily.

Over a period of a week, Coleridge took refuge in reading – chiefly Italian – which, although he had left Sicily, was still going to be useful to him as the language of Maltese government declarations. Doubtless, he would have felt frustrated and limited by his confinement. Fortunately, the spread of the fever had been halted and nobody aboard *L'Hirondelle* succumbed to the disease. Eventually, the moment came when all concerned were given *pratique*, that is to say a licence to disembark, by the designated *pratique*-master. When Coleridge reacquainted himself with Maltese affairs, he discovered that the staffing situation was still in a state of flux. Alexander Ball had approached Captain Leake to undertake a corn-buying expedition upon Chapman's return from the Crimea. Donald Sultana states that it was common practice to send a different agent to the same region every year. It seems that Leake was yet to accept the commission but, if he were to do so, Ball wanted Coleridge to accompany him. The trip would entail the handling of a considerable sum of government money. There was also talk of British involvement in Sardinia and the possibility of Ball relocating and taking Coleridge with him. All of these potential avenues of adventure would see the poet handsomely rewarded; as always, his financial situation was less than healthy and he was acutely aware of debts to be paid back in England.

With these prospective opportunities very much at the forefront of his mind, Coleridge's equilibrium was jolted further when he discovered that his old rooms in the Governor's Palace had been given to someone else. He gathered together the few possessions he had brought with him or otherwise accrued and moved across the street to the treasury building in what is now Republic Street. It started its life as the administrative hub at the heart of Malta's economy in 1744 when it was acquired by the Order of St John and designated the *Casa del Comun Tesoro*. The structure has since become the Casino Maltese – a somewhat misleading title as it refers to an exclusive members' club rather than a gambling establishment.

On the wall, to the right of the door as you face the entrance, is a plaque commemorating Coleridge's stay with the following words: 'Samuel Taylor Coleridge, renowned English poet and writer, worked here, 1804–1805.' This reveals that he would remain at the treasury building for the rest of his stay on the island, although it neglects to inform the casual onlooker that it also doubled as his residence. In fact, his work would take him to the palace and other notable addresses requisitioned by the British administration.

The Casino has a certain air of gravitas and presents a serious façade to the world. As if harking back to its past as a financial institution, the exterior eschews any fripperies or overly-ostentatious architectural features. Two arched grilled windows, often shuttered, flank the recessed door which is outlined by columns mimicking the role of balcony support. The balconies above the doors and windows are actually supported by simply turned stone brackets. They form the dividing line between the plastered lower half and the upper storeys of the building where the sandy-coloured brickwork is revealed.

The interior, which we were not able to personally access, is visible to all on the Casino's website. The institution has saved its more flamboyant side for the internal decor, the main feature of which is a magnificent, branched marble staircase leading from the entrance hallway where a Maltese Cross has been inlaid in the floor design. The other rooms, such as the reading room and dining room, are more reserved but equally elegant. The bar is located at the heart of an interior courtyard.

Coleridge was given a room that no longer exists in the current configuration but was essentially a garret with views over the open sea and harbours in one direction and the Città Vecchia escarpment in the other. He referred to it as his 'sky-chamber'[1] given the ceiling was frescoed with figures representing the four winds which he called 'vomit faces'.[2] If this sounds like he hated the space, it would be incorrect, as he found the huge windows entrancing, particularly with regard to the view they afforded him of the Mediterranean moon; 'the roundest and brightest moon I ever beheld . . . '[3] This midnight lunar musing would initiate many philosophical and internally troubling questions.

Sultana mentions that, in his frescoed attic, Coleridge was attended by a servant called Giuseppe and quite rightly laments the lack of detail with regard to the poet's retainer, as he points out we are denied any amusing asides. This is in considerable contrast to those made by the likes of Byron who was quite happy to mention his servants, such as Tita Falcieri. Often, it is these characters who enliven the backstory of the protagonists they serve. Falcieri's interesting and colourful life has been explored further by his distant relative, Claudia Oliver, in her detailed biography, *A Most Faithful Attendant*. If only we had the insights of Giuseppe to broaden the metaphorical hinterland of Coleridge's troubled nights, moon gazing from his lofty windows.

For the time being, Coleridge was rather in limbo. The possibility of the grain mission to the Crimea hovered on the horizon, which he had agonised over accepting, as did the prospect of other gainful employment from Ball. In addition, he was continuing to fulfil aspects of the role of Under-Secretary. On 23rd November, a substantial convoy arrived from England bringing no personal news except an alarming overview of his debts, specifically the doubling of his life insurance premium. According to Sultana, Coleridge was engaged to translate a testimonial from Chevalier Conte, who had arrived on one of the ships in order to request a post in Ball's administration. The poet, never enamoured of the ornate language used in Italian bureaucracy, took it upon himself to Anglicise the text in terms of tone as well as wording; the finished product is in the UK National Archives.

Chevalier Conte was far from the only non-Briton to seek gainful employment in the Maltese civil service or military. The arrival of the convoy also saw an escalation in the on-going row about the use of troops from the island in British military manoeuvres. General Villettes was in charge of what was to become the Royal Regiment of Malta, otherwise known as the Maltese Corps. The majority of soldiers were recruited from the island's provincial battalions, but the corps would also go on to include Sicilians and Spaniards. Their role and command structure was hotly debated – Villettes wanted only English officers at the helm but, in practise, the corps had English, Germans and Maltese employed in commanding roles.

Against Villettes' high-handed wish for control and desire to suppress salary levels was set Alexander Ball's plan for an expansion in their deployment and an increase in their pay. Perhaps in response to the general's antagonism, Ball considered the rank and file undisciplined and unruly. The dispute would eventually filter down to the common soldier who naturally felt unhappy at receiving less remuneration than their brothers-in-arms in the Royal Corsican Rangers, despite higher wage levels than the aforementioned provincial battalions. Coleridge and the governor would have seen an expansion in the Maltese Corps as a way of enfolding the average Maltese deeper into the embrace of the British establishment.

Similar attempts were made in the field of agriculture. To demonstrate this, Ball took the poet on a riding tour of the island's *casals*. A *casal* is the term used for a rural village parish and we can look to see how they were structured by turning to Attard, the *casal* on the doorstep of San Anton Palace, Ball's summer retreat. The population of Attard petitioned Monsignor Pietro Duzina to become a separate parish in 1575 and took advantage of its central position as a staging post between Notabile and Valletta to develop agriculturally. The settlement suffered during the 1798–1800 insurrection against the French; in particular, as Henry Frendo illustrates in *Attard: The Life of a Maltese Casale*, because there were two opposing houses, the Bonavitas and the Barbaros, the former supporting the insurrection and the latter behind the occupying forces. In 1798, the death toll rose by 58, a considerable 364% increase on the previous year – war and famine were to blame. Ball's initiative was designed to redevelop these areas.

Each *casal* had an appointed *luogotenente*, which Barry Hough and Howard Davis in *Coleridge's Laws: A Study of Coleridge in Malta*, call 'civil magistrates'.[4] It is a significant matter that Coleridge would now meet these *luogotenenti* on his tour of the island as his subsequent position in the administration would require him to issue these people with formal orders, although as we shall see, he would be happy to delegate. Coleridge characterised them as contented yeomen, perhaps a nod to the simple rural life he had observed in Somerset. The conditions he experienced though were far from the green rolling pastures and moorland of Nether Stowey. The fields were covered with rock-ridden soil;

the heat and wind turning them into dustbowls causing endless eye complaints among the locals.

The major flora consisted, in his eyes, of capers and prickly pears, both edible but perhaps not to his taste. He also remarked upon the magnificence of the stonework in such rural locations, stone being one resource that was not lacking. He attributed this to the legacy of the knights and their taste for architectural development. He was particularly taken with the parish church at Birkirkara, some five kilometres (three miles) to the east of Attard. He supposed the unfinished tower was due to a lack of money. In fact, the Parish Church of St. Mary had fallen into disrepair and, in 1787, the visiting Bishop Vincenzo Labini was shocked by its perilous state, remarking that the roof was dangerously close to collapsing. Today, the edifice is still lacking a tower and part of the frieze on the pitched roof, but is no longer deemed a danger and has not only been reinstated as a place of worship, but also listed as a Grade 1 national monument.

Aside from the stonework, Coleridge's attention was drawn by the plan for botanical development in each village. The legacy of this initiative can be seen in the list of crops and flora that Henry Frendo details in Attard. Amongst these are vines, tomatoes, watermelons, citrus and olives – a list far beyond Coleridge's scrubby capers and the barbed fruit of the Indian fig. In truth, he also noticed the sowing of corn and the end of the cotton harvest – both important to the local economy and prone to the vagaries of war. Doubtless, he was comparing his tour of the *casals* with Ball to the forays into the Sicilian countryside he undertook with Leckie. This period of time was accompanied by mild weather of the sort that, superficially at least, improved his mood. However, his notebook entries betray his deeper upset at the realisation that he was but a pawn in the imperial game, complaining of the way that powerful men made '*instruments* of their fellow-creatures'.[5]

Coleridge found further detail of concern whilst talking to Captain Leake. It seems Samuel Taylor had made errors of calculation with regard to the amount of fertile land available in Egypt whilst writing one of the previous reports for Ball. He had lifted his figures from Henry Brougham whom Leake knew to be inaccurate, which prompted him to re-write the paper and add an extensive appendix of exculpation. It is fair to say that this error rankled with Samuel Taylor who continued to explain himself, even on return to England. The fact that Ball had another employee check the statistics may well have contributed to Coleridge's on-going embarrassment. The man responsible for double-checking, Charles William Pasley, would nevertheless go on to become a friend of the poet's. Their burgeoning friendship, though, probably had more to do with Pasley making use of the telescope in the observatory above Coleridge's room in the Treasury.

The lead up to Christmas 1804 saw Coleridge remain undecided about his future. In a letter to his wife, he promised to send money home and pay his insurance premium. He raised his status to that of confidential secretary and spelt out the degree of responsibility he would undertake if required to travel to Odessa. In reality, he had decided to keep all the potential plates spinning, without discounting a return to England. We suspect the latter was a pacifier to avoid an angry response from Sara Coleridge. The real driving force behind any impending return was undoubtedly linked to his passion for Asra and a desire to see his children. The letter is set down in a stream of consciousness, twisting, turning and contradicting at every stage. He could come home; he could go to Sardinia; he could earn good money if things came to fruition, but ultimately, he was in an intractable situation. Caught between financial, emotional and physical instability, his addictions of mind and body hounded him without escape.

He could always turn for comfort to Wordsworth and the manuscript chiefly written out by Dorothy, William's sister, but also in the hands of Mary Wordsworth, Asra (Sara Hutchinson) and William himself. They copied out much more than just the first five books of *The Prelude*; there was also 'The Pedlar', forty-three sonnets and forty-one other works. It seems that Coleridge must have had the leaves bound whilst in the Mediterranean as the instructions written to the bookbinder were in Italian. The finished product is now known as *The Malta Notebook* and is on display at Wordsworth's Dove Cottage in Grasmere. An article subsequent to his stay in Malta, written by Coleridge in *The Friend*, reveals that he read one of William's poems from this text to Alexander Ball and his wife. The piece in question was *Peter Bell*.

This poem, although written in 1798, was not published until 1819; therefore, Coleridge was giving the Balls privileged access to a work hitherto largely unknown. He had promised the Wordsworths that he would prevent anyone copying verses from *The Malta Notebook*, but recitation appears to have been acceptable. *Peter Bell* is written with a degree of mock solemnity, starting with a prologue that details the poet's rovings around the earth and heavens in a boat of the imagination. The poet rejects fanciful subjects, instead choosing the seemingly mundane and hard-hearted purveyor of pots, Peter Bell. The original description of Peter tells of a man, cruel in thought and action: 'Full twenty times was Peter feared / For once that Peter was respected'.[6] His discovery of a dead man in the water, and a stubborn mule which he beats relentlessly in a bid to ride away, are the beginnings of the reawakening of his conscience and a softening of his attitudes.

In 1819, the poem received a less than favourable critical response. Byron, who famously rhymed 'Wordsworth' with 'Turdsworth', was prompted to write in his magnum opus, *Don Juan*, that he 'makes / Another outcry for 'a little boat', / And drivels seas to set it well afloat'.[7] The diarist and newspaper correspondent, Henry Crabb Robinson, thought that William had 'set himself back ten years by the publication of this unfortunate work'.[8] Sadly, we have no indication as to the way in which the work was received by the Balls, other than that recounted by Coleridge in *The Friend*:

> Works of Amusement, as Novels, Plays &c. did not appear even to amuse him: and the only poetical Composition, of which I ever heard him speak, was a Manuscript Poem written by one of my Friends . . . it was evident to me, that it was not so much the poetic merit of the Composition that interested him, as the Truth and psychological interest with which it represented the practicability of reforming the most hardened minds . . .[9]

There is no mention of the response from Lady Ball, who was the primary target of the recitation. We can assume that she was open to this kind of literary evening given she often crossed paths with Coleridge, exchanging conversation on matters unrelated to the government and politics. More than one biographer has questioned the veracity of her husband's reaction given that Coleridge, in the years subsequent to Malta, was prone to placing his words in the mouths of others. In this regard, one of the most scathing critics of this Coleridgean tendency was Thomas De Quincey:

> We really beg pardon for having laughed a little at these crazes of Coleridge; but laugh we did, of mere necessity, in those days, at [Dr Andrew] Bell and Ball, whenever we did not groan . . .

Coleridge, we are well convinced, owed all these wandering and exaggerated estimates of men – these diseased impulses, that, like the *mirage*, showed lakes and fountains where in reality there were only arid deserts – to the derangements worked by opium.[10]

De Quincey is, of course, talking here of the period during which Coleridge worked on *The Friend*, but there is some evidence that by mid to late December of 1804, he had begun to resort once again to laudanum and to increase his alcohol intake. His notebook for 23rd December recounts '*involuntary* intoxication'[11] which prompted an ill-advised drunken letter to Southey and much personal recrimination with regard to his addiction to opium. A further notebook entry compares the pains restricting his mental capacity to that experienced by an eagle encircled by a constricting serpent. His escape, which he claimed was never 'pleasure for its own sake',[12] was laudanum. De Quincey felt that Coleridge's addiction was detrimental to his poetry – 'a fountain choked up with weeds'[13] – but that it 'roused and stung by misery his metaphysical instincts into more spasmodic life'.[14]

Thomas De Quincey, the opium eater *par excellence*, was also inclined to speculate on Coleridge's initial dabbling with the drug as being something more than mere pain relief. In his treatise, *Coleridge and Opium Eating*, he even recounts the gossip that Gillman, the doctor in Highgate who aimed to wean Samuel Taylor off opium, was actually persuaded to partake by Coleridge himself: 'And scandal says (but, then, what will not scandal say?) that a hogshead of laudanum goes up every third month through Highgate tunnel'.[15]

All of this speculation prompts a vision of Coleridge, his laudanum-induced shining face 'as glorious as that of Æsculapius',[16] expounding the virtues of a converted Peter Bell to an enthralled Lady Ball and a bemused Alexander, who was politely listening but with much less enthusiasm for the poetic artistry or even the moral message indicated by the reciter. There is a copy of a portrait of Ball in the Maltese National Archive situated in Rabat. A visit to the archive is desirable for anyone on the Coleridge trail in Malta. We were surprised to find it located in a former Franciscan Convent which once incorporated the Santo Spirito Hospital complete with an intriguing little rotating wooden portal set into the bleached stone. On investigation, this small door became tainted with a great deal of sadness as it was the means by which babies were left to the care of the nuns. These unfortunate little bundles were anonymously placed in the niche and the doorway was revolved inwards for the child to disappear from sight.

Sadly, the archive holds no correspondence directly relating to Coleridge. Given he was part of the British Administration, the UK National Archives in Kew, as we have already noted, hold valuable documents. There is, however, information pertaining to John Stoddart with regard to letters in the CSG 03 section and some of his writings on the law of Malta in CSG 47/1. Correspondence regarding Ball is located in the GOV Despatches category. The photograph of Ball's portrait, held at Rabat, shows a man of middle-age, dressed in full naval regalia with golden epaulets on a brocade-edged dark blue jacket. He is wearing a ribboned medal and the overall impression is one of a meticulous, self-contained man. His face is narrow with a high forehead; his receding grey hair formed into a widow's peak. Large eyes, evading the onlooker's gaze, appear serious but do not convey either sadness or frippery. He seems a man little given to the extremes of emotion, traditionally associated with the Romantic poets.

Ball and Stoddart, who had first given Coleridge a roof over his head in Valletta, were at this point in 1804 moving closer in their aims and beliefs. Donald Sultana indicates that, initially, Ball had seen John Stoddart as a meddler in legal affairs who had the potential to line his own pockets. Stoddart, as the King's and Admiralty Advocate in the Court of Vice Admiralty, now had the opportunity to earn some serious money from the Spanish vessels detained in Valletta on the outbreak of war between Britain and Spain. There is a certain irony in this as the advocate was fulfilling the potential that Ball had once feared yet now seemed to accept and even praise. In the background, Coleridge began to take an interest in these legal matters, although he was yet to interact directly with the court. There is evidence that he was becoming increasingly antagonistic towards Stoddart and the resentment was mutual.

Over the Christmas period, Coleridge decided to read *De Juro Maritimo et Navali* by Charles Molloy, the Latin maritime law text used by the aforementioned Maltese court. In counterpoint to this straight-laced and ethical juridical tome, he also turned to Machiavelli's *Istiorie fiorentine*, with all its power struggles and political intrigue. It is difficult to escape the conclusion that Coleridge was flexing his intellectual muscle in order to keep abreast of the various debates and machinations that could ensue from the current state of Maltese politics; an indication, perhaps, that his mind was still fixing upon further employment on the island. Machiavellian thought clearly left a permanent mark on the poet as later paragraphs in *The Friend* are peppered with the Florentine's quotes: '"There are Brains of three races. The one understands of itself; the other understands as much as is shewn it by others; the third neither understands of itself nor what is shewn it by others"'.[17] In his garret in the Treasury, Coleridge would have undertaken this pigeon-holing exercise, allocating those he knew to the three categories.

Further to his reading habits and De Quincey's allusion to poetry 'choked up with weeds', there is additional self-criticism of the vocabulary he used, quoted by Sultana as being 'deformed with Germanisms'[18] owing to his extensive reading of the philosophers who wrote in that language. The background to his post-Christmas reading is an unhappiness lost in a haze of opium intake and alcohol, although he had the good sense to withdraw his drunken letter addressed to Southey from the packet of items he would despatch on the next available convoy, which included his corrected paper on Egypt. He had to wait until early January for a return convoy with much anticipated news from England. It was prevented from docking in Valletta by a raging *grigal*, the strong, bitter wind from the north-east, otherwise known as a *gregale*, *grecale* or *graigos*. It is said to originate from the island of Zakynthos, hence the Greek origins of the name, and has a cooling yet chaotic effect. Coleridge mistakenly reversed its direction, but was right about its properties. Like its Adriatic cousin, the *bora*, the *grigal* has a weapon-like intensity when attacking shipping.

The delay forced upon the convoy created much agitation and a further lowering in Coleridge's mood. The depressive effects of the alcohol and opium combined with the annoying and mood-deflating presence of the wind left him with the near-certain premonition of bad news in the letters he was anticipating. In fact, he was heartened to receive good news of John Wordsworth's prospects and surprised to hear that William and Dorothy were considering a move from Dove Cottage. News from Asra, though, left him with little optimism regarding their future, provoking musings on hope and the sensation of touch, tinged with much pessimism. Richard Holmes refers to a ciphered entry at this point in his notebook concerning 'eunuchs in all degrees'[19] which he feels may allude to Coleridge's fear that his drug habit would lead to impotence. The dread of bad dreams also returned which he medicated with more opium that could only lead to an ever decreasing circle of increased intake and terrifying nightmares.

In the midst of these waves of mental and physical fragility, stilled by moments of relief afforded by the improvement in the weather and the beauty of the Città Vecchia ridge, Coleridge was faced with a major decision. On 18th January, Macaulay, the Public Secretary, died and he was offered the position by Ball. There is good reason to believe that Ball expected Coleridge's appointment to be relatively brief and, indeed, Coleridge, on accepting the placement, described his new Public Secretary role as '*pro tempore*'. The person originally lined up to replace the aged Macaulay was Chapman but he was still stuck in the Crimea; hence, the notion that Coleridge was just filling in until Chapman's return which was expected to be at any moment. So confident of this was Samuel Taylor, that he wrote to the Wordsworths shortly after the Public Secretary's death saying that he would be back in England by the end of March.

It was assumed that Chapman would step into the roles of secretary and treasurer, but Coleridge refused to take on the post in the Treasury, an early indication that he knew this increase in administrative duties would be all-consuming. As Hough and Davis illustrate, the Public Secretary, alone, was central to the Maltese administration. Policy making and legal powers were directly in the hands of the Civil Commissioner (Ball) and his secretary was the person who headed the executive and ensured the smooth-running of the administration through which policy was delivered. We have noted a tacit tendency for some looking into Coleridge's life to skate over the Maltese years as if dabbling in law-making on a small Mediterranean island was unworthy of the great poet. However, like Michael John Kooy, who wrote the introduction to Hough and Davis' *Coleridge's Laws*, we feel that his decisions and proclamations had a direct practical impact on many people's lives. In fact, Kooy goes so far as to say that the research in the book proves that the legal proclamations known as *bandi* and *avvisi* were altogether 'destabilising'.[20] Despite Coleridge's poetic genius and talent for metaphysics, the role of Public Secretary was quite possibly the most responsible position he had ever held.

Although he had refused the additional Treasury duties, Coleridge was still in control of a team and acting as Ball's right-hand man, all of which meant he was handsomely remunerated. He could also take a seat in the *Segnatura* – essentially, the ruling council. He would now come into direct contact with the Court of Vice Admiralty, issue passports, administer sworn statements and the aforementioned *bandi* and *avvisi*, in addition to the onerous task he most despised, arbitrating in disputes. There were several government departments for which he acted as an overseer: Customs, the Almoner's Office, the Printing Office, the Tribunals, the Post Office, the Quarantine and Harbour Departments, the hospitals including those for orphans and invalids and, despite his refusal to act as a Treasurer, the Public Treasury. There was also the Università, not simply an educational institution as the name would suggest, but a key vehicle in the Maltese economy – an organization with local government functionality originally set up by the Grand Masters of the Knights. The Università monopolised the buying and supply of grain, as well as other indispensable food items. As we can see from all of the above, Coleridge was not merely dabbling in the publication of a few minor legal documents but was at the heart of decision making and the island's well-being. It is fair to say that he was not a little daunted by the prospect and was hoping Chapman would make a swift return.

Coleridge had been a pamphletist and opinion piece writer for newspapers in the past, during which time he had espoused views on many subjects of a political nature. Now, for the first time, he was charged with implementing actual policy. In a situation with many modern parallels, albeit of a considerably more serious nature, Coleridge's ideals were to clash with *realpolitik*. We have already hinted at the occasional divergence of opinion with Ball, but Coleridge's lionising of the governor in later years can be seen as a way of justifying his own actions as a Public Secretary. If Ball's opinions were 'unwarped by zealotry, and were those of a mind seeking after truth in calmness and complete self-possession',[21] as the poet would write in *The Friend*, then surely his own actions in government were as even-handed as they could be.

Before Coleridge could get to grips with his new role, he had to move once again. He came down from the dreaming, moonlit garret in the Treasury and transferred his possessions to a ground floor apartment which he described in his notebook as facing 'the piazzas and vast saloon built for the archives and library and now used as the garrison ballroom'.[22] The piazzas in question are the larger Misraħ San Gorg or (St George's Square) and the smaller Misrah Ir-Repubblika (Republic Square) which was then called the Piazza Tesoreria and subsequently Queen's Square. Coleridge found it congenial as it was a popular haunt for booksellers and an easy place for him to pick up inexpensive Italian editions of works that interested him. He mentions a dictionary written by Lorenzo Franciosini di Castelfiorentino who was the first Italian to translate *Don Quixote* as *L'ingegnoso cittadino Don Chisciotte della Mancia*. It is unclear, though, which of Franciosini's various lexicographical texts Coleridge had purchased, especially as he was considered an eminent hispanist.

Today, Misrah Ir-Repubblika still retains the statue of Queen Victoria – hence its previous incarnation – and is as busy as it would have been in 1805. The library, founded by Grand Master Emmanuel de Rohan-Polduc in 1776, continues to face the Casino Maltese and is the home to some of the *bandi* and *avvisi* directly related to Coleridge's tenure as secretary. The square is usually filled with outdoor, parasol-shaded tables from the sumptuously decorated Caffè Cordina which neighbours the Casino and forms the corner of Republic Street where it joins Misra San Gorg . The throng of Maltese street-life that had initially upset Coleridge's senses now came back to disrupt his increasingly scarce leisure hours. Hawkers, military gatherings and casual encounters conducted at high decibels all contributed to undermine the extended office hours he was now expected to keep.

One of his first tests of principle was a visit to some Spanish and French prisoners. Donald Sultana mentions Coleridge's poems 'The Dungeon' and 'The Devil's Thoughts' as illustrations of his hitherto fierce condemnation of poor prison conditions, and it is worth quoting from the former by way of showing the degree to which reality would have collided with his ideals: 'Is this the only cure? Merciful God! / Each pore and natural outlet shrivelled up / By Ignorance and parching Poverty, / His energies roll back upon his heart, / And stagnate and corrupt; till changed to poison, / They break out on him, like a loathsome plague-spot . . . '[23] The dungeon in question is medieval but the retaliatory poor conditions for prisoners in the Napoleonic wars were, in many ways, a hark back to the Middle Ages. The nature of punishment would continue to prick Coleridge's conscience at this time. Hough and Davis note that there are some instances where Alexander Ball's legal penalties went beyond customary Maltese law, i.e. the *Code de Rohan* instituted by the Knights of Malta, and were dependent upon the whim of the governor.

Specifically, we can look at the *avviso* dated 22nd May 1805 where the public at large were told of the punishment to be meted out to

Andrea Borg, Giovanni Hasciach and Saverio Bonello. The British had removed certain restrictions on Jewish immigration to the island which had led to threats against the community, in addition to the spreading of vicious rumours, notably the blood libel, that vengeful slander which claimed Jews killed Christian children for their rituals. The aforementioned three detainees were accused of inciting hatred and duly convicted. Bonello was only twelve at the time and Borg had been roaring drunk. It is difficult to escape the conclusion that they were scapegoats designed to set a harsh example should more civil disobedience become prevalent. Hough and Davis remark upon the speed with which the *avviso* was issued, given Coleridge's significant commitments, and feel that the punishment was directly from the pen of Ball rather than any court. The penalty was also beyond anything permitted by the *Code de Rohan*. Coleridge's *avviso* makes no mention of due process, simply saying that 'Ed è determinazione di S. E. di trattare nella medesima guisa . . .'[24] (And it is the determination of his Excellency, the Governor, to treat, in the same manner . . . )' (translation authors) anyone else engaged in such gossip. Coleridge was a champion of a separate judiciary and this ruling flies completely in the face of these values.

We can see from the date of the above *avviso* that Coleridge had not been given the opportunity to leave in March as he had intimated to his wife; Chapman was still detained abroad. Instead, he found himself walking an increasingly fine line between the demands of government and an ever-growing restlessness amongst the general Maltese population. Donald Sultana makes the claim that it was Coleridge's Protestantism that prevented him from making any Maltese friends given his numerous sneers at 'Catholic superstition'.[25] Whilst it is true that he was always dismayed to find religious iconography in government or health institutions, we tend to think that a lack of fraternisation between the British ruling class and the Maltese was, as Hough and Davis suggest, a consequence of friendships being officially discouraged. This feeds into Coleridge's observations in Gibraltar that British *sang-froid* and *hauteur* were generally disliked in the Mediterranean. Indeed, the poet was critical of such attitudes but was bound by his position.

Ball, in miscalculating the economy, had created a situation that required the reintroduction of certain taxes which the locals considered a broken promise. By March, excise duty on wine had been reinstated and the tax on spirits increased. The Maltese clamoured for some form of participation in government which would prevent Ball from making unilateral decisions. Coleridge was the chief means by which the administration could promote new initiatives to placate the populace. He was also in the unenviable position of having to present unpopular news in the best possible light, not to mention tackling the near impossible task of ensuring the island had a workable welfare system without a significant increase in the tax burden. Had Coleridge been given a free hand and limitless money, he would have been able to adhere more closely to his cherished principles and his insistence on the social function or idea attached to a given political institution.

The *bandi* and *avvisi*, as mentioned, were written in Italian. Although Coleridge had been progressing with the language and had been exchanging conversation with Barzoni, the journalist, there is every reason to think that he would have had some compositional help, albeit in translation, from the likes of Giuseppe Zamittello. Nevertheless, he admits that the writing of these and other documents such as public letters 'belongs to my talents rather than my *pro-tempore* Office'.[26] He was also tuning his ear to the sonorous values of the language which he called, in his notebook, a 'pomp of sound'.[27] The language in the proclamations, though, owes little to the literary output of Dante or Boccaccio and was designed to address the people directly. Doubtless, the legislative changes announced in this manner would have gone through multiple translations. Coleridge would have made his initial draft in English, perhaps attempting his own Italian version, which was then proofed by a more competent hand. Once published, the average Maltese was unable to read the text, due to both poor literacy levels and a lack of Italian. Somebody from each village, competent in the language of Dante, would have provided a verbal rendition for the gathered populace.

Hough and Davis feel that Coleridge tried to avoid a simple reiteration of facts in his published notices, instead trying to flesh them out with more narrative. One such example can be found in the case of Fortunata Tagliana, who had a Jewish soldier followed and beaten. The document does give the facts as Coleridge understood them, but also adds some interesting vignettes. Tagliana was exiled to Gozo where Coleridge expected that 'with the change in air' she would 'find a cure for her fanaticism'[28] (translation by Lydia Davis). Likewise, the notice written to prevent boats misusing an anchor positioned by way of warning in a narrow channel. The document ends with Coleridge stating that 'any person who continues to misuse this marker will have only themselves to blame if they are welcomed by rifle shots'[29] (translation Lydia Davis).

It was not long before Coleridge was confiding thoughts of overwork to his notebook. His life was settling into a dull routine of office administration, punctuated by often lonely evenings of spirits, laudanum and introspection. Outside the direct circle of the Balls, there was the occasional foray into Valletta's nightlife, notably his February trip to the Teatru Manoel, the city's baroque theatre whose interior grandeur is hidden behind a more modest façade. Situated in Triq it-Teatru l-Antik or Old Theatre Street, the theatre has admittedly lost some of its exterior decoration due to heavy-handed restoration in the twentieth century. Inside, the theatre-stalls are surrounded by four tiers of ornately decorated golden boxes rising to a ceiling that tricks the eye into believing it is a domed cupola. During the British period, opera was the main form of entertainment, although dramas by the likes of Goldsmith, Coleman and Morton were added to the repertoire in addition to Italian works. The actors were predominantly amateurs drawn from the floating populace. Coleridge showed his more prudish and priggish face regarding the work he had gone to see, considering the unnamed drama in question to be rather dissipated. Consequently, he left directly after the performance without staying for the comedy encore or drinks.

It was now a matter of course to end the day with opium and the evening of the theatre trip was no different. As with so many subsequent nights, a drug-induced escapist slumber was followed by remorse; although in this instance, he avoided the excruciating nightmares that could ensue. Sultana cites this occasion as the point at which he moved from intellectualising religious theory to his own perceived direct experience of Original Sin and Redemption. 'O me miserum,'[30] he cried on awaking the following morning. If the pleasure of sleep provoked remorse at drug use, the opposite seems to have been the case with regard to his nightmares. The almost puritanical fear of a pleasurable narcotic sleep caused much anguish but the nightmares seem strangely separated in his mind from opium use. Rather than seeing them as a direct result of addiction, he succumbed to opium as a means of 'sweet sleep',[31] thereby supposedly avoiding the night terrors. It would be nearly a decade after returning from Malta before he eventually admitted to himself and the wider world that the Fuseli-like incubus that intimidated him at night was found inside a laudanum bottle.

Coleridge's analysis and theorising with regard to his dream-states appear to be a way of explaining and partially controlling their existence. The opium plunged his mind to the depths of childhood anxiety which he examined through the most acute of his adult faculties. Charles Lamb, the poet's friend from his early days, made this pertinent observation in his 'Witches and Night-Fears' article from *The Essays of Elia*: 'Gorgons, and Hydras, and Chimæras dire – stories of Celæno and the Harpies – may reproduce themselves in the brain of superstition – but they were there before. They are transcripts, types – the archetypes are in us, and eternal'.[32] The poet's drug taking was the key that unlocked these archetypes and let them roam unfettered through his brain during the small hours. Also troubling his conscious and unconscious mind were the debts now beginning to crowd in and his mood was further depressed by the realisation that little of his correspondence had reached its intended target – falling victim to the briny depths in order to escape prying French eyes.

Personal debt was not his only concern. With hindsight, it is easy to see that the institution of the Università was in financial difficulty. An 1812 Royal Commission report found enough evidence to indicate ostensible debt levels had risen to significant figures. Ball was to admit that there had not been sufficient inspection of accounts. In 1805, purchased grain was deemed to be fit only for animal feed. There is no evidence to suggest Coleridge made direct decisions affecting the Università – if anything, there is a significant gap in documentation bearing his name in this respect. Some researchers have pointed out that this indicates he delegated to the likes of Zamitello, but was this through overwork, lack of experience or previous precedent? The taxing of the Università's grain was not desirable as it was deemed a staple and, in view of its poor quality, little justification could be made, hence Ball's excise duty on wine and Coleridge's emphasis on public health through reduced alcohol consumption – a nanny state inference that he did not apply to his own consumption. This was, though, more propaganda as political expediency trumped the moral high ground.

The Maltese countryside, specifically San Anton, continued to provide him with respite and inspiration. The springtime blossom and vibrant flora were a temporary reprieve from his increasingly dark mood which was sent into a downward slide at the end of March when he was confronted with the news that William Wordsworth's brother, John, had been lost at sea. It was Lady Ball who conveyed the news of the three-hundred souls who had perished on the *Earl of Abergavenny*. Coleridge was felled by the shock of this sudden news and immediately retreated to his home in the Treasury. There were tears, not just because of his own grief, but for John's brother and sister and, as he wrote in his notebook, even for Sara Hutchinson, given Asra had been connected to John as a possible future wife.

Lady Ball seems to have been surprised at the depth of feeling he showed in his mourning for William Wordsworth's brother and wrote to him, fearing that these emotions would have a detrimental effect on his general health and well-being. The tragic event started a chain reaction in Coleridge's mind which saw him catastrophize each and every scenario concerning those he loved and the fate that might befall them – who would be next to die? William, himself? Or, worse still, would it be Asra? Would he ever see England again? Would he perish at sea? Drugs and alcohol only exacerbated these dark and paranoid thoughts.

Richard Holmes, in his biography of the poet, tells us that Coleridge's period of mourning and consequent ill health lasted for a couple of weeks. As part of his rehabilitation, he went on a riding tour through the countryside up to the heights of Città Vecchia where he had a view over St Paul's Bay all the way around to Valletta. St Paul's, including the resort of Bugibba, is now a popular tourist destination and has been greatly developed since the nineteenth century. Looking down on the bay today, we saw the coast lined with brilliant white, homogenous apartment blocks and hotels spreading backwards into the hinterland. Essential for the modern Maltese economy, they nonetheless draw the eye away from the natural beauty of the Mediterranean *maquis* and the strident blue of the sea which, for a few precious minutes, diverted Coleridge away from his despondent thoughts.

The lighter duties during his time of grief soon gave way to the resumption of his hectic daily schedule, but the shock of John's death further accentuated his indecision and despair regarding his own future. He was most reluctant to return to his wife and had fallen into the routine of British colonial life in the Mediterranean. Although he continued to complain of the workload, his evenings were convivial enough when he was invited to the Balls' at the palace or San Anton where he could enjoy the limited but lively conversation and avoid being alone with his thoughts, which turned increasingly suicidal during April. The more his health deteriorated, the more opium he took and the more opium he took, the more his health deteriorated. Coleridge still seems to have been associating the drug with amelioration whereas, in reality, the cause and effect were one and the same. There are, though, moments of lucidity in his notebook where he fully confronts the issue, as with this Italian phrase: 'spera una delusione, loda un inganno'[33] ('he hopes for a deception, he praises a deceit').

Asra also dominated his thoughts and dreams, some of which were becoming increasingly sexualized but without the shame of the ensuing early morning reproof. As spring turned to summer, his notebook is peppered with passionate allusions; 'Joy & Love' go hand in hand with an 'awakened appetite'.[34] Asra does not necessarily make an appearance on each occasion, but the languid longing for her companionship must have inevitably contributed to the subconscious desire of his opium-filled nights. The onset of the Mediterranean summer and the subliminal workings of his mind form the background to a rare burst of poetry writing. Temporarily, the weeds untangled from De Quincey's choked fountain and the words began to flow. The verses became 'The Blossoming of the Solitary Date-Tree', a poem suggested by the Linnaen story of a date tree that could blossom but not bear fruit until a branch from another tree was transported from some distance to act as a pollinator. It is clearly a metaphor for Coleridge's incomplete self without the addition of Asra. The lines were most likely scribbled in the San Anton gardens where date palms still offer their shade. Coleridge would have felt solitary amidst the burgeoning fecundity of the landscape:

> The finer the sense for the beautiful and the lovely,
> and the fairer and lovelier the object presented to the
> sense; the more exquisite the individual's capacity of joy,
> and the more ample his means and opportunities of
> enjoyment, the more heavily will he feel the ache of
> solitariness, the more unsubstantial become the feast
> spread around him . . .[35]

Like so much of Coleridge's writing at this time, the original of the 'Date-Tree' was lost but, fortunately, he recreated the lines he had managed to recall. The landscapes of Malta and Sicily and his fate being amongst them are apparent in the words: 'Fields, forests, ancient mountains, ocean, sky, / With all their voices – O dare I accuse / My earthly lot as guilty of my spleen, / Or call my destiny niggard! O no! no!'[36] Despite the beauty he had been fortunate enough to experience, it could not override his need to be loved by the absent object of his desire:

> This is she tenfold gladder than before!
> But should disease or chance the darling take,
> What then avail those songs, which sweet of yore
> Were only sweet for their sweet echoes sake?
> Dear maid! no prattler at her mother's knee
> Was e'er so dearly prized as I prize thee:
> Why was I made for Love and Love denied to me?[37]

Fitfully, he was also considering some verses on Andalusia, rather in the epic vein, which never materialised as was the case with other writing projects whilst he was Public Secretary. Throughout the summer, his opinions of Malta vacillated from one extreme to the other, eventually settling on the notion of it being dull, as he described it to his wife in a letter. Despite protestations that he liked the heat, the August temperatures brought his skin out in rashes and, to add to nature's torments, he even experienced earth tremors. At San Anton, he was dosing himself with a mixture of castor oil, gin and water, in addition to more opium that Sultana suggests he purchased from the American fleet which had docked from Tripoli and Sicily. However, duty called him back to the heat of Valletta and his noisy rooms in the Treasury.

News had finally filtered through that Chapman was on the move in the Crimea which must have increased Coleridge's anticipation of a return home. The August holiday festival of St Roch, the island's plague protector, came and went with no sign of him showing enthusiasm for the celebration. Aside from a dislike of such saints' days, he felt a 'hollowness'[38] at watching the pleasure of others. His mind turned to the miracles of the saint which he treated with a degree of scepticism yet, with his newly acquired Trinitarian beliefs, he felt that 'still the doctrines remain binding on thee . . .';[39] Sultana says his drug addiction adhered him to the doctrines of the Fall, Grace and Redemption. As he struggled with his religious conscience, so he struggled with the increasingly ragged threads of political intrigue. He had been helping Pasley with a paper on the island of Lampedusa which was designed to combat William Eaton's controversial theory that it would provide a good exchange for Malta as a British base. Eaton, the Superintendent of Quarantine, had fallen out of favour with Ball and the governor was keen to quash any ideas Eaton could present to the government in London. Coleridge was also dealing with corruption in the dockyard that had led to threats of a duel between complainants – a concept that disgusted him as he considered it a throwback to the Middle Ages.

He had been self-medicating a stomach complaint with more opium and just as that had begun to subside, he developed an eye injury caused by an errant rope whilst disembarking from a boat. If this was not enough to contend with, he was subjected to summer temperatures that rose to the mid-thirties Celsius and above. There was no comfort to be derived from the botanical variation of San Anton, stuck as he was inside the Treasury building. Contemplating the impending end to his tenure as Public Secretary, there must have been an element of self-evaluation with regard to his utility in the role.

Coleridge's last *bando* (2nd September) was a proclamation advising against sheltering deserters from the Maltese battalions and stating that fines would be meted out to offenders by the Tribunal. Once more, he is the mouthpiece of punishment, the deliverer of bad news to the local populace. Whether he told them of tax reversals, permits, exile or monetary punishment, he had to maintain the fine line between implementing Ball's policies and issuing the diktats in a sugar-coated manner so as not to antagonise an already restless population. There were times, as we have illustrated in the punishments for the anti-Jewish disturbances, when Coleridge's principles clashed directly with his responsibilities. Arbitrary decisions to exceed codified punishments without due process did not sit well with his established liberal-leaning ethics. Ball had to be presented as a benign paternalist who only wanted to brighten the lives of his citizens; therefore, colonial interests had to be obfuscated lest the more astute became aware of the real purposes behind some of the legislation. We feel that the moral dilemmas that this presented can only have contributed, along with his overwork, to his increased use of opium.

Hough and Davis reach the conclusion that, through the poet's praise of Ball, he was, essentially, complicit in supporting the extra judiciary acts of the government, although they make the salient point that Coleridge did not necessarily express support for the policies. Once again, this presupposes a conflict of interest that must have caused him some late night soul-searching. Opium, through the medium of laudanum, was the escape and the curse. Emanuel Carrère, in his novel *Bravoure*, titled *Gothic Romance* in the English version, has one of the best evocations of opium and its stirring of the creative consciousness that we have encountered. The novel fictionalises the decline of John Polidori, Lord Byron's ill-fated doctor. Polidori has succumbed to laudanum addiction but finds its effects contradictory:

> At this point, his health was already in an extreme state of decline, and the drug would ward off his shaking spells, his awful stomach aches, and the violent spasms that agitated his eyes after a strong emotion. The opium took the edge off. In numbing his senses, it made him indifferent to a fate that seemed like someone else's . . . For it also encouraged intellectual activity that could be accomplished calmly, without qualms or prejudices, as in a laboratory . . . He developed brilliant theories, plots for novels or plays, and their futility only troubled him during the increasingly rare moments when he wasn't under the influence. He almost took pleasure in the nightmarish intervals when he'd be tortured by the recognition of his failures . . . [40]

Needless to say, the drug that once gave Polidori this blissful intellectual curiosity required increasing doses in order to have the same effect. Reeds clogged the river of his consciousness. For Polidori's 'laboratory' we can substitute Coleridge's religious theorising and metaphysical philosophising followed by nightmares and guilt.

Was there also guilt surrounding the accomplishments and quandaries in his role as Public Secretary? Did he shirk or delegate responsibilities that he should have personally undertaken, especially with regard to overseeing the Università, or was he simply swamped by duties in a job that he never really wanted and for which he was temperamentally unsuited? For his own mental health, however, he clearly made the correct decision to avoid engaging with the Treasury and, it could be argued, that he was also right in his choice to delegate tasks to the likes of Zamitello more than would have been the case for his predecessors. The difference in Coleridge's approach and that of his replacement, Chapman, is illustrated by the fact that Chapman fulfilled the full gamut of the role. Much to Coleridge's relief, news reached him that Chapman had docked in Valletta harbour on 6th September. Samuel Taylor could now think about packing up his belongings and organising his return home.

As we have seen previously, Coleridge always liked to have a travelling companion, and he arranged passage to Syracuse with a certain Colin Mackenzie who seems to have had an argument with Pasley, the poet's friend; therefore, the circumstances of his departure were not altogether smooth. There is also a silence in his notebooks at this time with regard to Ball. It is surprising that Coleridge would not have eulogised his farewell thoughts to a man he would later praise significantly in *The Friend*. Donald Sultana hints at an acrimonious end to their relationship but is clear to state that this cannot be inferred from anything Coleridge wrote or said. Dykes Campbell, in his biography, mentions 'a good foundation for certain rumours which reached Coleridge's friends, probably through Stoddart's letters'.[41] Coleridge's problematic relationship with Stoddart might explain this leaking or exaggeration of salacious gossip. We also detect, behind De Quincey's sardonic words concerning Ball and Coleridge's relationship, a degree of scepticism that all was not as it seemed. For Coleridge to admit, however, that he left on unfavourable terms, would tacitly have been to admit that his service had been tainted.

But this was of little matter now – he was finally leaving. With Chapman released from quarantine on 23rd September, it was up to him to deal with the issues of rotting corn and an increasingly restless clamour from the Maltese for a say in government. Coleridge was looking to reach Messina and, from there, to progress to Naples where he could eventually pass through the Veneto up towards Germany and then home. As usual, life had other plans.

CHAPTER FIVE

# The Grand Tourist Returns Home

Day after Thou brightest star of star-bright Italy!
Rich, ornate, populous, all treasures thine,
The golden corn, the olive and the vine.
*The Garden of Boccaccio*

Mirroring his 1804 journey, Coleridge crossed the relatively short distance from Valletta to Syracuse, only to find himself, once again, in quarantine. Much to his relief, the period of confinement lasted just two days. He headed inland away from the Syracusan dockside in search of the Leckies. Knowing them to be congenial company, he was more than happy to reacquaint himself with Britain's *de facto* kingpin in the south-east corner of the island. He travelled through the town under a clear moonlit sky. The heavens, just as they had in Malta, prompted mystic and melancholic thoughts. Unsurprisingly, he mused dreamily on the charms of Cecilia, his seductive opera diva who was still in the city preparing that season's programme of performances. She remained, however, a wistful memory as he made no attempt to rekindle their connection, despite visiting her for one last time.

Ever curious, he took the time to pay some close, rather politically incorrect, attention to the faces he saw in the street, making a comparison between the Maltese, with their uniformity of look, and the Syracusans who had a 'fearful variety'.[1] This statement needs unpacking somewhat; the 'variety' he refers to can be attributed to the waves of invaders who have swept through the island leaving their mark on the gene pool. Contrary to the stereotype, not all Sicilians have dark hair, brown eyes and olive skin. The Normans of Viking origin ruled the island for some considerable time, as did the French, and let us not

**12** The Greco-Roman Theatre, Taormina, Sicily (Andrew Edwards).

**13** The Lungarno, Pisa (Suzanne Edwards).

forget that one of the island's kings was the Holy Roman Emperor, Frederick II crowned in Mainz. Coleridge considered the 'variety' to be positive which makes it all the more surprising that he paired it with the adjective 'fearful'. As Donald Sultana asserts, 'fearful' applied to the many people he saw with the addled appearance of drug addicts.

We know from his walks with Leckie in the autumn of 1804 that this corner of Sicily had a considerable opium poppy crop. In the intervening months between this and his previous visit, Coleridge's laudanum consumption had started to affect many aspects of his life. The denizens he witnessed on the streets of Syracuse were now a stark reminder of a future all too imminent if he continued on this dangerous road. Coleridge's use of 'variety' also refers to the exacerbation of differences in appearance according to their level of addiction. He saw their hollow, haunted demeanour as ghosts of his future self if he allowed 'the tyger fangs'[2] of opium to take hold which, in truth, he knew they already had.

His stay at Tremilia was a mere four days as he needed to move on to Messina. There seems to be some confusion with regard to the identity of his travelling companion. The poet contradicted himself concerning this leg of the journey saying, on different occasions, that he was alone or was accompanied by Colin Mackenzie. Nonetheless, there are enough references to make the assumption he was accompanied at least part of the way by this new acquaintance. They passed a salt works at Augusta which he mentions in his notebook. For a near-contemporary description, we turn to a *Memoir Descriptive of the Resources, Inhabitants, and Hydrography, of Sicily and Its Islands* by a certain Captain Smyth who describes the area:

> The south side of the harbour of Augusta is formed by the promontory of Magnisi, which, though joined to the main by an isthmus, is generally called an island. It is of moderate height, and was the ancient peninsula of Thapsus, where the ill-fated Athenians landed previously to attacking the Epipolae. It appears well calculated for a grand lazaretto (should their commerce ever require it) for the ports of Syracuse and Augusta, being equidistant from both . . . The salt-works are at the end of the isthmus, and not far from them is a column erected by Marcellus in commemoration of his success over the Syracusans.[3]

We can see from this that, not only did Coleridge miss the Classical allusions, he also – perhaps of greater note – neglected making in-depth reference to the adverse working conditions of the labourers who toiled in the harsh environment of the salt pans. Salt and sulphur were the two industries that often drew opprobrium from shocked travellers who wrote of the terrible hardships endured by the men extracting the minerals. Leonardo Sciascia, the ever-prescient documenter of Sicily's ills, wrote a book in the 1950s entitled *Le parrochie di Regalpetra* (*The Parishes of Regalpetra*) but translated into English as *Salt in the Wound*. In the work, he describes the complaints of salt workers crippled with rheumatism who believe that they need to take as much sun as they can stand in order to dry the humidity they feel in their bones. These medical complaints led to days of absenteeism in an era when no work certainly meant no pay. He goes on to mention hyperhydrosis of the hands, comparing the handshake of a salt worker to the touch of a wet stone.

Salt and sulphur were rural industries and, having visited the Trapani salt pans ourselves, it is all too easy to romanticise the picturesque windmills and conical piles of the mineral shimmering under a meridional sun. Coleridge would go on to write pamphlets exhorting the British government and mill owners to improve the conditions for those labouring in Blake's 'dark satanic mills', especially the child labour force. Children also worked in appalling conditions in Sicily's mines, but perhaps he was too consumed by his own troubles to shoulder the pain of others at this point. To his relief, the scenery became more bucolic as he skirted Mount Etna. Both destroyer and provider, the volcano has blessed the villages at its foot with ample fertile soil, to such an extent that Coleridge harked back to his time in the Quantocks where lush valleys provided plenty of grazing for Somerset's renowned dairy herds. In terms of vegetation, he had swapped apples and pears for oranges and vines but the rural abundance felt the same. Still attuned to the physiognomy of the people, he was comforted by the seeming rosy good health of the local women in marked contrast to the drawn urban countenances of Syracuse.

His more upbeat frame of mind continued when he encountered Taormina's Roman theatre with its natural stage setting of Mount Etna rising above verdant hills and the curved bay of the Ionian shore. It was, he assured his notebook, perhaps the best view he had ever seen. In this fulsome praise, Coleridge was not alone. Henry Swinburne, the English writer, had included an extensive section on the town in his book of Sicilian travels. Coleridge, thanks to Leckie's library, had previously read from Swinburne's account and would have been familiar with this description:

> Everything belonging to it is drawn in a large sublime style; the mountains tower to the very clouds, the castles and ruins rise on mighty masses of perpendicular rock, and seem to defy the attacks of mortal enemies; Etna with all its snowy and woody sweeps fills half the horizon; the sea is stretched out upon an immense scale, and occupies the remainder of the prospect.[4]

Similarly, Johann Wolfgang von Goethe, the German polymath admired by Coleridge, had travelled the same roads in 1786. Samuel Taylor may have been aware that Goethe had visited Italy but he would not, at this point, have been privy to his diary as it was not published until 1816. In it, the German is overcome by the spectacle before him:

> Now, sitting down at the spot where formerly sat the uppermost spectators, you confess at once that never did any audience, in any theatre, have before it such a spectacle as you there behold. On the right, and on high rocks at the side, castles tower in the air – farther on the city lies below you; and although its buildings are all of modern date, still similar ones, no doubt, stood of old on the same site . . . and then the wide and extensive view is closed by the immense smoking volcano . . .[5]

Goethe was a serious man and not prone to fripperies, as we can see from his adverse reaction to a villa in Bagheria decorated with gurning, chimerical statues. He was a Classicist and, as such, in tune with the Ancient world – yet even he could not resist the lure of purple prose when confronted with the synergy created by man and nature. As always, it was the natural side of that equation which drew Coleridge; his notebook, as he approaches and spends time in Taormina, begins to feel like a travelogue as opposed to a metaphysical investigation. His mind turned to the Wordsworths and Asra, doubtless conjuring up their imaginary reaction to the scenes of beauty that he would have loved to have shared with them.

Clearly, words were not the only way of capturing this scene. Taormina's popularity began to soar when the German landscape artist, Otto Geleng, moved to the town and painted its renowned sites. His works were exhibited in Paris and Berlin, causing something of a stir. It was not long before the moneyed classes flocked to visit. An astute Geleng set up Taormina's first substantial hotel catering to these foreign visitors. Coleridge had no such luck in finding a place for refreshment; the only options were small inns, one of which was selected for a much-needed break. He perused the entries in the guest-book, finding some in German and one in English criticising a Catanese inn-keeper. The poet's hackles immediately rose; never a friend of the greedy, tight-fisted English variant of the species, he added his own comments condemning their predatory behaviour.

Taormina would be the magnificent punctuation in his journey between Syracuse and Messina where he arrived on 4th October. We know the name of the hotel he stayed at as he jotted it down in his note-book – it was the Albergo della Villa di Firenze. As might be expected given Messina's seismic reputation, the building no longer exists but we also failed to track down a print or artist's impression of the building. Nevertheless, we do know that Coleridge was every bit as impressed with Messina as he was with Taormina and decided to walk up into the hills behind the city to what is now known as Rione Gravitelli (the district of Gravitelli). The neighbourhood has merged completely with central Messina but for Coleridge it was a peaceful prospect. Diletta D'Andrea, in her article for *Incontri Mediterranei*, entitled 'Messina vista dagli inglesi' ('Messina as seen by the English'), emphasises how the beauty of the natural world before him actually acted as a dampener on his mood; he laments not having encountered it in a better frame of mind and health:

> Now too I see the whole town of Messina, its towers, & steeples, [ . . . ]. Now too I see the Faro, that fair tongue of land, & the sea & the mountains beyond it – [ . . . ] the open sea, which by the hither shore & the coast of Calabria appears shaped as a wedge with an indefinite base. The ships, the beautiful speronaras, the fishing boats, the white sails of the Mediterranean. Oh, even but 3 years ago how should I have hoped & schemed amid all this! But now I hope no more.[6]

These dashed hopes are personal, but also have a political edge, as D'Andrea illustrates. Sicily's position in the chess game of Anglo-French manoeuvring was increasingly precarious. It is at this point we gain an uncommon insight into Coleridge's relations with the Sicilians themselves. Throughout his time in Sicily, rare are the mentions he makes of individual islanders, excepting Cecilia Bertozzi. In Messina, he is introduced to a gentleman named Campolo who even invites him to his country house in the aforementioned district of Gravitelli with its view of the straits towards Calabria. Through a series of connections, he also encounters a blind mathematician called Iaci, previously known to Sir William Hamilton. Iaci gave Coleridge a book he felt would be of interest to the admiralty. The man had a great impact on the poet who, years later, would write about him in *The Friend*:

> I knew a profound mathematician in Sicily, who had devoted a full third of his life to perfecting the discovery of the Longitude, and who had convinced not only himself but the principal mathematicians of Messina and Palermo that he had succeeded; but neither throughout Sicily or Naples could he find a single Artist capable of constructing the instrument which he had invented.[7]

Coleridge referred to Iaci, or Father Antonio Maria Jaci (Professor of Physics and Mathematics at the Seminary of Messina), in terms of a favoured theory, believing that the daily necessities of life should be provided by fellow citizens, allowing those intent on perfecting their particular branch of industry to succeed. He goes on to lament the conditions in which the professor was to be found:

> The good old man, who is poor, old, and blind, universally esteemed for the innocence and austerity of his life not less than for his learning, and yet universally neglected, except by persons almost as poor as himself, strongly reminded me of a German epigram on Kepler, which may be thus translated: No mortal spirit yet had clomb so high / As Kepler – yet his country saw him die / For very want! the *minds* alone he fed, / And so the *bodies* left him without bread.[8]

In *The Friend*, Coleridge reiterates his commitment to spreading Iaci's theories, offering to pass the book (*L'Orizonte della longitudine*

...) to any scientist worthy of commenting upon it. At the time, he also offered to take a letter from the mathematician to Sir Joseph Banks, the President of the Royal Society. It is perhaps no coincidence that Coleridge found himself in the company of such a learned man in Messina as the city was, at the time, Sicily's most cosmopolitan metropolis. It was an entrepôt and, despite the poet's subsequent lamentations that there was no-one to build Iaci's device, he was more likely to have found someone in Messina than in any other southern Italian city.

For the time being, Coleridge was resigned to listlessly frittering his days in the local environs. There is nothing to suggest that he was unduly perturbed by this, alternating between the hills behind the city and the famed sickle-shaped harbour. Although ideally situated as Sicily's link to the continent, the narrow funnel of the strait separating the settlement from Reggio Calabria was, and remains, very treacherous. This reputation fed by swirling currents of water gave rise in Classical times to the legends that would have doubtless featured in Coleridge's thoughts. Looking out over the deceptively peaceful waters, how could he not have conjured visions of Odysseus or the Trojans in the *Aeneid*. On the Sicilian shore we have Charybdis, the sea monster, living under a rock and, on the Calabrian shore, the equally dangerous, Scylla. Move too close to one and, to escape, you are forced into the arms of the other. So it was for Odysseus who, trying to avoid Charybdis, lost six men to the voracious appetites of Scylla.

Coleridge's mind, though, was drawn to the more tangible dangers felt by those fighting at sea. Parallel to his days spent in languid leisure, the world was turning in a far less placid manner. King Ferdinand was calling on the Russians and English to land in Naples as a defensive force; meanwhile, off the coast of Cádiz, the Spanish and French were gathering where they were engaged by Nelson's battle fleet within sight of Cabo Trafalgar. Nelson won the battle but lost his life, dying on 21st October, Coleridge's birthday. Bizarrely, Samuel Taylor had mistakenly thought the previous day was his actual birthday and it caused a bout of self-loathing, not least as he could now see his stomach protruding outwards, calling it an 'abdomen prominent'[9]. If Coleridge had actually received news of Nelson's death on the very day, he would have been sent into an even deeper depression. Communication being what it was, he did not hear until many days later and was deeply affected as we shall see. He was not alone in his grief, many felt Nelson's death as a personal loss.

Coleridge found himself at the heart of the Kingdom of Two Sicilies, a land that had already honoured Nelson with a Duchy in 1799. Although he never visited the town of Bronte in the foothills of Mount Etna, the Duchy of the area was passed down to his relatives. By the 1920s, the territory was still in the feudal hands of Alexander Hood, a descendant of Nelson and the incumbent Duca di Bronte. For a writer like D H Lawrence, who spent two years in Taormina, the Admiral's reputation had already faded by the twentieth century and he considered Hood a figure of amusement. In a letter written to Lady Cynthia Asquith, he poked satirical fun at them both:

> Did you ever hear of a Duca di Bronte – Mr Nelson Hood – descendant of Lord Nelson (Horatio) – whom the Neapolitans made Duca di Bronte because he hanged a few of them? [ . . . ] We went to see him – rather wonderful place – mais mon Dieu, M'le Duc – Mr Hood I should say. But perhaps you know him.
>    Tell me where do Dukedoms lie
>    Or in the head or in the eye . . .[10]

The political fallout from battles in central Europe had made Coleridge's plan to progress from Trieste through the Südtirol to Germany a non-starter; although, once again, the speed with which news filtered south meant he was largely ignorant of these matters whilst at Messina. Just when and how he came to sail from Sicily is largely shrouded in mystery. Donald Sultana makes some educated deductions based on the fact that a British expedition had set sail from Malta under the command of General Craig. Did this prompt Coleridge to return to Syracuse and gain passage on one of the ships bound for Naples? Sultana seems to think so and Richard Holmes tends to agree. Sultana also speculates that Coleridge was still in touch with Mackenzie and it was he who may have influenced this decision. Nonetheless, he quotes Coleridge's future explanation to his brother that Naples was the destination owing to 'inducements'[11] received from the city's British representative, Elliot.

By whatever method he travelled, we can certainly place Coleridge in the Bay of Naples overlooked by that other dominant volcanic presence, Vesuvius, on 20th November. From the deck of his unnamed ship, he would have seen the city unfurling into its hinterland in a manner reminiscent of Catania. The bay, itself, would have been full of other ships – both those of Craig's command and Russian forces. Using his beloved Lakes as a reference point, he made the unlikely comparison between Skiddaw near Keswick and Vesuvius. We have become accustomed to Coleridge's dubious comparisons between landmarks in the Lake District and various formations he contemplated in the Mediterranean. However, on this occasion, if you take the profile of the two mountains, we have to agree there is a certain similarity in their outlines, despite Vesuvius' shifting volcanic rim.

Coleridge found accommodation at the Albergo del Sole which offered a view of Vesuvius. Unfortunately, this does little to locate the whereabouts of said institution as a large percentage of Naples has a view towards the mountain. Perhaps the only thing this tells us is that the hotel was not buried within the backstreets whose balconies look upon their neighbour's washing. The window of the establishment did, however, afford the view of a street scene he would later turn into an anecdote. A 'mountebank'[12] was extravagantly entertaining a crowd when he was interrupted by a streetwise little urchin, the kind of ragamuffin (or *scugnizzo*) the American troops used as messenger boys during their occupation of the city in the Second World War. As Coleridge settled into the *albergo*, nearby Castel-a-Mare was filling up with the disembarked Anglo-Russian forces who were, for the time being, confined to barracks. Not so Coleridge, who had sufficient opportunity to wander the city with John Moore's *View of Society and Manners in Italy* to hand.

Despite being in Naples, the Venetian story of the Foscari family peaked his interest. Doge Francesco Foscari had to abdicate when his son was found guilty of bribery and corruption. Moore picks up the story, somewhat haughtily, when the son has already been exiled:

> But the most affecting instance of the odious inflexibility of Venetian courts, appears in the case of Foscari, son to the Doge of that name.
>
> This young man had, by some imprudences, given offence to the Senate, and was, by their orders, confined at Treviso, when Almor Donato, one of the Council of Ten, was assassinated, on the 5th of November 1750, as he entered his own house.[13]

A reward was offered for finding Donato's murderer along with a pardon for crimes committed, should that be applicable. It seems that Foscari's footman had been seen loitering near Donato's residence and had subsequently fled Venice the following morning. Suspicion fell on his master as the instigator of the crime. The case became a *cause célèbre* and Foscari the Elder's portrait is the only one to be obliterated in the Doge's Palace. Coleridge was not the only Romantic poet to be attracted by the story. In 1821, Lord Byron, who had been living in Venice, penned *The Two Foscari*. Here we have Jacopo, the son, lamenting his fate, 'The soil! – Oh no, it is the seed of the soil / Which persecutes me; but my native earth / Will take me as a mother to her arms. / I ask no more than a Venetian grave . . . '[14]

Donald Sultana hints that Coleridge, himself, was considering the plot for a possible drama which, like so many of his projects, never came to fruition. Naples also abounds with the kind of stories Moore enumerated in his book. Virtually every corner of the old city could tell a salacious tale. In 1609, the painter, Caravaggio, emerged from the Osteria del Cerriglio, a tavern and house of ill repute behind the Church of Santa Maria La Nova, to find a group of armed men waiting to ambush him. Severely injured, he stumbled the streets in a daze. Many an aggrieved party had cause to try and kill the cantankerous artist. The elements of underlying violence and overt Catholicism, amply demonstrated through the reverence for saints and saintly images, would be motifs that both attracted and repelled Coleridge during his stay. Not for the first time, the religious architecture and iconography brought out his most virulent Protestantism.

We can compare Coleridge's comment that 'the principle of the Gothic architecture is infinity made imaginable'[15] with the kind of Baroque found in Naples, of which the cloister in the Monastero di Santa Chiara is a beautiful example. Placed within an originally Gothic structure, the cloister is laden with majolica tiles decorating everything from pillars to stone benches and path edges. This oasis of calm in a hectic city could lead the visitor to believe in the infinity of the Baroque. Indeed, the website of the cloister describes the space as a place where the two architectural infinities meet. Had Coleridge not been blinded by what he considered the superstitions of the Catholic faith, he could possibly have come to the same conclusion. Years later, in *Table Talk*, he had softened his opinions of the Neapolitans and their city. He also made a wry observation, comparing the nature of the

Spanish and Italian personalities. In a city where these two cultures meet head on, given centuries of Spanish Bourbon control, his comment is apt, albeit a sweeping generalisation:

> The genius of the Spanish people is exquisitely subtle, without being at all acute; hence there is so much humour and so little wit in their literature. The genius of the Italians, on the contrary, is acute, profound, and sensual, but not subtle; hence what they think to be humorous is merely witty.[16]

Perhaps nowhere in Italy is the wit and sensuality he speaks of more apparent than in Naples, a city that lives its life on the streets and doorsteps at a level of volubility beyond most of Europe. In the same section of *Table Talk*, however, he cannot resist a sideways jibe at the philosopher and historian, Giambattista Vico who, Coleridge postulates, could have achieved so much more had he not been a Papist at Naples and had been privy to the scientific advancements of the age.

Talk of Coleridge obtaining a sinecure from Elliot, the British representative, involving the delivery of despatches to London, quickly went cold. It appears that he was hoping for free passage under the auspice of an official mission but it was not to be. Soon finding himself free of commitment, he made the obligatory trip to see Virgil's tomb at Posillipo. Richard Holmes asserts that he was accompanied by Pasley who must have arrived on one of the British ships. Situated on a hill at the Piedigrotta entrance to the Grotto of Posillipo, the supposed tomb of the poet was sketched some fourteen years later by Turner who captures the arched entrance below a rounded upper storey with its crumbling stone softened by the encroaching vegetation. The view back to Naples and Vesuvius is worthy of Virgil who loved the location and composed the *Georgics* and the *Aeneid* whilst living in the city. He was moved to write the following as his own epitaph: 'Mantua me genuit, Calabri rapuere, tenet nunc Parthenope; cecini pascua, rura, duces',[17] which, as Coleridge would have known, translates as 'Mantua gave me life, the Calabrians took it away, Naples holds me now; I sang of pastures, farms, and commanders' (trans. Bernard Knox).

For a man so steeped in Classical verse, he was rather unmoved by the actual locations that had prompted the words he admired. His notebook turns instead to more modern notions of transgression before the eternal – 'È un peccato',[18] he records from the talk of a local girl regarding her confessor – her sin being felt more deeply thanks to the draconian attitudes of the priest. Coleridge needed no such clerical intervention to examine the faults of his own soul; the demon attraction of opium was the sin and confessor which led to lacerating remorse. If individual locations failed to hone his mind to the words of the past, the general aura of Naples certainly turned his thoughts to the Roman poets. Even before visiting Posillipo, his notes mention Martial and Claudian, the latter of whom he criticised for being unduly concerned with producing 'striking'[19] language, a criticism he would extend to the likes of Pope.

Further evidence of Coleridge's *laissez-faire* attitude to the tangible constructions of antiquity can be seen by the absence of reference to sites such as Herculaneum which was in the process of being excavated. His conversations with British officers were peppered with the enthusiasms of these military men for the discoveries made by archaeologists at Herculaneum. There is no evidence, however, to suggest that he visited the site but he almost certainly saw items recovered from the excavations at a museum in Portici. He did, though, pick up a list in Italian of the manuscripts written on papyrus that had been uncovered by a British scholar commissioned by the Prince of Wales.

At this point, the Coleridge trail goes cold. We know that he travelled further afield in Campania, specifically to Salerno and perhaps down into Calabria. Salerno, the old Norman capital of mainland southern Italy, is close to Paestum, the location of three incredibly well-preserved Greek temples. For those with a Classical education, Paestum was very much on the beaten track. Did Coleridge visit these temples? A passage in his 'Tribute to Spencer Perceval' intrigues us in this regard. Written in 1812, he compares Perceval's 'enduried' nobility to the 'stately Doric Columns each images & all constitute the enduring Strength of the Temple of Neptune'.[20] The notes to this passage in *The Collected Works of Samuel Taylor Coleridge, Volume 11* suggest he is referring to one of the temples at Paestum. There are two temples dedicated to Hera, the Greek Goddess of women, marriage, family and childbirth – the second of which was once thought to be dedicated to Poseidon who is, of course, Neptune under the Roman pantheon. When Coleridge correctly writes of the Doric order, of which this second temple is a magnificent example, is he recalling a visual image witnessed first-hand?

The purpose of Coleridge's expedition is uncertain. He may have joined the party out of curiosity and the desire to see a landscape he would not have the opportunity to visit again. Nonetheless, the group he was travelling with had a more concrete aim, namely reconnaissance, which would benefit future troop movements. Sultana tells us that they passed what would become the location for the Battle of Maida in which Coleridge's friend, Pasley, would participate. The battle took place in July 1806 between British and French expeditionary forces. In addition, the British contingent was supplemented by Sicilian forces and their combined strength defeated the French who also called upon recruits from the Italian mainland and Poland. These ghosts of war to come are illustrative of the historical context and present reality that Coleridge experienced in Naples. Alexander Ball's desire to engage the French on Italian soil was to be realised in 1806, but the Kingdom crumbled under French invasion and King Ferdinand IV fled to Sicily.

A further reminder of the bellicose world in which Coleridge lived was the shock to every Englishman on discovering that Nelson had died, knowledge of which the expedition received on returning to the city. It is difficult at a distance of over two hundred years to contemplate the overwhelming effect this news had on the British and, even more so, the English. Nelson was seen as the bulwark against Napoleon, the nation's great defender in a time of uncertainty and threat. With the development of mass media, modern attitudes are, one could argue, less one-dimensional in their appraisal and lionisation. The Neapolitans were also distressed given the investment Nelson had made in defending the king. Coleridge succumbed to the collective grief in a display of sincere national feeling. He would later reflect on these emotions in one of his essays:

> The tidings arrived at Naples on the day that I returned to that city from Calabria; and never can I forget the sorrow and consternation that lay on every countenance. Even to this day there are times when I seem to see, as in a vision, separate groups and individual faces of the picture. Numbers stopped and shook hands with me because they had seen the tears on my cheek, and conjectured that I was an Englishman; and several, as they held my hand, burst themselves into tears. And though it may awake a smile, yet it pleased and affected me, as a proof of the goodness

of the human heart struggling to exercise its kindness in spite of prejudices the most obstinate, and eager to carry on its love and honour into the life beyond life, that it was whispered about Naples, that Lord Nelson had become a good Catholic before his death. The absurdity of the fiction is a sort of measurement of the fond and affectionate esteem which had ripened the pious wish of some kind individual, through all the gradations of possibility and probability, into a confident assertion, believed and affirmed by hundreds.[21]

As well as admitting to his own feelings and painting a picture of the sense of grief spreading as if by contagion, Coleridge also highlights something akin to Gustave Le Bon's contagion theory promulgated in the mid-nineteenth century. Le Bon theorised that crowds exert a hypnotic influence on the individual, lending a certain anonymity and irrationality to the body of behaviour. The resulting emotional charge then spreads like an infection through a crowded city. This is evident in both Coleridge's description of the way tears flowed from those merely observing the poet's grief and in the manner in which an individual firmly wanted the Catholicisation of the resolutely Anglican Nelson. If Nelson was to be a hero in death, he had to reflect the beliefs held by those idealising his memory. This 'pious wish', trickling from its source, surged through the Neapolitan populace. It is a measure of Coleridge's feelings on the matter, even years later, that he was able to reign in his prejudices in order to remember, affectionately, the reaction in Naples, even if his words could be construed as rather patronising.

After this news of Nelson's death received on 14th December, the conflicts in Europe grew ever closer. Despite the loss at Trafalgar, the French were pressing the Austrians and Russians in central Europe; Napoleon's victory at Austerlitz could now open a southern front. Dire warnings filtered through to Naples of mass movements of French troops. Every bulletin had an impact on Coleridge's mental state and future plans. Perhaps he had the feeling that an English non-combatant in the city would be a target for the attentions of the invading French. He turned to literature as a salve, musing on the literary style of Renaissance panegyrics. In a more down to earth manner, he witnessed the enticements and amusements available to the troops, including opera at the San Carlo. It was not long before he was advised to accompany a certain 'Mr B' to Rome. There has been much speculation as to the identity of his fellow traveller, but it seems all of Coleridge's usual travelling companions in the Mediterranean can be discounted. On the face of it, the choice of Rome appears foolhardy, given he would be journeying north towards the advancing French. In reality, the direction was less important than the status of the city and its region which was then neutral.

Coleridge's role as a civilian was crucial in permitting this journey and it is clear that it was taken in some haste as most of his personal effects were left behind on the advice of the merchant, George Noble, who offered to take care of them in his absence. In addition to some travel notebooks, he made the rash decision to take some 'political'[22] papers with him which included some of the observations on strategy he had penned for Alexander Ball. This foolhardy move clearly identified him as a man who had been in the pay of the British in the Mediterranean, thereby opening himself up to the close attentions of the French should he be stopped at any point. As it turned out, the journey up through Gaeta and Garigliano to Fondi was relatively uneventful. He mentions the round towers of the latter destination in his notes. They belong to Fondi castle, a fourteenth century structure built over Roman defences which bolstered the town's premiere position on the Via Appia. Even in the first decade of the nineteenth century, Fondi was still a major stopping point on the southern route to Rome, despite a reputation for malarial marshes and brigands.

The travellers had left Naples on Christmas Day 1805. Fortunately, by 31st December, Coleridge was safely ensconced in accommodation in the vicinity of the Piazza di Spagna at the heart of the Eternal City. His intentions were purely touristic and, at this early stage, there is nothing to suggest that he saw Rome as anything other than an interim stop. The area he had chosen, apart from being central, was also popular with Grand Tourists and the kind of like-minded souls who would be drawn to Coleridge. He had plenty to occupy his time in the immediate environs of the Spanish Steps, at the top of which is the church of the Trinità dei Monti. He was to see the recent havoc caused by the invading Neapolitan army, in addition to a series of paintings portraying the miracles of saints; in truth, there would have been part of Coleridge's psyche that would have welcomed the iconoclastic destruction of these images which he deemed 'blasphemous'.[23] That is not to say he would have given voice to such thoughts had the soldiers undertaken the task but his benevolent warmth towards idolatrous Neapolitan Catholicism had now melted away.

More to his taste was the nearby Antico Caffè Greco with its bohemian clientele. The establishment was founded on Via dei Condotti in 1760. Nobody on the trail of the Romantics in Rome can fail to take a coffee at the Greco, and we were no exception. The walls are bedecked with art, occasionally separated with Baroque stuccowork decoration. The caffè even has an artist in residence, Stellario Baccellieri, who has been visually documenting its life for forty years. At the time of our visit, there were questions over its continued existence given the steep hike in rental costs. It is unthinkable to imagine that such a locale, witness to so many famous visitors, might no longer exist. It would take paragraphs to list all the notable figures who have passed through its doors, but they include the modern Hollywood set – Elizabeth Taylor, Audrey Hepburn, Orson Welles et al. – as well as artists and writers, past and present – Lord Byron, John Keats, Charles Dickens, Henry James, Stendhal, Goethe, Henrik Ibsen, Hans Christian Andersen and Renato Guttuso who portrayed the interior in a 1976 work. Not to be left out are a plethora of world famous composers such as Wagner, Liszt and Mendelssohn. There was even a section of the caffè renowned for gatherings of the Italian political elite, doubtless plotting policy and intrigue.

Coleridge was to meet an artistic crowd in its environs which was made up of the Scottish landscape painter, George Wallis, Thomas Russell, a Devonian art student, and Washington Allston, with whom he struck up a great friendship. Allston, an archetypical Romantic figure – a shade Byronic in looks with jet black wavy hair – was an American painter from South Carolina who had rubbed shoulders with the likes of Fuseli whilst a student at the Royal Academy in London. It has also been suggested by some that the circle included Washington Irving, the writer of *Sleepy Hollow* and several memoirs of travel in Europe. Unfortunately, Irving and Coleridge never crossed paths in Rome but the other Washington did know Allston and had this to say about his personality: 'Everything about him bespoke the man of intellect and refinement. His conversation was copious, animated, and highly graphic; warmed by a genial sensibility and benevolence, and enlivened at times by a chaste and gentle humour.'[24] In short, Allston was the perfect companion for Coleridge.

S. F. B. Morse was a pupil of Allston's in Rome and was a first-hand observer of Coleridge in conversation:

> ... Coleridge was a frequent, almost daily, visitor to our studio. For our entertainment while painting, we used to arrange in advance some question in which we were interested, and propound it to Coleridge upon his coming in. This was quite sufficient, and never failed to start him off on a monologue to which we could listen with pleasure and profit throughout the entire sitting.[25]

The two men, graphic and garrulous in their intellectual pursuits, walked miles across Rome engaged in discussion. Scholars have speculated that Coleridge tried to tempt Allston away from his sculptural inclination towards the Greek. The American greatly admired the Apollo Belvedere, then considered to be a Roman copy of a Greek original. He thought it 'the harmonious confluence of the pure ideas of grace, fleetness and majesty . . . '[26] Despite this professed admiration, he had a liking for Gothic imagery, witness his later painting, *Donna Mencia in the Robber's Cavern*, described by the *Knickerbocker* magazine as showing Donna Mencia 'supported by that hideous old hag, and looks very lovely in her distress . . . ',[27] in addition to her being 'very attractive to those lawless, satyr-like bandits grouped behind her . . . '

Coleridge can only have encouraged these Gothic thoughts, endeavouring to push them to the fore in Allston's artistic approach. The *Life and Letters of Washington Allston* records one interesting conversation on this theme, attributing the following to Coleridge: 'Grecian architecture is a thing, but the Gothic is an idea. I can make a Grecian temple of two brick-bats and a cocked hat.'[28] This throwaway line is illustrative of the disinterest he showed in venturing to Herculaneum whilst at Naples; the Classical word would always overshadow the Classical deed. Coleridge was also to frequent another circle of like-minded individuals but the two sets of friends were far from mutually exclusive as Allston's biographer, Sweetser, indicates, suggesting Allston knew Wilhelm von Humboldt, Madame de Staël and August Wilhelm Schlegel, whom Byron would later describe as a 'dousterswivel',[29] that is to say, a two-faced schemer.

Wilhelm von Humboldt was undoubtedly an acquaintance of Coleridge's in Rome. He enjoyed holding forth at his house, the

Palazzo Tomati, above the Piazza di Spagna. Coleridge, it must not be forgotten, was deeply steeped in German literature and had dabbled as a translator of Schiller. Knowledge of the playwright created immediate common ground between the English poet and Prussia's minister to the Vatican. Subsequently, Coleridge credited Humboldt with introducing him to Schlegel's works which he seems to have rated highly. It is worth, at this juncture, segueing to highlight a small controversy mentioned by Sultana and others. Both Schlegel and Coleridge would go on to deliver lectures about the merits of Shakespeare. The similarities in delivery between the two were such that the Englishman was accused of stealing content from the German. In defence, Coleridge claimed to have never read Schlegel, apart from some Spanish translations he had seen whilst in Rome. Contrary to this, Wellek in his *A History of Modern Criticism*, quotes a German Grand Tourist who wrote to Schlegel, himself, declaring that he had heard Coleridge praise August Wilhelm's translations of Shakespeare during his stay in the Eternal City. Not for the first or last time would Coleridge be accused of casually borrowing others' ideas without due attribution. We feel this is more absent-minded than intentionally deceitful.

Also part of Humboldt's gathering was Ludwig Tieck who was at the forefront of the German Romantic movement. We can imagine Coleridge dusting down his Devonian-inflected German or using his civil service Italian, laced with Renaissance dialogue learnt from the likes of Dante and Boccaccio, whilst engaging the literary crowd in Rome. Humboldt, however, spoke English and was well-versed in British literature, something which prompted the poet to regale him with lines from Wordsworth which he would always have ready to recite from memory. Tieck was not privy to this performance but poetry must have been at the heart of their conversation given Coleridge's notebook has a short translation from one of Ludwig's verses. There was a mutual respect and kindness between the writers.

What had started as an intended stay of a few weeks was now extending into months. By February, the French threat was closing in and Thomas Jackson, the English minister to the exiled court of Turin, had been forced to flee the city. The French were demanding the Papacy close its ports to British ships. The residency of British diplomats and government functionaries was now being seen by the French as a breach of the Vatican's avowed neutrality. As frequently happened with

Coleridge when pressing matters required urgent decision-making, he decided to avoid the situation altogether and disappear on a journey to the Roman *campagna* with his friend, Allston. The painter had a favourite country retreat at Olevano, a strenuous twelve-hour walk from the poet's accommodation or a few hours' ride in a carriage.

Olevano, or Olevano Romano to give the town its full title, lies in the Sabine Hills. Its taupe-coloured houses tumble down the slopes in a continuous flow creating a cohesive community from the apparent disorder. Allston had rented a property for the duration and was already more than familiar with the landscape which takes the form of a bowl with encircling highlands and scarps. He was working on his painting of *Diana and her Nymphs in the Chase*, a work that Coleridge much admired and described fully in his notebook. He was moved to Latin, stating that 'quam qui non amat, illum omnes et Musae et Veneres odere',[30] implying a viewer who did not fall in love with the work would be one who hates all the Muses and Venuses. Coleridge's description starts with mere detailed observation and builds into a full immersive reality, as if he is walking through the scene encountering the obstacles and relaying each sensation to the viewer. He climbs the 'Bowder stone' on the left reaching the 'prospect of the far valley' where he can view the 'sunshiny mountain all jagged and precipitous'.[31] Despite Allston tinkering with the image in Olevano, the landscape was taken from Swiss mountain scenery – a fact made obvious from the aforementioned 'jagged' peak.

Allston did, however, paint landscapes in the vicinity of his rented house and used his environs to inspire backdrops for his biblical and Classical subjects. He was able to feed from Coleridge's enthusiasm for the landscape and the breadth of knowledge he imparted; the American was to recall that 'the fountain of his mind was never dry'.[32] Once again, the Lakes feature as a touchstone by which the poet judged other landscapes. Whilst wandering the spring valleys bursting with flower, he mused 'Olevano – Am I at Keswick? – The woods all peopled with Knots of Primroses . . . O why is there no Lake? No River? – '.[33] The countryside was truly a tonic and he admitted, perhaps for the first time in many months, to having a more amiable mood. He and Allston were also joined by George Wallis and his young son, the romantically named Trajan, who chatted away in Italian. As the artists sketched, Coleridge took advantage of the balmy Roman spring, relaxing on the grass whilst composing mental pictures of the scenes before him.

At some point during their stay, Allston and Coleridge agreed that it would be the ideal opportunity for the former to paint the latter. The decision can be seen as Allston's ultimate affirmation of their friendship and the great esteem in which he held Coleridge. Sadly, the painting remained unfinished but enough was completed to gain a good impression of the intended effect. Allston was one of those painters who worked slowly and would return again and again to a piece before completion. Unfortunately, in this instance, once Coleridge had left Rome, the moment had passed and the canvas remains forever a work in progress. The poet is seated, his gaze looking away from the viewer into the distance – perhaps towards the Olevano hills. His dress is neither formal, nor casual, but has a relaxed Bohemian air, the silk scarves at his neck catch the light in a spirited flourish. His face shows no sign of tension or a clue to any deeper emotion but there is a quiet thoughtfulness to his features. The only signs of his Maltese excesses are the pallor and pudginess of face, the rounded features exacerbated by the Devonian yeoman contribution to his physique.

In 1811, Coleridge would recall the image as the best likeness that had been painted of him up to that point in time. Not everyone formed such a warm opinion. Robert Lowell, in his poem 'To Delmore Schwartz', thought that Coleridge's gaze was 'paranoid, inert'[34] attributing this to opium and his mental state. Lowell also interpreted his eyes as being subsumed by flesh and his lips as cracked and black. This last description is puzzling until we learn that he was not viewing the original but a badly reproduced copy. Hindsight and common knowledge of Coleridge's addiction inevitably colour subsequent interpretations but there is a scintilla of truth to Lowell's stinging observations. In many ways, Coleridge's own opinion of the nature of portraiture is the most appropriate way to interpret Allston's image of his friend from their time in Olevano: 'When you look upon a portrait, you must not compare it with the face when present, but with the recollection of the face. It refers not so much to the senses, as to the ideal sense of the friend not present.'[35]

Coleridge returned to Rome just in time for the Easter celebrations. He was now in the company of a Robert Sloane, another scion of the English merchant classes still operating in Italy. He accompanied Sloane on Maundy Thursday to St Peter's and returned again on Good Friday. Thursday's liturgy, he classed as 'mummery'[36] – a mummer was a disguised performer in a pantomime and, by extension, mummery was classed as a ridiculous or extravagant ceremonial procedure. As always, the theatre of Catholic ritual was not to his taste. This was not the case with regard to Michelangelo, whose Sistine Chapel he observed in detail on the Friday. He lauded the painter, along with Raphael, as representing the height of Renaissance art – a common if uncontroversial opinion. In a subsequent notebook entry, nearly two years in the future, Coleridge wrote: 'And truly – deeply, O far more than words can I express as I venerate the Last Judgement and the Prophets of Michael Angelo Buonoroti –'.[37]

He was less in awe of Raphael and, therefore, probably found him more accessible. In typically Grand Touristic fashion, he purchased some prints of the painter's frescoes in a burst of present buying, tacitly acknowledging that his time in Rome was drawing to a close. Napoleon's troops were occupying papal ports along both the Adriatic and Tyrrhenian coasts, thereby blocking maritime exit routes to the British. Naples had fallen and the noose was tightening. Fortunately for Coleridge, Thomas Russell, the Devonian art student, was able to lend him some money as his financial resources were running perilously low. Russell thought that Coleridge had fallen into a state of despair, particularly with regard to money. To what degree he was being sought by the French is open to question – Coleridge would later declare that his essays for the Morning Post had singled him out as a marked man. Contemporary accounts do not reflect this. Gone were the balmy days of Olevano and Coleridge slipped once again into depression, medicated and exacerbated by opium. The nightmares returned as reality sank in, but still he procrastinated, visiting Lord Bristol's painting collection and the Villa Farnasina with Allston.

The poet's increasing bitterness turned to the Italian language which he still admired in its literary form but execrated in the mouths of the Roman peasantry. In one of his most ludicrous statements on the matter, he felt that Italian sounded best in the mouth of an 'agreeably-voiced Englishman'.[38] Roman speech was nothing but 'the most ear-splitting chaos'.[39] Had an educated Roman visited an agricultural market in Exeter, he might have come to the same conclusion. Whilst Allston and Coleridge continued to visit Rome's contribution to the world's artistic patrimony, the American was still working on his friend's portrait. More Raphaels, Berninis and Canovas passed before their eyes, although Coleridge was never introduced to Canova by Allston, unlike Washington Irving. Allston eventually put his brushes down on the Olevano portrait when Coleridge was forced by circumstances to leave the city. There is no evidence to point to his imminent arrest, rather a blanket demand from the French that the British leave papal territory. This was resisted by the Vatican authorities, but the threat was real enough to force the evacuation of a good many British citizens. By 21st May, Coleridge was on the road to Florence with Thomas Russell.

The traditional route was via Terni and Perugia. Terni is about a third of the way to Florence and a convenient location for a stop. Coleridge and Russell allowed themselves the time to visit the Cascata delle Marmore, a man-made waterfall created on the orders of the Roman consul Manius Curius Dentatus who wanted to divert the stagnant waters of the marsh-laden Velino river. By the time of Coleridge's visit, subsequent works had been ordered and completed by the Papacy. He clambered the precarious slopes to the side of the falls, committing these words to his notebook: '. . . and the right Hand leaps down in a narrow plaunge [sic] torrent-like, the left Hand stream spreads out into a great breadth and then falls [over] a convex semicircular brown & mossy rock . . . '[40] According to Kathleen Coburn's comments on the text, Coleridge's strenuous feat of observation was considered a hazardous exercise by the locals. His issues were temporarily forgotten as he delighted in the subsequent scenery of 'oranges & flowering shrubs', 'vines & olive Trees/Corn, Wine, Oil!'[41] At the inn where they halted for refreshment, Coleridge described a pastoral scene worthy of Constable with carts drawn up at the entrance providing convenient beds for a woman and child who were stretched out, siesta-fashion, underneath chicken coops.

The route beyond Perugia took in the environs of Lake Trasimeno, Ossaia and Arezzo until they reached Florence towards the end of May. As Coleridge wandered the picturesque byways of rural Tuscany, his loved ones at home in England were hearing rumours, via letters from his old Maltese connection, Stoddart, that he had been spotted in Rome mixing in German and American artistic circles. Their preoccupations were not satisfied directly by Coleridge who had still not written to anyone explaining his whereabouts. On arrival in Florence, the two travelling companions were to meet a contact recommended by Allston, Pietro Benvenuti, who, despite his name, was not over-effusively welcoming. In a letter to Allston, dated 17th June and addressed to the Pittore Americano (Caffè Greco), Coleridge complained of Benvenuti's treatment but also gave the rationale behind it:

> Benvenuti received me with almost insulting coldness, not even asking me to sit down . . . However, within the last 7 or 8 days he has called and made this amende honorable . . . yesterevening the Truth came out he had been bored by Letters of recommendation, & until he received a Letter from Mr Migliorini looked upon me as a *Bore* which however he might and ought to have got rid of in a more gentlemanly manner . . . [42]

Even allowing for intervening trips, we can tell from this letter that Coleridge's stay in the city was not a matter of hours, but days. His Florentine itinerary requires some intuitive deduction as his notes are scant, but it seems he acquired a guidebook called *La Galerie de Florence*. We were able to track down an 1803 copy which gives a detailed list of the many paintings to be found in what is now known as the Uffizi Gallery. We know that Coleridge saw the Tribuna of the Uffizi, an octagonal room designed by the architect Buontalenti for Francesco I, as he writes of Parmigianino's *Madonna and Child with Saint* which was displayed in this room. The guidebook calls the Tribuna a place where the paintings chosen are 'de plus precieux dans la Galerie',[43] in other words, the most precious canvasses. Despite Coleridge's worries regarding his current predicament and future prospects, he was sufficiently jolted from his anxieties to record his presence in such an august institution.

By 5th June, he had arrived in Pisa after travelling through 'a lovely plain'[44] then noting, but not expanding on, the Piazza dei Miracoli, with its cathedral, baptistery and famous tower; he simply calls it a 'grand & wild mass'.[45] Underneath this entry in his notebook, he then lists the painters whose work he must have seen, including Buffalmacco, Giotto and Benozzo Gozzoli. There is no further elaboration but his thoughts would return to them at a later date, especially to Giotto. Coleridge is now moving ever closer to the dreaded return journey by boat to England. Two days after arriving in Pisa, he finds himself in Livorno, commonly referred to by the English as 'Leghorn' and checks in to the Arms of England hotel. It is of little surprise that the town had an establishment with such an Anglicised name, as Livorno had long been a centre of British merchant activity. Nonetheless, owing to the situation with the French, their presence at the port would not have gone unnoticed. British ships were scarce; consequently, Russell had negotiated passage on an American vessel called the *Gosport*. They were also waiting for Wallis and his family to join them.

The spectre of his outward voyage to Malta now resurfaced to haunt him causing a considerable darkening of his mood and thoughts of suicide: 'so deep and black is my Despair'.[46] He returned to the sad demise of John Wordsworth, wishing that he could have taken his place so that John would have been able to marry his beloved Asra. To relieve this agonising turmoil, his laudanum consumption increased still further, but he knew it would 'degrade the Being'.[47] By doing so, he was also feeding the issue he most feared, that of suffering the stifling constipation experienced after leaving Gibraltar for the crossing to Malta. Perhaps through fear or due to procrastination, Russell and Coleridge surprisingly returned to Florence where Wallis was still expected. It is during this period that Coleridge penned the aforementioned letter to Allston, in which he admitted his melancholic feelings and thoughts of self-harm that were only prevented by the image of his children and the fear of God.

Benvenuti was more solicitous, but the art professor's attentions were scant consolation and failed to enhance his mood. There is virtually no mention of the city's illustrious sites, although, still fixated on language matters, he complained of the Florentines' speech as being equivalent to the act of gargling and had nothing of an educated Roman's 'sweet' diction. The ugliness he detected in Florentine pronunciation extended to the women whom he thought 'Junos' in comparison with the Roman 'Venuses' and 'Graces'.[48]

The road to Livorno led through Pisa so, once more, Russell and the poet packed up, leaving Florence for the city of the leaning tower. They took accommodation at the Globe Inn where a biblical thunderstorm raged outside. As lightening pierced the night sky and the Arno was phantasmagorically lit, Coleridge longed to be struck down. The apocalyptic bleakness of this June evening found its way into verse in one of his last notebook entries in Italy. In many ways, these four short lines are a metaphor for his whole Mediterranean misadventure. What began with resolution and the brightness of hope, had descended into the death-rattle of near leafless branches, wind-stripped by the whims of life; June had become a desolate December: 'Come, come, thou bleak December wind, / And blow the dry Leaves from the Tree! / Flash, like a love-thought, thro' me, Death! / And take a life, that wearies me.'[49]

The following day, 23rd June 1806, Russell and Coleridge boarded the *Gosport* at Livorno. Joseph Cottle, in his *Reminiscences of Samuel Taylor Coleridge and Robert Southey*, claimed that Captain Derkheim had obtained a false passport for Coleridge and that he had to pass as an American steward to avoid the attentions of the authorities. Whether this is true or not, Derkheim did take the precaution of stating the pair were American citizens. There is little to back up Coleridge's later fanciful notion that Napoleon had a warrant out for his arrest. Rather, an existential promise of danger seems to have hovered over their departure.

Coleridge was more concerned with his constipation and had purchased the kind of syringe used for enemas, which were indeed to be administered by Derkheim during the voyage. To the great regret of posterity, some of Coleridge's papers were thrown overboard during the trip when the panicked captain spotted the attentions of a Spanish privateer. Two notebooks and Coleridge's *Observations on Egypt* survived. He had also purchased a good many editions of Italian Renaissance poetry which were to be incorrectly packed in Russell's luggage and would also go temporarily astray. Coleridge's sluggish system, humiliation and regret blocked his written output throughout the long journey home. It was fifty-five days of hell, which led him to vow that, unless it was for a matter of hours, he would never sail again. Such were the scars left by this most traumatic of sea journeys.

CHAPTER SIX

# Lectures and Legacy

> The haunt obscure of old Philosophy,
> He bade with lifted torch its starry walls
> Sparkle, as erst they sparkled to the flame
> Of odorous lamps tended by Saint and Sage.
> *A Tombless Epitaph*

The *Gosport* docked at Stangate Creek in the River Medway, Kent, on 17th August. This minor customs post and quay was actually a common landing point for returning Grand Tourists. Some eighteen years later, Lord Byron would return here from exile in an even worse state than Coleridge, having been embalmed and shipped back in a barrel after dying in the Missolonghi swamps whilst supporting the cause of Greek independence. Coleridge was the returning reluctant civil servant, having worked in the engine room of Empire, a role he increasingly saw as intriguing on behalf of prominent men. He swore to avoid this fate in the future; although he would admit in a letter to Stuart that he had gained much insight into the minds of such characters.

The immediate question for Coleridge was how to deal with his domestic arrangements, specifically whether he could face a return to his wife or perhaps arrange some kind of separation. Almost inevitably, he procrastinated and prevaricated, eventually deciding to spend some time in London reacquainting himself with people and places. It is difficult to see this as anything other than a displacement activity given the length of time he had been away. Richard Holmes, in his biography, *Darker Reflections*, makes a telling observation of the man during this period, saying that the thirty-four year old had crossed a threshold whilst in the Mediterranean, moving into gloomier waters. The bright skies and clear horizons of the Middle Sea, once so full of promise and

**14** Manuscript draft of *The Ancient Mariner*, lines 201-12 (written in 1806), by Samuel Taylor Coleridge
(The British Library: https://www.bl.uk/collection-items/a-variant-version-of-the-ancient-mariner-lines-201-12).

**15** The former residence of the Gillman family, Highgate, London (Suzanne Edwards).

**16** St Michael's Church, Highgate, London (Andrew Edwards).

opportunity for the poet, had turned into the 'sunless sea'[1] of his Kubla Khan opium reverie.

When agonising over his health and future on the *Gosport*, he must have mused on the 'Ancient Mariner'. It would lead to a new stanza full of pain and foreboding that he would later jot down in October:

With never a whisper in the main
Off shot the spectre ship:
And stifled words & groans of pain
Mix'd on each {murmuring / trembling} lip
[And] We look'd round & we look'd up
And Fear at our hearts as at a Cup.[2]

This manuscript from his notebook, kept at the British Library, is headed with this Latin tag: 'Sic perit Ingenium, / Ingenii (aliter Genii) ni / pignora vitam Perpetuam / statuant – ', which starts by decrying that 'Wit is lost'.[3] From these depths, Coleridge tried to make sense of his Mediterranean experience by proposing to write a travelogue detailing his time in Malta and Italy, the latter of which was much enlightened by the period he spent in Rome with Allston. Another potential avenue he wanted to explore was a lecture series. Knowing he had to contact his wife, and after much encouragement from Mary Lamb, he decided to pen a letter. Any talk of a separation was avoided but the practical nature of the text dictated a schedule which would see him in London, thereby instigating a natural degree of distance that spoke volumes, despite his lukewarm suggestion that she and the children could come down to visit him after his proposed fleeting trip to see them in the Lakes.

It is thanks to this letter that we know he also intended to work on an essay, tentatively entitled '"Reflections Moral and Political grounded on Information obtained during two years Resident in Italy and the Mediterranean"',[4] and that his lecture series was to be on the Fine Arts. Like so many of Coleridge's projects, they would not materialise in the exact manner projected. For the time being, he was anticipating an income of £400 for his lectures, enabling him to remain in London and send money to his family. Coleridge's chaotic financial management always over-estimated potential income and underestimated expenses, but he was not without offers of support, particularly from those who would open their homes to him such as Thomas

Clarkson, the anti-slavery campaigner and Quaker. When the poet finally extracted himself from the hubbub of London, deciding to depart for Keswick and his wife, he was immediately side-tracked by stopping in Bury St Edmund's to renew his friendship with Thomas. The metaphysical machinations of his Maltese nights were fertile ground for Clarkson's theological hypothesising. He posed Coleridge a series of questions on the nature of God and the soul which led to Samuel Taylor distracting himself with a three thousand word essay in reply.ABSTRACT thought was infinitely preferable to the harsh glare of the reality that awaited him in the Lake District. It was 26th October, 1806 before he finally decided to make the remainder of his journey. He stopped at Penrith, expecting to find Asra but, instead, met Wordsworth who informed him that she, along with the rest of his household, were going to Coleorton via Kendal. In this latter destination, they were all reunited but the Wordsworths' shock at seeing their friend was palpable.

The years of Maltese and Italian dissipation had left their mark. He was fatter, puffy of face and, as Dorothy remarked in a letter, much changed in his conversation. Gone were the witty asides about mutual friends and his own life; instead, his discussions were peppered with allusions to Alexander Ball and, notably, the intrigues of the political classes, particularly with reference to British policy in the Mediterranean. Clearly, with the benefit of hindsight, Coleridge was now reassessing his role in the grand game of power which had led him to feel uneasy, even when seated at the breakfast table in San Anton. Perhaps owing to this lack of spark in his conversation or his general poor health, Wordsworth was not enamoured of Coleridge's idea to lecture in London. There is a degree of patronising paternalism in the Wordsworths' wish to protect and organise their friend. It must have been obvious to them that his drinking and drug abuse had greatly increased – they, and only they, could save Coleridge from himself.

From Kendal, he went to Greta Hall for the inevitable confrontation with Sara Coleridge and, more happily, the reunion with his children. Initially, things were calm as he regaled them and Southey of his Mediterranean exploits. All hell broke loose, however, when Coleridge's long-held desire for a separation was finally mentioned. In explanation to the Wordsworths, he castigated Sara for her 'temper, and selfishness, her manifest dislike of me'.[5] The use of the word 'selfish' is rather preposterous, coming as it does from a man who had disappeared for the best part of three years with scant communication and irregular remittance of money, whilst her dislike could be seen as sheer frustration at his chaotic personality and addictions. Putting aside their individual merits and failings, they had clearly reached an impasse, which only exacerbated Coleridge's opium taking. To his credit, though, his children were uppermost in his mind and it was having their best interests at heart which eventually began to assuage Sara. However, boils that plagued his skin were the physical manifestation of her rages.

The Christmas of 1806 was spent at Coleorton with the Wordsworths. Coleridge took along his son, Hartley, and entrusted him into the care of Asra, who was already helping to look after the Wordsworths' children. It was a happy return but there were tensions. Asra's sister, Mary, was married to William, but there was also a spark between Asra and Wordsworth. Needless to say, Coleridge was still fervently holding a candle for Miss Hutchinson. This somewhat dysfunctional set-up was inflamed by an incident that would haunt Coleridge for years. Biographers have tried to extract the truth from the opaque references to the event. Molly Lefebure, in *A Bondage of Opium*, recounts how Samuel Taylor had become convinced of a relationship between Asra and William which seemed to be confirmed one Saturday morning after Christmas when Coleridge thought he saw the pair in bed together.

Was this really the case? Richard Holmes tells us that Coleridge may well have been up all night and had wandered into Asra's room early in the morning. It is fair to speculate that he had taken much opium and had also been drinking. The notebook he had been keeping at the time breaks into lacerations of distress. He would also continue to refer back to the incident in future scribbled entries, witness this lamentation from 1808: 'O that miserable Saturday morning! The thunder-cloud had long been gathering, and I had been now gazing, and now averting my eye from it . . . But then was the first Thunderpeal!'[6] The contemporary description of the event was ripped out of the notebook, leaving us all to guess at the truth. However, even if we had Coleridge's words, was it reality or merely a vision? Wordsworth may well have been paying Asra an innocent visit but their closeness was undeniable. Coleridge's despair was also exacerbated by the fact that Asra had become cool towards him, to the extent that she avoided being alone with him. She had absolutely no intention of returning his affection, however innocent. Holmes goes on to cite Coleridge writing some considerable time later that 'I knew the horrid phantasm to be a mere phantasm',[7] but also that he had seen Asra's 'beautiful breasts uncovered'.[8] The fog remains to this day but the incident unquestionably rocked his foundations.

In that most stereotypically British way of proceeding, the episode was brushed under the carpet and never openly discussed. The wound was sutured by a pact of silence, as is evidenced by Coleridge's effusive poem to Wordsworth written in the January. Yet he would also commit words to paper that refer to his ever-increasing confusion with regard to his relationship with William. In 'The Tropic Tree', he seems to conjure the Mediterranean arboreal atmosphere of San Anton as a metaphor for the stout rootedness of Wordsworth: 'As some vast Tropic tree, itself a wood, / That crests its head with clouds . . . ', but would go on to introduce a Muslim mystic subservient to his idol: 'High in the Fork the uncouth Idol knits / His channel'd brow; low murmurs stir by fits / And dark below the horrid Faquir sits . . . '[9] Coleridge had reduced himself to a worshiper, yet both characters appear to be flawed.

Despite appearances on the surface, the underlying tensions inevitably remained and Coleridge must have been looking for an excuse to escape. Russell, the artist he had met in Rome, had regaled Coleridge's family in Devon with tales of their Italian travels. The extent to which the poet's troubles with opium were underplayed is hard to ascertain, but George Coleridge cannot have heard the full story as he was prepared to invite his brother to Ottery in a bid to save the school he was running. Samuel Taylor saw this as a means of honourable extrication. Coleridge now sought to re-establish himself in Devon but, firstly, wrote a letter to George explaining his marital difficulties, the contents of which undermined the plan as it shocked his brother who then decided to withdraw the offer.

Sara and his two younger children were, however, already on their way to Bristol whilst Coleridge headed for London with Hartley. Whilst in the capital, his thoughts turned to *Osorio*, his Spanish play but, as Richard Holmes wryly explains, Coleridge had typically lost his only manuscript copy. The sole recourse he had was to ask William Godwin if it was lying around at the back of his bookshop amongst the copious files he kept. Luckily, the text was found, although plans for its performance were buried under the melee of the months to come. Coleridge then headed west to reunite with the family in Bristol, eventually ending up back in Nether Stowey. He simmered with resentment towards Wordsworth and the misunderstanding with his brother, to the extent that he neglected to eulogise his benefactor, Tom Wedgewood. The pottery magnet had died whilst Coleridge had been in Malta and Tom's brother had now asked Samuel Taylor to pen some words. Luckily, he managed to hold on to the valuable annuity.

During his stay in the West Country, he met a character for the first time who would become something of a perverse mirror to the travails of his own life, twisting, distorting and reflecting the destructive hold of opium. In the unlikely location of Bridgwater, a young, slender and diminutive man approached and engaged him in conversation. Coleridge took him for a drink and dazzled him with his meandering wordsmithery. At one point, the topic turned to laudanum and the young man, a certain Thomas De Quincey, revealed he had taken the drug. De Quincey would famously go on to write *Confessions of an English Opium-Eater* and was clearly not dissuaded, at this early stage, by Coleridge's revelation that he was under 'hideous bondage'.[10] As Frances Wilson points out in *Guilty Thing: A Life of Thomas De Quincey*, many biographers have cast doubt on De Quincey's retelling of Coleridge's supposed confession. However, Wilson thinks that the recollection is plausible as both men would have been behaving in character if one had confided in an acolyte and the other lent a willing ear.

De Quincey would subsequently give Coleridge money anonymously and reappear in his life at a later date. For the time being, it was enough that he recognised the man's 'powers so majestic', even if they were 'already besieged by decay'.[11] As the two men went their separate ways, Coleridge finished his stay in Somerset alone with Tom Poole in Nether Stowey, still trying to combat his opium use with dilute solutions of quince substituting the lemons of Malta. He wandered the Quantocks in fine weather, gazing into the blue as he had in Valletta, streamlining his existential thoughts into 'one submissive gaze', desperately trying to find substance in the 'molten Being never cooled into a Thing . . .'[12]

Owing to the missing writings from his stay in the Mediterranean – some still waiting to be shipped home and some lying on the seabed – it was proving difficult for Coleridge to plan a lecture series based on the Italian and Maltese culture he had seen; consequently, he changed tack focussing instead on poetry, literary criticism and the imagination. Originally intent on decamping to London, as so often happened in Coleridge's life, he found himself, instead, as the cosseted guest of a family – this time, the Morgans. He was looked after by John Morgan, his wife Mary and her sister Charlotte. Richard Holmes is correct in drawing parallels between these two young women and the Hutchinson sisters, Mary and Sara (Asra). Indulged but suffering, he eventually left for London and his long-awaited Royal Institution lectures. The lead up to the first talk was inauspicious, with the strain of preparation and the nervous anticipation of delivery causing more opium intake and wracking pains.

The first lecture was either acceptable or lacking heart and soul, depending on whose opinion was sought. Years later, through his own opium-addled lens, De Quincey would recall a man whose 'lips were baked with feverish heat, and often black in colour' and who failed to give 'extempore illustration'.[13] At the end of that first evening, Coleridge returned to his lodgings with feelings of intense nausea. Two subsequent lectures were postponed because of diarrhoea and bouts of vomiting. He knew he had to hone his method, curtail his rambling and try to stick to his notes. The third lecture would prove more of a success, seeing Coleridge explore Shakespeare's *Venus and Adonis,* and the fourth would focus on the heights of poetic imagination. At this juncture, it seemed that Coleridge had finally found, for the first time since returning from the Mediterranean, a *raison d'être* that suited his talents and would bring in some income.

The lectures continued until the end of May 1808 with an increasingly deeper analysis of the imagination. Richard Holmes highlights one particular analogy – that of the comparison between ghosts and stage illusion. Holmes explains how Coleridge underlined the difference between a fake ghost and a hallucination coming from within. The former produced a sudden shudder, whilst the latter was a dream-like state that would intensify and fill the mind. Coleridge was, as his biographer indicates, speaking from experience as these vivid hallucinatory apparitions had infiltrated his Maltese nights. It is difficult to tell whether he had planned this analogy or if it was merely tangential; nevertheless, these deviations proved popular, especially as he took the unusual step of interweaving personal experience. After the decision to streamline the lectures according to his notes, he could not resist the temptation to extemporise considerably once his confidence had returned.

The final lecture of the series focused on the subject of education, for which he was criticised in certain quarters as many considered it not to be part of his remit or experience. However, Coleridge made a powerful and remarkably liberal defence of progressive state education. He most strongly disagreed with the idea of rote learning laced with reprimands for those who shirked or struggled. He championed an approach that placed to the fore the imagination of the learner who, he felt, should be nurtured rather than punished. Some of this feeling must have arisen because of his own bitter experiences whilst at the Christ's Hospital School. Coleridge may have been lucky to receive such an education, given he had no aristocratic silver spoon, but it was far from a happy few years and the institution, at the time, could not have been considered progressive.

There were further lectures planned for June but it seems they were never delivered or only delivered in part. The writer, Edward Jerningham, from the Norwich family who would befriend John Polidori, Byron's unfortunate doctor, tells us that Coleridge had his lecture quotations stolen which, naturally, impacted his delivery. If Coleridge was not self-sabotaging, then fate would always seem to intervene and deal him a losing hand. He spiralled downwards from the heights of public acclaim, turning to prodigious quantities of opium which only served to fuel his depression and wilder thoughts. Lonely and dispirited, he wrote rash letters and poured his drug-induced opinions into notebook entries. He uses the Italian verb '*sfogarmi*'[14] to describe his need to get things off his chest or blow off steam. In the same passage, he obsessively rails against many of his close acquaintances, from Tom Poole to Wordsworth, Southey and even his own family, particularly owing to the festering open wound caused by George's rejection.

Almost as quickly as the depression had descended when his lectures fizzled to an anti-climax, his mood began to lift after a trip to Margate and the invigoration of sea air coupled with good companionship. He now settled on the idea of creating a weekly publication in which he would expound his ideas and develop fully some of the themes of his lectures as well as the metaphysical preoccupations he had grappled with in Malta. He set about the task of gathering information for a prospectus that would explain the concept, a useful device for gaining support and potential subscriptions. In many ways, London was the best base for attempting such an enormous project – a project that would have been significant for anyone, let alone someone as chaotic and easily distracted as Coleridge who had the added complication of being drug-dependent.

Knowing he had to address this latter issue, he sought out various doctors, eventually being recommended a Quaker physician who put him on a regime of decreasing levels of laudanum in an attempt to ween him from dependency. With a potential remedy in sight and connections established for his new project, which would become *The Friend*, he made the incredible decision to return to the Lake District. Predictably, his journey was not direct and he disappeared for a month before appearing at Grasmere. It was 1st September when Coleridge walked into Allan Bank, Wordsworth's residence. He was given a study and bedroom where he would remarkably bring *The Friend* to life. It is easy to understand why Wordsworths and Asra remained sceptical about the publication and its viability, not to mention Coleridge's ability to stick to the demands of such a rigorous schedule.

Interspersed with his vigorous attempt to progress the project, were periods of languorous longing for the ever-saintly Asra, still placed firmly on her pedestal. No longer, however, did she seem tolerant of his unrealistic affections, although she would become his amanuensis when the magazine came to fruition. For the publication to be official, he needed stamped paper which was expensive and much more difficult to find in the Lake District. He also busied himself with the promotional necessities which meant he had to send out his prospectus and canvas for subscribers. Coleridge planned a magazine that would not pander to the gossipy tastes of the age but would serve to invite readers to broaden their intellectual horizons and creativity of thought. He fully intended to engage in metaphysical philosophising, drawing heavily from his beloved German authors. The prospectus included this weighty proposition: 'Sources of Consolation to the afflicted in Misfortune, or Disease, or speculative Gloom, from the Exertion and right Application of the Reason, the Imagination and the Moral Sense . . .'[15] He was, indeed, expecting much from his readership, not least by employing this, his own method of literary healing.

It was during this time that Coleridge's behaviour became increasingly irregular, waking late, spending much time alone in his room and eating at unusual hours. Laudanum was used to alleviate the pressures of his schedule which, in turn, caused the inevitable crash, where days would be wasted forcing him to write through the night. He also had to make frantic dashes over the fells to ensure additions of *The Friend* were released on time to the subscribers he had managed to garner, amongst whom were Captain Pasley (his colleague from Malta), Henry Crabb Robinson, Walter Savage Landor and Thomas De Quincey, now well and truly in the Wordsworths' good books. Just as they were complaining of the louche habits and chaotic lifestyle of their resident opium addict, they invited another guest into their life who was already in thrall to the drug.

De Quincey was persuaded to take on the lease of the then vacant Dove Cottage where he could be close at hand. He was an informed observer of Coleridge, understanding better than anyone the turbulence caused by opium; although, at this stage in his life, he was still able to mask its worst effects. Coleridge borrowed hundreds of volumes from De Quincey who had piled his books from floor to ceiling in the confines of his cottage. Frances Wilson, in *Guilty Thing*, makes the pertinent point that the pair gazed with envy at each other – Coleridge saw himself ensconced at Dove Cottage, surrounded by books and with the attentions of Asra, whereas De Quincey imagined a project such as *The Friend* to stimulate his mind – both were flights of fancy.

It is difficult to characterise Coleridge's project, except to say that it, inevitably, had a niche audience owing to its obscure subject-matter. In a letter to Southey, he even described his own writing as being a product of his 'lucubrations'.[16] Appropriately enough, for a magazine that was often produced by the light of a wick in the wee small hours, lucubration derives from the Latin *lucubrare*, which means to work by lamplight but, essentially, refers to intensive study with pedantic overtones. Significantly, Coleridge did lighten later episodes of *The Friend*, particularly when he added travellers' tales and the character of Satyrane who, as Richard Holmes indicates, provides a conduit for Coleridge to write in another voice. There seems to be something of the heteronym in this approach, preceding by many years the multiple literary personas of Fernando Pessoa.

*The Friend* would change again when Coleridge heard the news of the death of Alexander Ball. As we have previously seen, he dedicated many pages to the life of his former employer and friend, whose death affected him greatly. To modern ears, the poet's writing on Ball's life occasionally strays into the realm of hero worship, witness this comparison with Nelson:

> If it had pleased Providence to preserve his life, and to place him on the same course on which Nelson ran his race of Glory, there are two points in which Sir Alexander Ball would most closely have resembled his illustrious Friend. The first is, that in his enterprizes and engagements he would have thought nothing done, till all had been done that was possible: 'Nil actum reputans, si quid supresset agendum'. The second, that he would have called forth all the talent and virtue that existed within his sphere of influence, and created a band of Heroes . . . [17]

De Quincey, who opined on these 'wandering and exaggerated estimates of men'[18] was convinced these obsessions with certain figures were the workings of opium.

As *The Friend* eventually came to a close, the Wordsworths were at the end of their despairing tether with their erratic house guest. To make matters worse, Asra left to stay with her brother in Wales. The endeavours of writing so intensively had distracted Coleridge away from his children but now it was time to pay them some attention. He was delighted to discover that his daughter, Sara, had a facility for languages. He employed his own knowledge of Italian to write a little dialogue for her which she had soon surpassed and, within a year, was reading Italian texts without difficulty. The children were a happy release from the worries that plagued him. With the demise of his great project came the question as to what he should do next. He retreated to Greta Hall.

The increased drug dependency which deadened his preoccupations now manifested itself in physical obsessions. The habit of compulsively washing, which he had picked up in the sticky heat of Malta, began to creep into his daily life. Holmes sees this as connected with opium guilt and it does appear as if he is seeking to cleanse his very soul. At the height of Coleridge's frenzy and confusion, his attention turned to the Spanish mystic, Saint Teresa of Avila, who was immortalised in ecstatic revelation by the sculptor, Bernini. Coleridge calls her imagination 'fever-kindled'[19] – an epithet he could apply to his own tortured nights. To make matters worse, the split from Wordsworth was imminent. It was all prompted by the plan that Coleridge travel down to London with a Mr and Mrs Montagu. Basil Montagu was a London barrister and an admirer of Samuel Taylor, so much so, he decided to invite the poet to spend the winter at his London residence. Wordsworth became aware of the plan and, based on his own recent experience, was sure that the Montagus would not be able to tolerate Coleridge's unsociable behaviour.

Before the party's departure, Wordsworth took Mr Montagu aside and advised him against having Coleridge as a house guest. Consequently, when they arrived in London, Coleridge was dropped at another of the Montagus' properties, rather than accompanying Basil and his wife to their own residence. It was after a raucous dinner with Pasley, where they reminisced about Malta, that a loose-tongued Coleridge confronted Montagu, asking for an explanation regarding the change in plans. Nobody has been able to verify exactly what happened next, but it seems that the barrister lost all semblance of lawyerly balance and informed the distraught poet that Wordsworth had specifically told him to relay his views regarding Coleridge's recent behaviour; the upshot of this being the distressing news that his old friend had little hope of him slaying his demons and achieving anything in the future. It was nothing short of a character assassination. Did Montagu really have Wordsworth's authority to reveal their conversation, or was he using William as a shield behind which he could renege on his commitments?

A distraught Coleridge decamped to a hotel where he turned to drink and opium-filled introspection. His life seemed to be in free-fall with some of his firmest connections apparently irretrievably severed. He had a wife whose company he could only tolerate in small doses, children he barely saw and now a long-standing literary friendship left in tatters. Nothing appeared on the horizon as a tolerable solution to either his emotional difficulties or his authorial prospects. Whilst at his lowest ebb, a knight would ride to his defence. The degree to which Coleridge was esteemed by others is telling, particularly when all was lost, as he always found a champion willing to pick him up, dust him down and attempt to set him on the right course. In this instance, it was John Morgan who, together with his wife and sister-in-law, would play a significant role in the years ahead.

Ensconced with the Morgans in Hammersmith, Coleridge gradually emerged from the gloom to re-forge social connections and begin some journalistic work. Charles Lamb often acted as the conduit for introductions to new friends, one of whom was the journalist, Henry Crabb Robinson. Now able to engage Samuel Taylor in conversation, rather than discuss his works from a distance, he found they shared common ground, not least of which was study at a German university. Robinson was well-travelled and appreciated Coleridge's Mediterranean reminiscences, especially as Samuel Taylor was able to drop the names of Tieck and Humboldt from his time in Rome. Robinson also once wrote, 'If I have a pet in the South, it is Sicily'.[20] Clearly, the two men had much to talk over. These convivial dinners with Henry and others were a welcome distraction, yet, so often, they brought up topics and memories that set in motion painful self-analysis. One evening, as he was sitting listening to Angelica Catalana sing, he was once again in the audience at Syracuse listening to Bertozzi. Afterwards, in his notebook, he copied out some words from an aria by Metastasio, 'Teneri miei sospirii senza gioia, senza speme'[21] ('Tender my sighs without joy, without hope') – an apt description of his current state of mind.

Coleridge increasingly found himself at political odds with the conservative *Courier* newspaper for which he was writing and this contributed to his reputation for fair-weather political commitment amongst the young radicals, such as Leigh Hunt and, especially, William Hazlett, who would prove to be a critical nemesis. Coleridge did consider resigning and writing elsewhere but missed his opportunity to do so which only compounded his supposed connection to the establishment. It could be argued that, at this time, he needed to prioritise money over morals and attempt to re-establish himself. There was also the small matter of ensuring he had a daily routine to keep his addiction at bay, although writing to deadlines for a paper he little respected did nothing for his self-esteem. There were periods of collapse and turmoil. He was also acutely aware that his behaviour at the Morgans', mostly tolerated in a benign manner, occasionally caused scenes that must have offended the two women. His letters and speeches of *mea culpa* are filled with histrionic apologies and exaggerated excuses.

Coleridge realised, though, that this benevolent and accepting family were his only life-raft. John Morgan would go on to act as his amanuensis and help with his literary endeavours which included a return to the lecture circuit and the acceptance for performance of his Spanish play, *Osorio*, now re-christened *Remorse*. The play was a great success at Drury Lane and included an incantation scene with a choir of monks and boatmen 'sailing' across the stage. The incantation ended with the lines: 'Hush!, the cadence dies away / On the quiet moonlight sea: / The boatmen rest their oars and say, / Miserere Domine!'²² The January 1813 premiere brought rapturous applause and subsequent performances – the money rolled in and his star was, once more, in the ascendant. Coleridge knew he owed a debt to Morgan and when the family went through their own difficulties, he moved heaven and earth to help them.

Morgan's business had become a victim of the post Napoleonic War slump and creditors were at the door; so much so, that John escaped to Ireland in order to avoid them. Coleridge put together a rescue plan which saw his Maltese administrative experiences come to fruition. He wrote to creditors, pleaded with the bank and instituted his own series of lectures in Bristol – the proceeds of which were to go straight to the Morgans. Doubtless, some of his Drury Lane income also went to help his friends. Remarkably, the chaotic and hopeless Coleridge largely succeeded in rescuing their finances. Before John Morgan returned from Ireland, Samuel Taylor had paid up everything in London and moved Mary and her sister, Charlotte, to the West Country. It was all to come at a price; after this period of intense activity he nose-dived, once again, into the depths of opium.

Near Bath, living – perhaps scandalously to the locals – with Mary and Charlotte, Coleridge appears to have behaved in such a manner as to greatly embarrass himself and offend the ladies. We can imagine the tense atmosphere. The Morgan women had undergone months of uncertainty with John away and the threat of destitution around the corner; Coleridge had been frantically working on their behalf but also taking large amounts of laudanum and drinking heavily. Once the worst had passed, the steam from the pressure cooker had to find release. There were outbursts and harsh words. What was Coleridge expecting of the women, and did his behaviour overstep the bounds of decorum, particularly with regard to Charlotte? There is nothing to suggest physical impropriety, but much was said by Coleridge that he later regretted. Molly Lefebure thinks their reluctance to accord with all of his future wishes and plans was at the heart of the conflict, which could imply a lack of appreciation for his titanic efforts. Richard Holmes suggests these fractious moments were followed by the worst opium overdose he had ever experienced. Remarkably, the breach would be healed with alarming speed.

Initially, it was Josiah Wade in Bristol who came to his rescue. He was treated by Wade's personal physician and stayed with his friend for nine months. It was during this time that he began to heal his relationship with the Morgans, now settled in Ashley, Wiltshire. He also re-established his connection with Washington Allston who had his own troubles – not least of which was overwhelming grief from the early death of his wife. Allston had come to England with the intention of making a splash at the Royal Academy, but success was elusive. He was now at Clifton in the West Country planning an exhibition which, when it came to fruition, Coleridge reviewed in glowing terms. His essay for a Bristol newspaper included memories of their Roman interlude, notably Raphael's fresco in the Villa Farnesi. Morton Paley in *Samuel Taylor Coleridge and the Fine Arts* is clear that his review produced 'a discerning formal analysis of an image'[23] with regard to his account of Allston's *Dead Man Restored*. The American was immensely grateful for his old friend's backing.

This was the period that saw Allston paint his second portrait of Coleridge, a very different image from the one painted during the sunny days in Olevano. The intervening years had seen Samuel Taylor's hair fade to grey but still retain its volume. The composition of the image differs in the turn of the head away from the viewing artist; however, both portraits find Coleridge's eyes gazing into the middle distance – the later portrait has a sense of many hidden thoughts and none of the incomplete uncertainty of the first. Allston's 1814 image appears tinged with sadness; a sense of looking backwards rather than an anticipation of the future. The poet's full mouth is gently turned down at the corners exposing a vulnerability that could easily be missed by those not familiar with his recent traumatic past. Allston was happy with the portrait and Coleridge was sufficiently trusting of his friend to believe the picture was a faithful portrayal. It must be said, though, that he was seldom happy with representations of himself, lamenting that his appearance lacked a certain strength of masculinity.

His concentration on Allston's works and reminiscences of Italy helped his convalescence, as did the rapprochement with the Morgans. By the autumn of 1814, he had moved in with them once again and was reading avidly from Cervantes and Goethe, in addition to formulating an idea for what would become his *Biographia Literaria*. In an effort to resuscitate his career, he wrote to Lord Byron in the hope of gaining his favour. He was honest enough to plead his less fortunate lot and to distance himself, to a degree, from Southey and Wordsworth, both of whom had been subjects of Byron's sardonic verse as, indeed, had Coleridge himself, admitting as much in the letter. Byron's *English Bards and Scotch Reviewers* had this to say of Samuel Taylor, with his Lordship's tongue placed firmly in his cheek:

> Shall gentle Coleridge pass unnoticed here,
> To turgid ode, and tumid stanza dear?
> Though themes of innocence amuse him best,
> Yet still obscurity's a welcome guest.
> If inspiration should her aid refuse,
> To him who takes a Pixy for a Muse,
> Yet none in lofty number can surpass,
> The Bard who soars to elegize an ass.
> How well the subject suits his noble mind,
> "A fellow feeling makes us wondrous kind."[24]

No offence had been taken and it seems Byron had a great deal of respect for Coleridge's work. The reply contained much praise and an apology for his teasingly satirical verses. He was happy to receive any manuscripts and to recommend them for publication.

With the approval of Britain's ascending star of the literary world, the mariner now had wind in his sails. He began in earnest to write the *Biographia* which would evolve way beyond its initial concept. Happy again to have John Morgan as his amanuensis, the words flowed, covering the gamut of topics from autobiography to philosophical analysis, literary criticism and paternal advice for those starting on their authorial journey. He delved into the well of his extensive reading and experience for the text. His reading of Dante whilst in the Mediterranean comes to the fore when he compares the Italian with contemporary writers of English who 'strive to be in the fashion, and trick themselves out in the soiled and over-worn finery of the meretricious muse'. He champions the Renaissance author and his philosophy of language:

> Nay, even of those who have most rescued themselves from this contagion, I should plead inwardly guilty to the charge of duplicity or cowardice if I withheld my conviction that few have guarded the purity of their native tongue with that jealous care which the sublime Dante, in his tract 'De la nobile volgare eloquenza', declares to be the first duty of a poet.[25]

Almost in the next breath, Coleridge jumps to landscape painters applying the same view in parallel to the visual arts. His experience of Italian art leads him to opine that a 'visual language formed by the substitution of figures for words' created 'beauty and harmony of the colours, lines and expression with which the objects are represented'. The representation of similar subjects by many artists was the 'trial and test of the artist's merit'.[26] In a whirl of interlinking thought, he brings the subject back to Italy's Renaissance poets and their generalised imagery of 'sun, moon, flowers, breezes, murmuring streams . . .' with each writer fashioning the same concepts 'according to his judgement or fancy'. For Coleridge, these Italians of the past 'placed the essence of poetry in the *art*'.[27]

He harks back to his time in Florence by referring to a work of Giovambatista Strozzi that he was able to peruse whilst in the city. He writes out in Italian nine verses of Strozzi's 'Madrigale', lauding the work in the following manner: 'I have seldom met with compositions that possessed, to my feelings, more of that satisfying entireness, that complete adequateness of the manner to the matter which so charms us in Anacreon, joined with the tenderness, and more than the delicacy of Catullus.'[28] He offers the verses with no translation, being discouraged by what he calls the 'different genius'[29] of English. Coleridge clearly states his feeling that, in Italian, there is a greater distinction between prose and poetry, attributing this to the diversity of dialects which have produced their own poetic idioms. This is a mature reflection on the linguistic variety to be found in Italy and the poetically-driven language traditions. Indeed, had Coleridge been more fully aware of the Sicilian School of poetry, headed by the likes of the thirteenth century poet, Jacopo da Lentini, when living on the island, he might have investigated further and been less scathing of the quality of the islander's Italian.

The *Biographia* was substantially finished by July 1815 and, as Richard Holmes mentions, Coleridge saw the text as a form of dialogue with Wordsworth. The two poets had reached a type of accommodation after their rift, but their relationship was far removed from the heady days they had experienced in Somerset. In fact, Coleridge had received a letter from William asking him not to publish the conversational poem 'To William Wordsworth' that Samuel Taylor had written at the time of the Asra 'incident'. Wordsworth knew that Coleridge was planning a poetry collection, *The Sibylline Leaves*, to accompany his prose text. Despite Coleridge's hurt at the rather formal and chilly letter, he could not help but illustrate Wordsworth's genius in the *Biographia* – but not without criticism – as we can see from this example noting their differences on the theory of imagination: '... after a more accurate perusal of Mr Wordsworth's remarks on the imagination in his preface to the new edition of his poems, I find that my conclusions are not so consentient with his as, I confess, I had taken for granted.'[30]

The Bristol publisher made adjustment after adjustment to the deadline as Coleridge continued to tinker with and modify the draft. Reminiscent of his Shakespeare lectures, it is easy to see how accusations of plagiarism were made after publication as the text is littered with his favourite German sources without the necessary acknowledgements. Much debate still surrounds the extent to which this was deliberate or mere oversights arising from his vast digestion and absorption of knowledge throughout the years. He was writing at a pace, at times letting his mind run on a theme as his consciousness streamed onto the paper through the pen of Morgan. There must, however, have been some awareness as the *Biographia* is not without attributions, but they are selective and full of omissions. To what extent Coleridge's use of opium can explain these lapses, which could be classed as a lack of attention to the minutiae of text production, is open to question. Although, it is clear that the furious pace of the work and the ever-expanding nature of its structure helped to moderate the poet's days and reduce his intake to more modest levels – at least until the work was completed.

Gutch, the publisher, who seems not to have employed the most efficient printer in the book trade, had been accumulating expenses as Coleridge prevaricated on the nature of the text and its length. The book would not actually see the light of day until 1817 when Coleridge was firmly ensconced at his final residence in Highgate, London; even then, it would not be released by Gutch who, in the intervening months, had complained of its unfinished nature, presenting the poet with a hefty invoice for expenses accrued. It was this near completion of his prose and poetry work, in addition to the play, *Zapolya*, written for the Drury Lane Theatre, that redirected his thoughts to London. In many ways, Coleridge knew he could not end his days in the provincial backwater of Wiltshire but, equally, where was he to find the finances to move from the reassuring hearth of the Morgans?

His friend, William Sotheby, applied to the London Literary Fund asking if they would consider giving a grant to Coleridge. Additionally, Sotheby made contact with Lord Byron. Both the institution and his Lordship provided monies which were enough to facilitate a move to the capital. Unsurprisingly, the stress of the relocation provoked another relapse and Coleridge was soon calling John Morgan for help. To Morgan's credit, he came to London and, it is a testament to the loyalty the poet inspired, that John rushed to the assistance of a man who had just abandoned their family home when the prospect of literary achievement had provided better prospects. Morgan found a doctor who was able to make a recommendation to a colleague, namely James Gillman of the Royal College of Surgeons. Gillman was to prove the steadying influence Coleridge needed and, in truth, probably extended the poet's life by some years. Initially, he was invited to Highgate for a chat and, during what was essentially an interview, Coleridge treated the doctor and his wife with conviviality and courteousness. It was agreed that, to ameliorate his opium addiction, Samuel Taylor would lodge with the Gillmans as a form of in-house patient.

At the same time, Coleridge was writing a letter to Lord Byron that would be enclosed with his play, *Zapolya*. Remarkably, he made admissions to Byron that were more frank and open in manner than the circumlocutions he penned to his friends. In apology for the lateness of submission, he laments the 'wretched state of my mind and body',[31] going on to confess the degree of his laudanum addiction and the fact that his mind was often poisoned by the habit. He was also at pains to stress that he was seeking a cure at Highgate. Perhaps this frankness was not so remarkable when considering the rumours swirling around London about Byron's own lifestyle and peccadillos. Coleridge may have considered that if there was anyone who would not seek to judge him, it was Byron. In any event, Byron read the play immediately and invited Coleridge to come and meet him at his residence in Piccadilly. Sadly, there is no detailed record of this momentous occasion, but subsequent snippets reveal Byron's encouragement with regard to publishing 'Christabel' and 'Kubla Khan'. Coleridge was also taken aback by Byron's striking appearance, comparing his eyes to 'the open portals of the sun' and claiming that he had never seen 'so beautiful a countenance'.[32]

The initial months at Highgate were regimented as Gillman sought to decrease his dosage but, inevitably, Coleridge tried to smuggle in elicit quantities of laudanum which the doctor put a stop to when he found out. There was no recrimination and rancour as Samuel Taylor seems to have recognised he was in sound medical hands rather than receiving the well-meaning but amateurish attentions of his friends. That is not to say, however, that Gillman and his wife remained aloof acquaintances. Coleridge realised that the doctor shared some of his theoretical interests and the pair actually worked on texts together for the Royal College of Surgeons. He would become a valued member of the household, much appreciated by Gillman's wife and an erudite mentor to their children.

As Coleridge settled in to a more ordered life, his productivity increased. John Murray, owing to the good auspice of Byron, published 'Christabel' in a volume with 'Kubla Khan' in 1816. Reactions were mixed, even in the same review — admiration and disapproval sat side by side. 'Christabel' would become a favourite of those gathered at the Villa Diodati near Geneva during the stormy nights of that summer. Byron read the poem aloud and Percy Bysshe Shelley ran screaming from the room at the point where the narrator exclaims 'Behold! her bosom and half her side — / A sight to *dream of*, not to tell! / O shield her! shield sweet Christabel!'[33] Polidori, Byron's doctor, ran after the stricken poet in order to calm him. The poem had caused Shelley to have a vision of a woman with eyes in place of nipples.

'Kubla Khan' was prefaced with Coleridge's now famous third person explanation of 'the fragment'. It contains the following description of how he was disturbed and thus prevented from completing the poem after his opium-fed dream: 'On awakening he appeared to himself to have a distinct recollection of the whole, and taking his pen, ink, and paper, instantly and eagerly wrote down the lines that are here preserved. At this moment he was unfortunately called out by a person on business from Porlock . . . '[34] Alethea Hayter, in her book *Opium and the Romantic Imagination*, is sceptical concerning the strict veracity of Coleridge's explanation. She points out that the poet's usual drug-fed dreams contained incidents from his past or concerned his family and friends. There were also figures from legend and history but little in the way of detailed or fantastical landscape. By way of illustration, in her book she includes a photo of Piranesi's *Imaginary Prisons* as an example of the subconscious opium imagination at work, as recognised by both Coleridge and De Quincey. She is more convinced that Xanadu was the product of a waking reverie. De Quincey is quite explicit on the experiences of the opium-eater which could evoke a strong desire to escape crowds: 'He naturally seeks solitude and silence, as indispensable conditions of those trances, or profoundest reveries, which are the crown and consummation of what opium can do for human nature.' Coleridge would never admit, perhaps even to himself, that opium produced these trance-like moments that might lead to sublime creation – his guilt would not allow him to fully accept the role the drug played.

If Murray's volume was not universally praised, it certainly became a talking point, even more so after Thomas Moore's review. Moore was supposed to laud the text upon Byron's instruction but decided, instead, to demolish it in the *Edinburgh Review*. There is good reason to think that this hindered sales and dissuaded Murray from pursuing other projects with Coleridge. With his Bristol publisher of the *Biographia* demanding money for expenses and Murray's disinterest, Coleridge fell into the hands of Gale and Fenner who bought up his copyrights and issued the *Biographia Literaria* and the *Sibylline Leaves*. Returning to the opinions of Lord Byron, Richard Holmes raises the intriguing possibility that something written in the former work may have triggered Byron's thought processes when it came to the creation of his masterwork, *Don Juan*. In Chapter XXIII, Coleridge raises the subject of the Spanish libertine who he feels is worthy of further investigation. Knowing the work to be popular in Spain, he characterises him thus:

> Rank, fortune, wit, talent, acquired knowledge, and liberal accomplishments, with beauty of person, vigorous health, and constitutional hardihood – all these advantages, elevated by the habits and sympathies of noble birth and national character, are supposed to have combined in *Don Juan*, so as to give him the means of carrying into all its practical consequences the doctrine of a godless nature as the sole ground and efficient cause not only of all things, events, and appearances, but, likewise, of all our thoughts, sensations, impulses, and actions.[35]

With a summary such as this, how could anyone resist? The Byron scholar, Peter Cochrane, tells us, via Hobhouse's diary, that Byron was reading the *Biographia* in Venice during the October of 1817. Cochrane goes on to draw similar conclusions to Holmes, namely that the essay from Chapter XXIII was likely to have prompted Byron to use the Spanish anti-hero as his main protagonist. Our minds return to the square in Gibraltar where Coleridge first encountered Spaniards 'with their cloaks, falling down very elegantly, and in groups often compose excellently'[36] – a model for any Don Juan.

Sadly, Coleridge's publishing woes did not end with Gale and Fenner who went bankrupt leaving him without revenues, apart from those gained from Murray's volume. Luckily, the Gillmans stood by him and sent him down to the coast at Ramsgate to take his mind off the situation and to avoid more surreptitious trips to the backdoor of the local pharmacy in search of illicit laudanum. Added to the poet's troubles was a feeling that history was about to repeat itself. His son, Hartley, who had achieved a Cambridge degree and been appointed to a fellowship, was now being dismissed for his dissolute behaviour. It seems that Coleridge's eldest son had inherited the addiction gene, although, in this instance, it was his love of alcohol that contributed to his chaotic behaviour. Coleridge endeavoured to ride to the rescue, writing to the university authorities but to no avail. The scandal, as the poet saw it, affected him deeply, reminding him of his own faults and failings. There were scenes between father and son, the former trying to establish the truth, the latter denying the allegations. There would, eventually, be a rift between the two as Hartley drifted northwards, trying his hand as a schoolmaster but without much conviction. In this black mirror, Coleridge saw his own inability to fulfil his potential and achieve the works he intended.

There was no choice but to reconcile himself to circumstances and to count the blessings that had led him to Highgate. These years of deep thought culminated in the text *Aids to Reflection* in 1825. Coleridge now happily received the acclaim of the young acolytes who came to visit him and listen to his travel stories, philosophising and opinions. He had ploughed a path distinct from the establishment destinies of Southey and Wordsworth. Byron said of Southey, 'Although 'tis true that you turn'd out a Tory at / Last, – yours has lately been a common case . . . ';[37] yet, this specific accusation could not be levelled at Coleridge whose conservatism had a small 'c'. Even during his Highgate years, he was penning his support for those campaigning against child labour in the cotton mills. There were many regrets, though, not least of which was the wound inflicted by Hartley's dismissal and his own inability to shake the demon of addiction. Gillman was never totally successful in removing opium from his life.

In many ways, Coleridge's sojourn in the Mediterranean was the turning point, after which he tacitly acknowledged that his life would always progress hand in hand with the drug that he admitted to Byron had poisoned his imagination. The Maltese nights, full of opium-fueled dreams of Asra, set the pattern for a longing that would never be fulfilled. His fantasy notion of the perfect woman, the muse to his settled domestication and ordered existence, was just that – an unattainable fiction. Had Coleridge ever had the opportunity to consummate his relationship with Sara Hutchinson, and had society been able to accept such an arrangement, his addiction would have surely ruined any future together. However, without these sustaining thoughts of another possible life, the void he felt might have become unbearable.

The Mediterranean sojourn also taught him that he was wholly unfit for a salaried existence. When Hartley lost his fellowship, part of Coleridge's lament also centred around his own feelings of missed opportunity. Somewhere inside, he imagined himself as an academic don, teaching and writing papers for posterity. This is one more projection of another life for which he was unsuited; it is enough to witness the demands of ordered hours and pressured decisions that impacted his mental health in Malta and forced him to seek solace in laudanum. Our most favoured image of Coleridge in the Mediterranean has little to do with strategising for Alexander Ball but sees him in his star chamber, gazing to the heavens and setting off fireworks in his own mind – the Greeks, astrology, language, theology and philosophy.

Many of the works he perused whilst abroad between 1804 and 1806 could have been purchased and read whilst he was still in London. There is, though, much to be said for discovering the texts of a culture whilst *in situ*. Coleridge read the Renaissance poets whilst staring at the works of their artistic contemporaries; both would re-emerge in his lectures and his *Biographia*. The Latin world provided a counterpoint to his principal attachment to the Teutonic world, with his philosophy of the Romantic imagination acting as the umbrella for both. His meeting with Allston was also a key to later thought; it gave him the time and opportunity to observe and question an artist at work. He could compare and contrast their respective creative processes and inspirations. His notes on Allston's painting, *Diana and her Nymphs in the Chase*, are some of the most striking and thoughtful he wrote in Italy. Despite this, Coleridge would always retain his disregard for the ruins of the Classical world he observed; the words of the Ancients were still alive to him, their buildings a mere remnant.

Italy would return to him in 'The Garden of Boccaccio' completed in 1827. He invoked the journey he had personally taken from Florence to Pisa encompassing the beauty of stretches along the Arno:

> The brightness of the world, O thou once free.
> And always fair, rare land of courtesy!
> O Florence! with the Tuscan fields and hills,
> And famous Arno, fed with all their rills;
> Thou brightest star of star-bright Italy!
> Rich, ornate, populous, all treasures thine,
> The golden corn, the olive and the vine.[38]

The poem was a gesture for his gracious hostess, Ann Gillman. She and her husband were the last in a long line of affectionate friends who had sustained Coleridge in his hour of need. In his last years, he would become the sage of Highgate. His door was open to the likes of John Stirling and John Stuart Mill, the latter of whom would go on to be one of the most influential contributors to the world of classical liberalism. He also received visits from leading émigrés including Gabriele Rossetti (the poet father of Dante Gabriel) who would become a professor of Italian at King's College. Increasingly, Coleridge would find these visits difficult as his heart began to fail. Gone were the rambles up and down Highgate Hill and he even found moving across his room exhausting. On 25th July, 1834, maintaining conversation to the last, he slipped away. Coleridge was originally buried in the crypt of Highgate school, eventually being re-united in death with his wife. There was a subsequent move to St Michael's Church, Highgate, where part of his memorial plaque humbly reads, in his own words, 'A poet lies, or that which once seem'd he. / – O, lift one thought in prayer for S.T.C.; / That he who many a year with toil of breath / Found death in life, may here find life in death!'

In a final twist to the Coleridge story, despite the memorial and inscription, the actual site of his remains were uncertain. In 2018, during renovation underneath St Michael's Church, they were rediscovered in a former seventeenth-century wine cellar that had been covered in rubble and dust. During previous restoration and expansion, the cellar had been incorporated into the church's crypt. Some wry commentators have affectionately noted the irony of this bibulous location. Plans are afoot to convert the crypt into a more fitting memorial where people will be able to pay their respects, and scholars can study the continuing influence and significance of Samuel Taylor Coleridge's life and works.

# Notes

ONE  **Departure on the *Speedwell***

1 Coleridge, S. T., *Samuel Taylor Coleridge: Poems Selected by James Fenton* (London: Faber and Faber, 2006), 45.
2 Coleridge, S. T., *Samuel Taylor Coleridge: Poems Selected by James Fenton*, 13.
3 Coleridge, S. T., *The Collected Works of Samuel Taylor Coleridge, Volume 11 – Shorter Works and Fragments: Volume II* (Princeton: Princeton University Press, 2019), 59.
4 Coleridge, S. T., *Letters of Samuel Taylor Coleridge: Volume 2*, editor Coleridge, E. H. (London: W. Heinemann, 1895), 458.
5 Coleridge, S. T., *Collected Letters: Volume 2*, editor Griggs, E. L. (London: Clarendon Press, 1966), 929.
6 Dykes Campbell, J., *Samuel Taylor Coleridge: A Narrative of the Events of His Life* (London: Macmillan, 1894), 122.
7 Coleridge, S. T., *Samuel Taylor Coleridge: Poems Selected by James Fenton*, 58.
8 Wordsworth, W., *Poetical Works: Volume 10*, editor Knight, A. (Edinburgh: W. Paterson, 1889), 14.
9 Davy, H., *The Collected Works of Sir Humphry Davy: Volume 1* (London: Smith Elder, 1839), 449.
10 Coleridge, S. T., *Unpublished Letters of Samuel Taylor Coleridge Including Certain Letters Republished from Original Sources: Volume 1*, editor Griggs, E. L. (New Haven: Yale University Press, 1933), 318.
11 Lamb, C. and Lamb, M. A., *The Letters of Charles and Mary Anne Lamb*, editor Marrs, E. (Ithaca, Cornell University Press, 1976), 136.
12 Coleridge, S. T., *The Notebooks of Samuel Taylor Coleridge: Volume 2 1804 – 1808*, editor Coburn, K. (Abingdon: Routledge, 2002), 2013.
13 Coleridge, S. T., *Letters of Samuel Taylor Coleridge: Volume 2*, editor Coleridge, E. H., 470.
14 Southey, R., *The Story of His Life Written in His Letters*, editor Dennis, J. (Boston: D. Lothrop Company, 1887), 166.
15 Southey, R., *The Story of His Life Written in His Letters*, 133.
16 Southey, R., *The Poetical Works of Robert Southey: Complete in one volume* (London: Longmans, 1847), 731.
17 Byron, G. G. (Lord), *Letters, Journals and Other Prose Writings of Lord Byron: Volume II* (New York: George Dearborn, 1837), 555.

18  O'Connell, M., *Byron and John Murray: A Poet and his Publisher* (Liverpool: Liverpool University Press, 2014), 79.
19  Byron, G. G. (Lord), Byron: Poetical Works (London: Oxford University Press, 1967), 183.
20  Coleridge, S. T., *Unpublished Letters of Samuel Taylor Coleridge: Volume 2*, editor Griggs E. L. (New Haven, Yale University Press, 1933), 38.
21  Byron, G. G. (Lord), *Byron: Poetical Works*, 190.
22  Cervantes, M., quoted in Duffield, A. J., *Don Quixote: His Critics and Commentators* (London: C. Kegan Paul & Co, 1881), 29.
23  Coleridge, S. T., *Notebooks: Vol. 2*, 2026.
24  Fraser, W. W., *A Letter Addressed to the Governor of Gibraltar Relative to the Febrile Distempers of that Garrison* (London: Callow & Wilson, 1826), 49.
25  Coleridge, S. T., *Notebooks: Vol. 2*, 2045.
26  Coleridge, S. T., *Notebooks: Vol. 2*, 2045.
27  Coleridge, S. T., *Notebooks: Vol. 2*, 2045.
28  Coleridge, S. T., *Notebooks: Vol. 2*, 2034.
29  Waring, G., *Letters from Malta and Sicily, addressed to a young naturalist* (London: Harvey and Darton, 1843), 23.
30  Coleridge, S. T., *Notebooks: Vol. 2*, 2045.
31  Sanchez, M. G., *The Prostitutes of Serruya's Lane and other Hidden Gibraltarian Stories* (Gibraltar: Rock Scorpion Books, 2007), 12.
32  Coleridge, S. T., *Confessions of an Inquiring Spirit*, editor Nelson, H. (Boston: James Munroe & Company, 1841), 18.
33  Coleridge, S. T., *Notebooks: Vol. 2*, 2045.
34  Coleridge, S. T., *Notebooks: Vol. 2*, 2045.
35  Coleridge, S. T., *The Complete Works of Samuel Taylor Coleridge: The Poetical and Dramatic Works*, editor Shedd, W. (New York: Harper & Brothers, 1884), 883.
36  Blasco Ibáñez, V., quoted in *Gibraltar Through the Spanish Eye*, editor Tubino, F. M. (Amazon Media, 2012), 1046 .
37  Téllez Rubio, J. J., *Gibraltar en el tiempo de los espías* (Seville: Fundación José Manuel Lara, 2005), 31.
38  Téllez Rubio, J. J., *Yanitos: Viaje al corazón de Gibraltar (1713–2013)* (Seville: Centro de Estudios Andaluces, 2013), 22.
39  Coleridge, S. T., *Notebooks: Vol. 2*, 2074.
40  Coleridge, S. T., *Notebooks: Vol. 2*, 2071.
41  Coleridge, S. T., *Notebooks: Vol. 2*, 2091.
42  Brydone, P., *Travels in Sicily and Malta* (Aberdeen: George Clark & Son, 1848), 194.
43  Dumas, A. (père), *Pascal Bruno*, editor Hook, T. (London: Henry Colburn, 1837), 4.

44  Benza, Dr., *The Penny Cyclopaedia of the Society for the Diffusion of Useful Knowledge* (Limonia: Charles Knight, 1839), 345.
45  Piccolo, L., *Collected Poems of Lucio Piccolo*, trans. Swann, B. (Princeton: Princeton University Press, 1972), 97.

TWO  **Strategising for Nelson in Malta**

1  Byron, G. G. (Lord), *Byron: Poetical Works* (London: Oxford University Press, 1967), 61.
2  Coleridge, S. T., *The Notebooks of Samuel Taylor Coleridge: Volume 2 1804 – 1808*, editor Coburn, K. (Abingdon: Routledge, 2002), 2100.
3  Nelson, H. (Viscount), *Letters and Despatches of Horatio, Viscount Nelson*, editor Knox Laughton, J. (London: Longmans Green, 1886), 1801.
4  Coleridge, S. T., *The Friend: A series of essays to aid in the formation of fixed principles in politics, morals and religion: Volume II* (London: Edward Moxon, 1863), 279.
5  Coleridge, S. T., *The Friend: A series of essays* (London: Gale and Curtis, 1812), 421.
6  Brydone, P., *Travels in Sicily and Malta* (Aberdeen: George Clark & Son, 1848), 125.
7  Coleridge, S. T., *Notebooks: Vol. 2*, 2137.
8  Coleridge, S. T., *Unpublished Letters of Samuel Taylor Coleridge Including Certain Letters Republished from Original Sources: Volume 1*, editor Griggs, E. L. (New Haven: Yale University Press, 1933), 321.
9  De Quincey, T., *The Treasury of Modern Biography: Issue 92*, editor Cochrane, R. (London, 1878), 141.
10  Coleridge, S. T., *Notebooks: Vol. 2*, 2431.
11  Byron, G. G. (Lord), *Byron: Poetical Works* (London: Oxford University Press, 1967), 629.
12  Coleridge, S. T., *The Collected Works of Samuel Taylor Coleridge, Volume 11 – Shorter Works and Fragments: Volume II* (Princeton: Princeton University Press, 2019), 145.
13  Brydone, P., *Travels in Sicily and Malta*, 127.
14  Brydone, P., *Travels in Sicily and Malta*, 127.
15  Coleridge, S. T., *Notebooks: Vol. 2*, 2144.
16  Coleridge, S. T., *Notebooks: Vol. 2*, 2141.
17  Coleridge, S. T., *The Statemen's Manual* (London: Gale and Fenner, 1816), 17.
18  Coleridge, S. T., *The Statemen's Manual*, 28.
19  Hazlitt, W., *The Selected Writings of William Hazlitt: Political Essays*, editor Wu, D. (London: Pickering & Chatto, 1998), 110.
20  Coleridge, S. T., *Notebooks: Vol. 2*, 2101.

21 Coleridge, S. T., *Unpublished Letters of Samuel Taylor Coleridge Including Certain Letters Republished from Original Sources: Volume 1*, 31.
22 Coleridge, S. T., *Notebooks: Vol. 2*, 2434.
23 Coleridge, S. T., *Notebooks: Vol. 2*, 2434.
24 Coleridge, S. T., *The Works of Samuel Taylor Coleridge: Prose and Verse* (Philadelphia: T. Cowperthwait, 1845), 14.

THREE   Sicily and the Prima Donna

1 Luque, A., *Borges in Sicily: Journey with a Blind Guide*, trans. Edwards, A. (London: Haus, 2019), 38.
2 Coleridge, S. T., *The Notebooks of Samuel Taylor Coleridge: Volume 2 1804 –1808*, editor Coburn, K. (Abingdon: Routledge, 2002), 2171.
3 Coleridge, S. T., *Notebooks: Vol. 2*, 2171.
4 Ferrara, F., *Storia generale dell'Etna* (Catania, 1793), 67.
5 Coleridge, S. T., *Notebooks: Vol. 2*, 2171.
6 Coleridge, S. T., *Notebooks: Vol. 2*, 2171.
7 Coleridge, S. T., *Notebooks: Vol. 2*, 2172.
8 Coleridge, S. T., *Notebooks: Vol. 2*, 2172.
9 Dykes Campbell, J., *Samuel Taylor Coleridge: A Narrative of the Events of His Life* (London: Macmillan, 1894), 146.
10 Ferrara, F., *Storia generale dell'Etna*, 4.
11 Ferrara, F., *Storia generale dell'Etna*, 4.
12 Swinburne, H., *Travels in the Two Sicilies in the Years 1777, 1778, 1779, and 1780. Volume II* (Dublin: Luke White, 1787), 344.
13 Swinburne, H., *Travels in the Two Sicilies in the Years 1777, 1778, 1779, and 1780. Volume II*, 345.
14 Swinburne, H., *Travels in the Two Sicilies in the Years 1777, 1778, 1779, and 1780. Volume II*, 345.
15 Ferrara, F., *Storia generale dell'Etna*, 38.
16 Ferrara, F., *Storia generale dell'Etna*, 43.
17 Ferrara, F., *Storia generale dell'Etna*, 246.
18 Brydone, P., *Travels in Sicily and Malta*, 85.
19 Brydone, P., *Travels in Sicily and Malta*, 68.
20 Brydone, P., *Travels in Sicily and Malta*, 68.
21 Brydone, P., *Travels in Sicily and Malta*, 68.
22 Cottle, J., *Reminiscences of Samuel Taylor Coleridge and Robert Southey* (London: Houlston and Stoneman, 1848), 318.
23 Coleridge, S. T., *Notebooks: Vol. 2*, 2176.
24 Dykes Campbell, J., *Samuel Taylor Coleridge: A Narrative of the Events of His Life*, 146.
25 Leckie, G. F., quoted in D'Andrea, D., 'Gould Francis Leckie and the

'insular strategy' of Great Britain in the Mediterranean, 1800–1815', *Journal of Mediterranean Studies*, Volume 16 1/2 (2006): 82.
26 Monterosso, M., *Massæ, massari e masserie siracusane* (Siracusa: Maura Morrone, 2001), 22.
27 Fidone, E., 'Schinkel and the Mediterranean', *Karl Friedrich Schinkel Aspekte seines Werkes (Aspects of his Work)*, editor Peik, S. (Stuttgart: A. Menges, 2001), 30.
28 Schinkel, K. F., quoted in Fidone, E., 'Schinkel and the Mediterranean', *Karl Friedrich Schinkel Aspekte seines Werkes*, 30.
29 Coleridge, S. T., *Notebooks: Vol. 2*, 2195.
30 Leckie, G. F., quoted in D'Andrea, D., 'Gould Francis Leckie and the 'insular strategy' of Great Britain in the Mediterranean, 1800–1815', 84.
31 Greenough, G. B., *Diario di un viaggio in Sicilia, 1803*, trans. Giliberti, E. (Palermo: A. Lombardi, 1989), quoted by Russo, I. in *Noitiziario Storico di Augusta* (2002), 7.
32 Greenough, G. B., *Diario di un viaggio in Sicilia*, quoted by Russo, I. in *Notiziario Storico di Augusta* (2002), 8.
33 Greenough, G. B., *Diario di un viaggio in Sicilia*, quoted by Russo, I. in *Notiziario Storico di Augusta* (2002), 8.
34 Coleridge, S. T., *Notebooks: Vol. 2*, 2179.
35 Coleridge, S. T., *The Collected Works of Samuel Taylor Coleridge, Volume 11 – Shorter Works and Fragments: Volume II* (Princeton: Princeton University Press, 2019), 145.
36 Coleridge, S. T., *Samuel Taylor Coleridge: Poetry Selected by James Fenton* (London: Faber and Faber, 2006), 13.
37 Coleridge, S. T., *The Collected Works of Samuel Taylor Coleridge, Volume 11 – Shorter Works and Fragments: Volume II*, 145.
38 Coleridge, S. T., *Notebooks: Vol. 2*, 2212.
39 Coleridge, S. T., *Collected Letters: Volume 2*, editor Griggs, E. L. (London: Clarendon Press, 1966), 1168.
40 Coleridge, S. T., *Notebooks: Vol. 2*, 2195.
41 Brydone, P., *Travels in Sicily and Malta*, 105.
42 Irving, W., *Notes and Journal of Travel in Europe 1804 -1805* (New York: The Grolier Club, 1920), 101.
43 Coleridge, S. T., *Notebooks: Vol. 2*, 2246.
44 Coleridge, S. T., *Notebooks: Vol. 2*, 2246.
45 Coleridge, S. T., *Samuel Taylor Coleridge: Poetry Selected by James Fenton*, 13.
46 Coleridge, S. T., *Notebooks: Vol. 2*, 2261.
47 Coleridge, S. T., *Notebooks: Vol. 2*, 2261.
48 Leckie, G. F., *An Historical Survey of the Foreign Affairs of Great Britain, with a View to Explain the Causes of the Disasters of the Late and Present Wars: Volumes 1–2* (London: J. Bell, 1808), 2.

49  Leckie, G. F., *An Historical Survey of the Foreign Affairs of Great Britain*, 6.
50  Leckie, G. F., *An Historical Survey of the Foreign Affairs of Great* Britain, 10.
51  Baker, S., *Written on the Water: British Romanticism and the Maritime Empire of Culture* (Charlottesville: University of Virginia Press, 2010), 201.
52  Leckie, G. F., *An Historical Survey of the Foreign Affairs of Great Britain*, 10.
53  Coleridge, S. T., *Unpublished Letters of Samuel Taylor Coleridge Including Certain Letters Republished from Original Sources: Volume 1*, editor Griggs, E. L. (New Haven: Yale University Press, 1933), 328.
54  Leckie, G. F., *Essay on the Practice of the British Government* (London: A. J. Valpy, 1812), XIV.
55  Jeffrey, F., *Contributions to the Edinburgh Review by Francis Jeffrey* (London: Brown Green and Longmans, 1846), 145.
56  Jeffrey, F., *Contributions to the Edinburgh Review*, 145.
57  Moore, T., *The Poetical Works of Thomas Moore* (London: Brown Green and Longmans, 1855), 124.
58  Coleridge, S. T., *Notebooks: Vol. 2*, 2193.
59  Loreto, A., *Musica e musicisti a Siracusa nel XIX secolo* (Palermo: Istituto siciliano studi politici ed economici, 1998), 121.
60  Coleridge, S. T., *Notebooks: Vol. 2*, 2192.
61  Coleridge, S. T., *Notebooks: Vol. 2*, 2196.
62  Coleridge, S. T., *Notebooks: Vol. 2*, 2245.
63  *The Notebooks of Samuel Taylor Coleridge: Volume 3 1808–1819*, editor Colburn, K. (Abingdon: Routledge, 2002), 3404.
64  D'Agostini, M. E., *Il Paese altro: presenze orientali nella cultura tedesca moderna* (Naples: Bibliopolis, 1983), 106.
65  Coleridge, S. T., *Notebooks: Vol. 2*, 2222.
66  Fortis, A., *Viaggio in Dalmazia dell'abate Alberto Fortis: Volume primo* (Venice: Alvise Milocco, 1774), 84.
67  Coleridge, S. T., *The Works of Samuel Taylor Coleridge: Prose and Verse* (Philadelphia: T. Cowperthwait, 1845), 456.
68  Decatur, S., quoted in Mackenzie, A. S., *Life of Stephen Decatur, a Commodore in the Navy of the United States* (Boston: Little Brown, 1846), 295.

FOUR   **A Hand in Maltese Affairs**

1  Coleridge, S. T., *The Notebooks of Samuel Taylor Coleridge: Volume 2 1804 – 1808*, editor Coburn, K. (Abingdon: Routledge, 2002), 2370.
2  Coleridge, S. T., *Notebooks: Vol. 2*, 2268.

3  Coleridge, S. T., *Notebooks: Vol. 2*, 2402.
4  Hough, B. and Davis, H., *Coleridge's Laws: A Study of Coleridge in Malta* (Cambridge: Open Book Publishers, 2010), 40.
5  Coleridge, S. T., *Notebooks: Vol. 2*, 2271.
6  Wordsworth, W., *Peter Bell: A Tale in Verse* (London: Longman Hurst Rees Orme and Brown, 1819), 16.
7  Byron, G. G. (Lord), Byron: Poetical Works (London: Oxford University Press, 1967), 697.
8  Crabb Robinson, H., *The Diary of Henry Crabb Robinson: An Abridgement* (Oxford: Oxford University Press, 1967), 60.
9  Coleridge, S. T., *The Friend: A series of essays* (London: Gale and Curtis, 1812), 343.
10  De Quincey, T., *The Collected Writings of Thomas De Quincey: Volume 5* (Edinburgh: Adam and Charles Black, 1890), 199.
11  Coleridge, S. T., *Notebooks: Vol. 2*, 2367.
12  Coleridge, S. T., *Notebooks: Vol. 2*, 2368.
13  De Quincey, T., *The Collected Writings of Thomas De Quincey: Volume 5*, 207.
14  De Quincey, T., *The Collected Writings of Thomas De Quincey: Volume 5*, 207.
15  De Quincey, T., *The Works of Thomas De Quincey, "The English Opium Eater" Including All His Contributions to Periodical Literature: Volume 11* (Edinburgh: Adam and Charles Black, 1862), 108.
16  De Quincey, T., *The Works of Thomas De Quincey, "The English Opium Eater" Vol. 11*, 108.
17  Coleridge, S. T., *The Friend: In Three Volumes, Conducted by S.T. Coleridge: Volume 1* (London: William Pickering, 1850), 157.
18  Sultana, D., *Samuel Taylor Coleridge in Malta and Italy* (Oxford, Basil Blackwell, 1969), 254.
19  Coleridge, S. T., *Notebooks: Vol. 2*, 2398.
20  Kooy, J., in Hough, B. and Davis, H., *Coleridge's Laws: A Study of Coleridge in Malta*, XIX.
21  Coleridge, S. T., *The Friend: A series of essays* (London: Gale and Curtis, 1812), 342.
22  Coleridge, S. T., *Notebooks: Vol. 2*, 2583.
23  Coleridge, S. T., *The Works of Samuel Taylor Coleridge: Prose and Verse* (Philadelphia: T. Cowperthwait, 1845), 91.
24  Hough, B. and Davis, H., *Coleridge's Laws: A Study of Coleridge in Malta* (Cambridge: Open Book Publishers, 2010), 213.
25  Coleridge, S. T., *Notebooks: Vol. 2*, 2420.

26  Coleridge, S. T., *Letters of Samuel Taylor Coleridge: Volume 2*, editor Coleridge, E. H. (London: W. Heinemann, 1895), 495.
27  Coleridge, S. T., *Notebooks: Vol. 2*, 2431.
28  Coleridge, S. T. (trans. Davis, L.), in Hough, B. and Davis, H., *Coleridge's Laws: A Study of Coleridge in Malta*, 337.
29  Coleridge S. T. (trans. Davis, L.), in Hough, B. and Davis, H., *Coleridge's Laws: A Study of Coleridge in Malta*, 331.
30  Coleridge, S. T., *Notebooks: Vol. 2*, 2437.
31  Coleridge, S. T., *Notebooks: Vol. 2*, 2055.
32  Lamb, C., *Essays of Elia* (Paris: Baudry's European Library, 1835), 74.
33  Coleridge, S. T., *Notebooks: Vol. 2*, 2534.
34  Coleridge, S. T., *Notebooks: Vol. 2*, 2600.
35  Coleridge, S. T., *The Works of Samuel Taylor Coleridge: Prose and Verse*, 216.
36  Coleridge, S. T., *The Works of Samuel Taylor Coleridge: Prose and Verse*, 216.
37  Coleridge, S. T., *The Works of Samuel Taylor Coleridge: Prose and Verse*, 216.
38  Coleridge, S. T., *Notebooks: Vol. 2*, 2647.
39  Coleridge, S. T., Notebooks: Vol. 2, 2640.
40  Carrèrre, E., *Gothic Romance* (New York: Macmillan, 1984), 12.
41  Dykes Campbell, J., *Samuel Taylor Coleridge: A Narrative of the Events of His Life* (London: Macmillan, 1894), 147.

FIVE  The Grand Tourist Returns Home

1  Coleridge, S. T., *The Notebooks of Samuel Taylor Coleridge: Volume 2 1804 – 1808*, editor Coburn, K. (Abingdon: Routledge, 2002), 2679.
2  Coleridge, S. T., *Notebooks: Vol. 2*, 2679.
3  Smyth, W. H., *Memoir Descriptive of the Resources, Inhabitants, and Hydrography, of Sicily and Its Islands, Interspersed with Antiquarian and Other Notices* (London: John Murray, 1824), 162.
4  Swinburne, H., *Travels in the Two Sicilies in the Years 1777, 1778, 1779, and 1780. Volume II* (Dublin: Luke White, 1787), 361.
5  Goethe, J. W., *Goethe's Travels in Italy: Together with His Second Residence in Rome and Fragments on Italy*, trans. Morrison, A. and Nisbet, C. (London: G. Bell and Sons, 1885), 285.
6  Coleridge, S.T., quoted in 'Messina vista degli inglesi (1770 – 1815)', *Incontri Mediterranei*, vol. I–II (2003): 236.
7  Coleridge, S. T., *The Friend: A series of essays* (London: Gale and Curtis, 1812), 231.
8  Coleridge, S. T., *The Friend: A series of essays* (London: Gale and Curtis, 1812), 231.
9  Coleridge, S. T., *Notebooks: Vol. 2*, 2701.

10　Lawrence, D. H., *Letters By David Herbert Lawrence*, compiler Aldington, R. (London: Penguin Books, 1950), 134.
11　Coleridge, S. T., *Unpublished Letters of Samuel Taylor Coleridge Including Certain Letters Republished from Original Sources: Volume 1*, editor Griggs, E. L. (New Haven: Yale University Press, 1933), 362.
12　Coleridge, S. T., *Notebooks: Vol. 2*, 2717.
13　Moore, J., *A View of Society and Manners in Italy With Anecdotes Relating to Some Eminent Characters: Volume 1* (London: Strahan and Cadell, 1781), 161.
14　Byron, G. G. (Lord), *Byron: Poetical Works* (London: Oxford University Press, 1967), 494.
15　Coleridge, S. T., *Specimens of the Table Talk of the Late Samuel Taylor Coleridge: Vol. I*, editor Coleridge, H. N. (New York: Harper & Brothers, 1835), 103.
16　Coleridge, S. T., *Specimens of the Table Talk of the Late Samuel Taylor Coleridge: Vol. I*, 24.
17　Various, *Italy: A Handbook for Travellers, Southern Italy, Sicily, The Lipari Islands* (Coblenz: Baedeker, 1867), 91.
18　Coleridge, S. T., *Notebooks: Vol. 2*, 2731.
19　Coleridge, S. T., *Notebooks: Vol. 2*, 2728.
20　Coleridge, S. T., *The Collected Works of Samuel Taylor Coleridge, Volume 11 – Shorter Works and Fragments: Volume II* (Princeton: Princeton University Press, 2019), 288.
21　Coleridge, S. T., *The Friend: A series of essays* (London: Gale and Curtis, 1812), 442.
22　Coburn, K. (ed.), *The Notebooks of Samuel Taylor Coleridge: 1804–1808: Text. Notes. 2 v* (New York: Pantheon Books, 1957), 1911.
23　Coleridge, S. T., *Notebooks: Vol. 2*, 2760.
24　Irving, W., *Life and Works of Washington Irving*, editor Stoddard, R. (New York: Pollard & Moss, 1880), XVIII.
25　Allston, W. and Flagg, J. B., *The Life and Letters of Washington Allston* (New York: C. Scribner's Sons, 1892), 63.
26　Allston, W. and Flagg, J. B., *The Life and Letters of Washington Allston*, 65.
27　Various, *The Knickerbocker; Or, New-York Monthly Magazine: Volume 14* (New York, 1839), 173.
28　Allston, W. and Flagg, J. B., *The Life and Letters of Washington Allston*, 65.
29　Byron, G. G. (Lord), *The Works of Lord Byron: Letters and Journals*, editor Coleridge, E. H. (London: John Murray, 1904), 429.
30　Coleridge, S. T., *Notebooks: Vol. 2*, 2796.

31 Coleridge, S. T., *Notebooks: Vol. 2*, 2831.
32 Allston, W. and Flagg, J. B., *The Life and Letters of Washington Allston*, 64.
33 Coleridge, S. T., *Notebooks: Vol. 2*, 2817.
34 Lowell, R., *Robert Lowell: Essays on the Poetry*, editors Deese, H. and Axelrod, S. (Cambridge: Cambridge University Press, 1986), 97.
35 Coleridge, S. T., *Reports of Coleridge's Lectures*, editor Raysor, T. M. (London: Constable & Company Limited, 1930), 81.
36 Coleridge, S. T., *Notebooks: Vol. 2*, 2828.
37 Coleridge, S. T., *The Notebooks of Samuel Taylor Coleridge: Volume 3 1808–1819*, editor Colburn, K. (Abingdon: Routledge, 2002), 3286.
38 Coleridge, S. T., *Notebooks: Vol. 2*, 2813.
39 Coleridge, S. T., *Notebooks: Vol. 2*, 2813.
40 Coleridge, S. T., *Notebooks: Vol. 2*, 2849.
41 Coleridge, S. T., *Notebooks: Vol. 2*, 2849.
42 Coleridge, S, T., *Letters of Samuel Taylor Coleridge: Volume 2*, editor Coleridge, E. H. (London: W. Heinemann, 1895), 498.
43 Various, *La Galerie de Florence* (Florence: Galleria degli Uffizi, 1803), 81.
44 Coleridge, S. T., *Notebooks: Vol. 2*, 2856.
45 Coleridge, S. T., *Notebooks: Vol. 2*, 2856.
46 Coleridge, S. T., *Notebooks: Vol. 2*, 2860.
47 Coleridge, S. T., *Notebooks: Vol. 2*, 2860.
48 Coleridge, S. T., *Notebooks: Vol. 2*, 2862.
49 Coleridge, S. T., *Notebooks: Vol. 2*, 2866.

## SIX  Lectures and Legacy

1 Coleridge, S. T., *Samuel Taylor Coleridge: Poetry Selected by James Fenton* (London: Faber and Faber, 2006), 13.
2 Coleridge, S. T., *Manuscript draft of The Ancient Mariner, lines 201–12*, https://www.bl.uk/collection-items/a-variant-version-of-the-ancient-mariner-lines-201-12.
3 Coleridge, S. T., *Manuscript draft of The Ancient Mariner, lines 201–12*, https://www.bl.uk/collection-items/a-variant-version-of-the-ancient-mariner-lines-201-12.
4 Coleridge, S. T., *Letters of Samuel Taylor Coleridge: Volume 2*, editor Coleridge, E. H. (London: W. Heinemann, 1895), 508.
5 Coleridge, S. T., *Collected Letters: Volume 2*, editor Griggs, E. L. (London: Clarendon Press, 1966), 1200.
6 Coleridge, S. T., *The Notebooks of Samuel Taylor Coleridge: Volume 2 1804–1808*, editor Coburn, K. (Abingdon: Routledge, 2002), 3328.

7 Coleridge, S. T., *The Notebooks: Vol. 2*, 2975.
8 Coleridge, S. T., from Notebook IV, as quoted in Holmes, R., *Coleridge: Darker Reflections* (London: HarperCollins, 1998), 85.
9 Coleridge, S. T., as quoted in Bradford, R., *Literary Rivals: Feuds and Antagonisms in the World of Books* (London: Biteback Publishing, 2014), 54.
10 De Quincey, T., *The Collected Writings of Thomas De Quincey: Volume 2* (Edinburgh: Adam and Charles Black, 1889), 150.
11 De Quincey, T., *The Collected Writings of Thomas De Quincey: Volume 2*, 162.
12 Coleridge, S. T., *The Notebooks: Vol. 2*, 3159.
13 De Quincey, T., *The Works of Thomas De Quincey, "The English Opium Eater" Including All His Contributions to Periodical Literature: Volume 11* (Edinburgh: Adam and Charles Black, 1862), 99.
14 Coleridge, S. T., *The Notebooks of Samuel Taylor Coleridge: Volume 3 1808–1819*, editor Colburn, K. (Abingdon: Routledge, 2002), 3305.
15 *The Friend: A series of essays to aid in the formation of fixed principles in politics, morals and religion: Volume II* (London: Edward Moxon, 1863), 319.
16 Coleridge, S. T., *The Collected Works of Samuel Taylor Coleridge, The Friend, Volume 4 (Part II)* (Princeton: Princeton University Press, 1969), 495.
17 Coleridge, S. T., *The Friend: A series of essays* (London: Gale and Curtis, 1812), 420.
18 De Quincey, T., *The Works of Thomas De Quincey, "The English Opium Eater" Including All His Contributions to Periodical Literature: Volume 11*, 96.
19 Coleridge, S. T., *The Notebooks: Vol. 3*, 3911.
20 Crabb Robinson, H., *Diary, Reminiscences and Correspondence* (Boston: Houghton, Mifflin and Company, 1869), 315.
21 Coleridge, S. T., *Notebooks: Vol. 3*, 4106.
22 Coleridge, S. T., *The Complete Works of Samuel Taylor Coleridge: The Poetical and Dramatic Works*, editor Shedd, W. (New York: Harper & Brothers, 1884), 373.
23 Paley, M. D., *Samuel Taylor Coleridge and the Fine Arts* (Oxford: Oxford University Press, 2008), 149.
24 Byron, G. G. (Lord), *Byron: Poetical Works* (London: Oxford University Press, 1967), 116.
25 Coleridge, S. T., *Biographia Literaria or Biographical Sketches of My Literary Life and Opinions* (New York: Crocker and Brewster, 1834), 188.
26 Coleridge, S. T., *Biographia Literaria or Biographical Sketches of My Literary Life and Opinions*, 189.
27 Coleridge, S. T., *Biographia Literaria or Biographical Sketches of My Literary Life and Opinions*, 189.

28 Coleridge, S. T., *Biographia Literaria or Biographical Sketches of My Literary Life and Opinions*, 190.
29 Coleridge, S. T., *Biographia Literaria or Biographical Sketches of My Literary Life and Opinions*, 190.
30 Coleridge, S. T., *Biographia Literaria or Biographical Sketches of My Literary Life and Opinions*, 165.
31 Coleridge, S. T., *Unpublished Letters of Samuel Taylor Coleridge: Volume 2*, editor Griggs, E. L. (New Haven: Yale University Press, 1933), 165.
32 Coleridge, S. T., *The Table Talk and Omniana of Samuel Taylor Coleridge* (London: George Bell & Sons, 1884), 279.
33 Coleridge, S. T., *Samuel Taylor Coleridge: Poetry Selected by James Fenton*, 25.
34 Coleridge, S. T., *Samuel Taylor Coleridge: Poetry Selected by James Fenton*, 12.
35 Coleridge, S. T., *Biographia Literaria or Biographical Sketches of My Literary Life and Opinions*, 324.
36 Coleridge, S. T., *Notebooks: Vol. 2*, 2045.
37 Byron, G. G. (Lord), *Byron: Poetical Works*, 635.
38 Coleridge, S. T., *The Complete Works of Samuel Taylor Coleridge: The Poetical and Dramatic Works*, 319.

# Bibliography

Allison, R. J., *Stephen Decatur: American Naval Hero, 1779–1820* (Boston: University of Massachusetts Press, 2005).
Allston, W. and Flagg, J. B., *The Life and Letters of Washington Allston* (New York: C. Scribner's Sons, 1892).
Attard, J., *Ghosts of Malta* (Valletta: PEG Publications, 1997).
Baker, S., *Written on the Water: British Romanticism and the Maritime Empire of Culture* (Charlottesville: University of Virginia Press, 2010).
Benza, Dr., *The Penny Cyclopaedia of the Society for the Diffusion of Useful Knowledge* (Limonia: Charles Knight, 1839).
Bosredon de Ransijat, J., *Journal du siège et blocus de Malte* (Paris: Valade, 1801).
Bradford, R., *Literary Rivals: Feuds and Antagonisms in the World of Books* (London: Biteback Publishing, 2014).
Brydone, P., *Travels in Sicily and Malta* (Aberdeen: George Clark & Son, 1848).
Byron, G. G. (Lord), *Byron: Poetical Works* (London: Oxford University Press, 1967).
——, *The Works of Lord Byron: Letters and Journals,* editor Coleridge, E. H. (London: John Murray, 1904).
Carrèrre, E., *Gothic Romance* (New York: Macmillan, 1984).
Cassar, P., 'The First Documented Case of Drug Addiction in Malta – Samuel Taylor Coleridge', *Hyphen,* Volume 3, No. 2 (1982).
Coburn, K. (ed.), *The Notebooks of Samuel Taylor Coleridge: 1804–1808: Text. Notes. 2 v* (New York: Pantheon Books, 1957).
Cochrane, P., *"Romanticism" – and Byron* (Newcastle: Cambridge Scholars Publishing, 2009).
Coleridge, S. T., *Biographia Literaria or Biographical Sketches of My Literary Life and Opinions* (New York: Crocker and Brewster, 1834).
——, *Collected Letters: Volume 2,* editor Griggs, E. L. (London: Clarendon Press, 1966).
——, *Confessions of an Inquiring Spirit,* editor Nelson, H. (Boston: James Munroe & Company, 1841).
——, *Letters of Samuel Taylor Coleridge: Volume 2,* editor Coleridge, E. H. (London: W. Heinemann, 1895).
——, *Manuscript draft of The Ancient Mariner,* lines 201–12,

https://www.bl.uk/collection-items/a-variant-version-of-the-ancient-mariner-lines-201-12 (accessed 18/11/21).

——, *Reports of Coleridge's Lectures*, editor Raysor, T. M. (London: Constable & Company Limited, 1930).

——, *Specimens of the Table Talk of the Late Samuel Taylor Coleridge: Vol. I*, editor Coleridge, H. N. (New York: Harper & Brothers, 1835).

——, *The Table Talk and Omniana of Samuel Taylor Coleridge* (London: George Bell & Sons, 1884).

——, *The Collected Works of Samuel Taylor Coleridge, The Friend, Volume 4 (Part II)* (Princeton: Princeton University Press, 1969).

——, *The Collected Works of Samuel Taylor Coleridge, Volume 11 – Shorter Works and Fragments: Volume II* (Princeton: Princeton University Press, 2019).

——, *The Complete Works of Samuel Taylor Coleridge: The Poetical and Dramatic Works*, editor Shedd, W. (New York: Harper & Brothers, 1884).

——, *The Friend: A series of essays* (London: Gale and Curtis, 1812).

——, *The Friend: A series of essays to aid in the formation of fixed principles in politics, morals and religion: Volume II* (London: Edward Moxon, 1863).

——, *The Friend: In Three Volumes, Conducted by S.T. Coleridge: Volume 1* (London: William Pickering, 1850).

——, *The Notebooks of Samuel Taylor Coleridge: Volume 2 1804 – 1808*, editor Coburn, K. (Abingdon: Routledge, 2002).

——, *The Notebooks of Samuel Taylor Coleridge: Volume 3 1808–1819*, editor Colburn, K. (Abingdon: Routledge, 2002).

——, *Samuel Taylor Coleridge: Poetry Selected by James Fenton* (London: Faber and Faber, 2006).

——, *The Statemen's Manual* (London: Gale and Fenner, 1816).

——, *The Works of Samuel Taylor Coleridge: Prose and Verse* (Philadelphia: T. Cowperthwait, 1845).

——, *Unpublished Letters of Samuel Taylor Coleridge Including Certain Letters Republished from Original Sources: Volume 1*, editor Griggs, E. L. (New Haven: Yale University Press, 1933).

——, *Unpublished Letters of Samuel Taylor Coleridge: Volume 2*, editor Griggs, E. L. (New Haven: Yale University Press, 1933).

Corona, D., 'S. T. Coleridge's Colonial Gaze: Sicily in his Mediterranean Writing', *Travels and Translations: Anglo-Italian Cultural Transactions*, Volume 167 (2013).

Cottle, J., *Reminiscences of Samuel Taylor Coleridge and Robert Southey* (London: Houlston and Stoneman, 1848).

Crabb Robinson, H., *Diary, Reminiscences and Correspondence* (Boston: Houghton, Mifflin and Company, 1869).

——, *The Diary of Henry Crabb Robinson: An Abridgement* (Oxford: Oxford University Press, 1967).

D'Agostini, M. E., *Il Paese altro: presenze orientali nella cultura tedesca moderna* (Naples: Bibliopolis, 1983).

D'Andrea, D., 'Gould Francis Leckie and the 'insular strategy' of Great Britain in the Mediterranean, 1800–1815', *Journal of Mediterranean Studies*, Volume 16 1/2 (2006).

———, 'Messina vista degli inglesi (1770–1815)', *Incontri Mediterranei*, vol. I–II (2003).

Davy, H., *The Collected Works of Sir Humphry Davy: Volume 1* (London: Smith Elder, 1839).

De Quincey, T., *Confessions of an English Opium-Eater and Other Writings* (Oxford: OUP, 1996).

———, *The Collected Writings of Thomas De Quincey: Volume 2* (Edinburgh: Adam and Charles Black, 1889).

———, *The Collected Writings of Thomas De Quincey: Volume 5* (Edinburgh: Adam and Charles Black, 1890).

———, *The Treasury of Modern Biography: Issue 92*, editor Cochrane, R. (London, 1878).

———, *The Works of Thomas De Quincey, "The English Opium Eater" Including All His Contributions to Periodical Literature: Volume 11* (Edinburgh: Adam and Charles Black, 1862).

Duffield, A. J., *Don Quixote: His Critics and Commentators* (London: C. Kegan Paul & Co, 1881).

Dumas, A. (père), *Pascal Bruno*, editor Hook, T. (London: Henry Colburn, 1837).

Dummett, J., *Syracuse: City of Legends* (London: I. B. Tauris, 2010).

Dykes Campbell, J., *Samuel Taylor Coleridge: A Narrative of the Events of His Life* (London: Macmillan, 1894).

Ferrara, F., *Storia generale dell'Etna* (Catania, 1793).

Fidone, E., 'Schinkel and the Mediterranean', *Karl Friedrich Schinkel Aspekte seines Werkes (Aspects of his Work)*, editor Peik, S. (Stuttgart: A. Menges, 2001).

Fortis, A., *Viaggio in Dalmazia dell'abate Alberto Fortis: Volume primo* (Venice: Alvise Milocco, 1774).

Fraser, W. W., *A Letter Addressed to the Governor of Gibraltar Relative to the Febrile Distempers of that Garrison* (London: Callow & Wilson, 1826).

Frendo, H., *Attard: The Life of a Maltese Casale* (Attard: Attard Local Council, 1997).

Goethe, J. W., *Goethe's Travels in Italy: Together with His Second Residence in Rome and Fragments on Italy*, trans. Morrison, A. and Nisbet, C. (London: G. Bell and Sons, 1885).

Greenough, G. B., *Diario di un viaggio in Sicilia, 1803*, trans. Giliberti, E. (Palermo: A. Lombardi, 1989).

Gregory, D., *Malta, Britain, and the European powers, 1793–1815* (London: Associated University Presses, 1996).

Harding, A. J., *Coleridge and the Idea of Love: Aspects of Relationship in Coleridge's Thought and Writing* (Cambridge: Cambridge University Press, 1974).

Hayter, A., *A Voyage in Vain: Coleridge's Journey to Malta in 1804* (London: Faber and Faber, 2009).

——, *Opium and the Romantic Imagination* (Wellingborough: Crucible, 1988).

Hazlitt, W., *The Selected Writings of William Hazlitt: Political Essays*, editor Wu, D. (London: Pickering & Chatto, 1998).

Hogarth, G., *Memoirs of the Opera in Italy, France, Germany, and England* (London: R. Bentley, 1851).

Holmes, R., *Coleridge: Darker Reflections* (London: HarperCollins, 1998).

——, *Coleridge: Early Visions* (London: Flamingo, 1999).

Hough, B. and Davis, H., *Coleridge's Laws: A Study of Coleridge in Malta* (Cambridge: Open Book Publishers, 2010).

Irving, W., *Life and Works of Washington Irving*, editor Stoddard, R. (New York: Pollard & Moss, 1880).

——, *Notes and Journal of Travel in Europe 1804 -1805* (New York: The Grolier Club, 1920).

Jeffrey, F., *Contributions to the Edinburgh Review by Francis Jeffrey* (London: Brown Green and Longmans, 1846).

Lamb, C., *Essays of Elia* (Paris: Baudry's European Library, 1835).

Lamb, C. and Lamb M. A., *The Letters of Charles and Mary Anne Lamb*, editor Marrs, E. (Ithaca: Cornell University Press, 1976).

Lampedusa, G. T. di, *The Leopard*, trans. Colquhoun, A. (London: Collins and Harvill Press, 1960).

Lawrence, D. H., *Letters By David Herbert Lawrence*, compiler Aldington, R. (London: Penguin Books, 1950).

Leckie, G. F., *An Historical Survey of the Foreign Affairs of Great Britain, with a View to Explain the Causes of the Disasters of the Late and Present Wars: Volumes 1–2* (London: J. Bell, 1808).

——, *Essay on the Practice of the British Government* (London: A. J. Valpy, 1812).

Lefebure, M., *Samuel Taylor Coleridge: A Bondage of Opium* (London: Quartet Books, 1974).

Loreto, A., *Musica e musicisti a Siracusa nel XIX secolo* (Palermo: Istituto siciliano studi politici ed economici, 1998).

Lowell, R., *Robert Lowell: Essays on the Poetry*, editors Deese, H. and Axelrod, S. (Cambridge: Cambridge University Press, 1986).

Luque, A., *Borges in Sicily: Journey with a Blind Guide*, trans. Edwards, A. (London: Haus, 2019).

Machiavelli, N., *Opere di Niccolò Machiavelli: Istorie Fiorentine* (Florence, 1796).

Mackenzie, A. S., *Life of Stephen Decatur, a Commodore in the Navy of the United States* (Boston: Little Brown, 1846).
McKee, C., *Edward Preble: A Naval Biography 1761–1807* (Annapolis: Naval Institute Press, 2014).
Molloy, C., *De Jure Maritimo Et Navali; Or, A Treatise of Affairs Maritime and of Commerce* (London: J. Bellinger and George Dawes, 1682).
Moore, J., *A View of Society and Manners in Italy With Anecdotes Relating to Some Eminent Characters: Volume 1* (London: Strahan and Cadell, 1781).
Moore, T., *The Poetical Works of Thomas Moore* (London: Brown Green and Longmans, 1855).
Monterosso, M., *Massæ, massari e masserie siracusane* (Siracusa: Maura Morrone, 2001).
Nelson, H. (Viscount), *Letters and Despatches of Horatio, Viscount Nelson*, editor Knox Laughton, J. (London: Longmans Green, 1886).
Norwich, J. J., *Sicily: A Short History from the Ancient Greeks to Cosa Nostra* (London: John Murray, 2015).
O'Connell, M., *Byron and John Murray: A Poet and his Publisher* (Liverpool: Liverpool University Press, 2014).
Oliver, C., *A Most Faithful Attendant: The Life of Giovanni Battista Falcieri* (Bretwalda Books, 2018).
Paley, M. D., *Samuel Taylor Coleridge and the Fine Arts* (Oxford: Oxford University Press, 2008).
Piccolo, L., *Collected Poems of Lucio Piccolo*, trans. Swann, B. (Princeton: Princeton University Press, 1972).
Russo, I., 'Dal Seicento all'Ottocento. Il Grand tour. Augusta sotto la penna del viaggiatore straniero', *Noitiziario Storico di Augusta* (2002).
Sanchez, M. G., *The Prostitutes of Serruya's Lane and other Hidden Gibraltarian Stories* (Gibraltar: Rock Scorpion Books, 2007).
Sciascia, L., *Salt in the Wound*, trans. Green, J. (New York: The Orion Press, 1969).
Smyth, W. H., *Memoir Descriptive of the Resources, Inhabitants, and Hydrography, of Sicily and Its Islands, Interspersed with Antiquarian and Other Notices* (London: John Murray, 1824).
Southey, R., *The Poetical Works of Robert Southey: Complete in one volume* (London: Longmans, 1847).
———, *The Story of His Life Written in His Letters*, editor Dennis, J. (Boston: D. Lothrop Company, 1887).
Sultana, D., *Samuel Taylor Coleridge in Malta and Italy* (Oxford: Basil Blackwell, 1969).
Sweetser, M. F., *The Life of Washington Allston* (Boston: Houghton, Osgood & Co., Boston, 1879).

Swinburne, H., *Travels in the Two Sicilies in the Years 1777, 1778, 1779, and 1780. Volume II* (Dublin: Luke White, 1787).

Téllez Rubio, J. J., *Gibraltar en el tiempo de los espías* (Seville: Fundación José Manuel Lara, 2005).

——, *Yanitos: Viaje al corazón de Gibraltar (1713–2013)* (Seville: Centro de Estudios Andaluces, 2013).

Tubino, F. M. (ed.), *Gibraltar Through the Spanish Eye* (Amazon Media, 2012).

Various, *La Galerie de Florence* (Florence: Galleria degli Uffizi, 1803).

Various, *Italy: A Handbook for Travellers, Southern Italy, Sicily, The Lipari Islands* (Coblenz: Baedeker, 1867).

Various, *The Knickerbocker; Or, New-York Monthly Magazine: Volume 14* (New York, 1839).

Waring, G., *Letters from Malta and Sicily, addressed to a young naturalist* (London: Harvey and Darton, 1843).

Wellek, R., *A History of Modern Criticism: The Romantic Age* (London: Cape, 1955).

Wilson, F., *Guilty Thing: A Life of Thomas De Quincey* (London: Bloomsbury, 2016).

Wordsworth, W., *Peter Bell: A Tale in Verse* (London: Longman Hurst Rees Orme and Brown, 1819).

——, *Poetical Works: Volume 10*, editor Knight, A. (Edinburgh: W. Paterson, 1889).

Wortley, E. C. E., *The Sweet South: Impressions of Spain* (London: John Barclay, 1856).

Zuccato, E., *Coleridge in Italy* (Cork: Cork University Press, 1996).

We would like to acknowledge the extensive and detailed work of previous biographers of Coleridge, in particular the works of Richard Holmes and Donald Sultana, and to thank Samuel Baker and Michela d'Angelo for their invaluable correspondence.

# Index

Acton, Sir John, 38
Adye, Major, 16, 21–23, 45, 51, 61, 80
*Aeneid*, 28, 118, 122
Alarcón, Pedro Antonio de, 23
Alemán, Mateo, 39
Algeciras, 14
Algiers, 40
Alighieri, Dante, 101, 129, 155
Allan Bank, 148
Allison, Robert, 80
Allston, Washington, 127–128, 130–133, 135, 141, 154, 162
Alpheus, 4–5, 68
Andersen, Hans Christian, 127
Arethusa, 4, 68
Arezzo, 133
Arno, River, 135, 163
Artemis, 4, 68
Ashley, 154
*Aspekte seines Werkes*, 64–65
Asquith, Lady Cynthia, 119
Asra, 7–8, 18, 21, 26, 39, 45, 77–79, 92, 96, 104–105, 115, 135, 142–144, 146, 148–150, 156, 162; see also Hutchinson, Sara
Attard, 37, 90–91
Attard, Joseph, 37
*Attard: The Life of a Maltese Casale*, 90
Augusta, 65, 69, 113
Austerlitz, 125

Baccellieri, Stellario, 127
Bagheria, 115
Baker, Samuel, 73
Balearic Islands, 25
Ball, Lady, 93–94, 104
Ball, Sir Alexander, 9, 34–41, 43, 46–47, 50, 56, 62, 66, 73, 81–82, 87, 89–95, 97–98, 100–101, 103, 107, 109, 126, 142, 149–150, 162
Balsamo, Abate, 73
Banks, Sir Joseph, 118
Barzoni, Vittorio, 41, 43, 101
Bath, 153
Battle of Maida, 124
Beaumont, George, 8
Beckford, William, 12
*Beheading of St. John the Baptist*, 37
Belmonte, Prince, 73
Bentinck, Lord, 74
Benvenuti, Pietro, 133
Benza, Dr, 27
Bertozzi, Cecilia, 76–79, 117
Birkirkara, 91
    Parish Church of St. Mary, 91
Bishop Middleton, 7
Blake, William, 114
Blasco Ibáñez, Vicente, 22
Boccaccio, Giovanni, 101, 129
Bonanno, Baron Giuseppe, 65
Bonaparte, Napoleon, 9, 124, 136
*Bondage of Opium, A*, 143
Bonello, Saverio, 100
Borg, Andrea, 100
Bosredon de Ransijat, Jean de, 34
*Bravoure (Gothic Romance)*, 108
Brent, Charlotte, 146, 153
*Bride of Abydos, The*, 13
Bridgnorth, 49
Bridgwater, 145
Bristol, 1, 48, 132, 144, 153–154, 157, 160
*Britain, and the European Powers, 1793–1815*, 85
Brougham, Henry, 91
Brydone, Patrick, 27, 36–37, 43, 60–61, 66, 71
Buffalmacco, 134

## 184  Index

Bugibba, 104
Buonarotti, Michelangelo, 132
Bury St Edmund's, 142
Byron, Lord (George Gordon), 12–13, 31–32, 43, 48, 75, 78, 89, 93, 108, 121, 127–128, 137, 147, 154–155, 158–162

Cabo da Roca, 11
Cabo de São Vicente, 13
Cabo Ortegal, 10
Cabo Trafalgar, 118
Cádiz, 13, 15, 118
Cambridge, 1, 4, 18, 161
Canova, Antonio, 132
Capo Passero, 83
Caravaggio (Michelangelo Merisi), 33, 37, 70–71, 121
Carrère, Emanuel, 108
Cascais, 13
Cascata delle Marmore, 133
Cassar, Dr Paul, 69
Castel-a-Mare, 120
Catalana, Angelica, 152
Catania, 4, 25, 57, 120
   Castello Ursino, 57
Catullus, 156
Cervantes, Miguel de, 13–14, 154
Chapman, Edmund, 40, 50–51, 97–98, 100, 106, 109
*Childe Harold*, 12–13, 75
Christ's Hospital School, 4, 26, 147
Cicero, 72
Città Ferdinand, 45
Città Vecchia, 40, 88, 97, 104
Clarkson, Thomas, 141–142
Claudian, 123
Clifton, 154
Coburn, Kathleen, 133
Cochrane, Peter, 160
Code de Rohan, 99–100
Coleorton, 142–143
*Coleridge and Opium Eating*, 94
*Coleridge and the Idea of Love*, 79
*Coleridge in Italy*, 41
*Coleridge's Laws: A Study of Coleridge in Malta*, 90

Coleridge, George, 144
Coleridge, Hartley, 143–144, 161–162
Coleridge, Samuel Taylor, 1, 4–29, 31–51, 56–58, 60–83, 85, 87–109, 111, 113–137, 141–164
WORKS
'A Tombless Epitaph', 137
'Christabel', 82, 158–159
'Dejection: An Ode', 8
'Fears in Solitude', 29
'Kubla Khan', 4, 44, 68, 71, 141, 158–159
'Religious Musings', 49
'The Blossoming of the Solitary Date-Tree', 105
'The Devil's Thoughts', 99
'The Dungeon', 99
'The Eolian Harp', 53
'The Garden of Boccaccio', 111, 163
'The Mad Monk', 4–5, 27
'The Rime of the Ancient Mariner', 1, 141
'The Tropic Tree', 144
'To William Wordsworth', 156
'Tribute to Spencer Perceval', 123
'What is Life?', 85
*Aids to Reflection*, 161
*Biographia Literaria*, 154, 160
*Collected Works of Samuel Taylor Coleridge, Volume 11, The*, 123
*Confessions of an Inquiring Spirit*, 18
*Friend, The*, 35, 92–94, 96, 98, 109, 117, 148–150
Notebook (STC Vols 2 & 3), 1, 4–5, 7, 9–10, 14, 16, 18–19, 21, 26, 39, 42, 58, 63, 65, 68, 70, 74, 76–79, 83, 91–92, 94, 96, 98, 101–102, 104–105, 113–116, 122–123, 126, 129–130, 132–135, 141, 143, 147, 152, 162
*Observations on Egypt*, 136
*On the Constitution of the Church and State*, 37
*On the Law of Nations*, 80

*Osorio (Remorse)*, 20, 25, 144, 152
*Sibylline Leaves, The*, 156, 160
*Statesman's Manual, The*, 46–47
*Table Talk and Omniana of Samuel Taylor Coleridge, The*, 121–122
Coleridge, Sara (daughter of STC), 150
Coleridge, Sara (wife of STC), 6, 9, 21, 26, 77, 79, 92, 100, 104, 106, 137, 141–144, 151, 163
*Coleridge: Darker Reflections*, 48
*Confessions of an English Opium-Eater*, 41, 145
Cordoba, Leonetto della, 33
Corona, Daniela, 40, 82
*Corsair, The*, 13
Cottle, Joseph, 136
Court of Vice Admiralty, 95
Courtenay, William, 12
Crabb Robinson, Henry, 93, 149, 151

D'Agostini, Maria Enrica, 78
D'Andrea, Diletta, 63, 73, 116
Davis, Howard, 90, 97, 99–101, 107
Davy, Humphrey, 8–9
*De Juro Maritimo et Navali*, 95
*Dead Man Restored*, 154
Decatur, Captain Stephen, 80–82
Denison, William, 67–69
Dent, Lieutenant John H, 77
Dentatus, Manius Curius, 133
Derkheim, Captain, 136
Devon, 1, 12, 48, 68, 144
*Diana and her Nymphs in the Chase*, 130
Diana, Antonino, 48
*Diary of a Journey in Sicily, 1803*, 5
Dickens, Charles, 127
*Don Juan*, 93, 160–161
*Don Quixote*, 13–14, 99
*Donna Mencia in the Robber's Cavern*, 128
Douro, River, 11
Dove Cottage, 92, 96, 149
Dumas, Alexandre (père), 27
Dummett, Jeremy, 56
Durham, 7
Duzina, Monsignor Pietro, 90

Dykes Campbell, James, 58, 109

*Earl of Abergavenny*, 104
Eaton, William, 85, 87, 107
*Edinburgh Review*, 74, 160
Edward, Prince (Duke of Kent and Strathearn), 14, 17
Elliot, Hugh, 56, 119, 122
Empedocles, 4
*English Bards and Scotch Reviewers*, 75, 155
Epipoli, 64–65, 67, 72
Erice, 4
*Essay on the Practice of the British Government*, 74
*Essays of Elia*, 103
Estrecho Natural Park, El, 14

Ferdinand IV, King of Naples, 38, 56, 124
Ferrara, Francesco, 58
Ferrol, 10
*Feverish Distempers of that garrison*, 15
Figueira da Foz, 11
Findlay, Captain, 10, 13, 18, 24–25
Florence, 133–135, 156, 163
   Uffizi, 134
Fondi, 126
Fortis, Alberto, 79
Franciosini di Castelfiorentino, Lorenzo, 99
Fraser, Hugh, 15
Frendo, Henry, 90

Gaeta, 126
Gagliardi, Rosario, 69
Gale and Fenner (publishers), 160–161
*Galerie de Florence, La*, 134
Galicia, 10
Garigliano, 126
Geleng, Otto, 116
*Ghosts of Malta, The*, 37
*Giaour, The*, 13
Gibraltar, 13–14, 16–19, 21–25, 33–34, 38, 45, 48, 56, 80, 85, 87, 100, 135, 161

Gibraltar (continued)
  Casemates Square, 23
  Europa Point, 14, 16, 22
  Griffiths' Hotel, 16, 18
  Main Street, 16
  Playa del Algarrobo, 19
  Sandy Bay, 19
  Serruya's Lane, 17, 33
  St Michael's Cave, 19–20, 23
*Gibraltar en el tiempo de los espías*, 24
Gillman, Ann, 163
Gillman, James, 94, 158–159, 161–162
Giotto, 134
Godwin, William, 8, 144
Goethe, Johann Wolfgang von, 115, 127, 154
*Gosport*, 135–137, 141
Göttingen, 1, 5, 32, 66
Gozo, 45, 101
Gozzoli, Benozzo, 134
Grasmere, 14, 92, 148
Greenough, George Bellas, 5–6, 66–67
Gregory, Desmond, 85
Greta Hall, 6, 142, 150
Greville, Colonel, 75
Guadiana, River, 13
Guglielmi, Pietro Alessandro, 76
*Guilty Thing: A Life of Thomas De Quincey*, 145
Gutch (Publisher), 157
Guttuso, Renato, 127
*Guzmán de Alfarache*, 39

Hamilton, William, 56, 117
Harding, Anthony John, 79
Härz Mountains, 1, 60
Hasciach, Giovanni, 100
Hayter, Alethea, 159
Hazlitt, William, 47
Hepburn, Audrey, 127
Hephaestus, 4
Herculaneum, 123, 128
*Historical Survey of the Foreign Affairs of Great Britain, An*, 72
*History of Modern Criticism, A*, 129

Hobart, Lord, 50
Hogarth, George, 76
Holmes, Richard, 18, 48, 61, 82, 96, 104, 119, 122, 137, 143–144, 146, 149–150, 153, 156, 160
Hood, Alexander, 119
Hough, Barry, 90, 97, 99–101, 107
Humboldt, Wilhelm von, 128–129, 152
Hutchinson, Sara, 7–8, 18, 21, 26, 39, 45, 77–79, 92, 96, 104–105, 115, 135, 142–144, 146, 148–150, 156, 162; *see also* Asra

Ibsen, Henrik, 127
*Imaginary Prisons*, 159
*Incontri Mediterranei*, 116
Ireland, Mrs, 10, 21, 29
Irving, Washington, 71, 127, 132
*Istiorie fiorentine*, 95

Jaci, Father Antonio Maria, 117
Jackson, Thomas, 129
James, Henry, 127
Jefferson Hogg, Thomas, 78
Jeffrey, Francis, 74
Jerningham, Edward, 147

Keats, John, 127
Kendal, 142
Keswick, 14, 120, 130, 142
Klopstock, Friedrich Gottlieb, 41–42
Knights of St John Hospitaller, 29, 31–34, 43, 50, 91, 98–99
Kooy, Michael John, 97

*L'Hirondelle*, 81–82, 85, 87
La Coruña, 10
La Línea, 17, 22–23
Labini, Bishop Vincenzo, 91
Laing, Reverend Francis, 49
Lake District, 1, 6, 14, 60, 120, 142, 148
Lake Trasimeno, 133
Lamb, Charles, 8, 21, 103, 151
Lamb, Mary, 141
Lampedusa, Giuseppe Tomasi di, 67

Landolina, Giovanni Battista, 69
Landor, Walter Savage, 149
Latomie, The, 4, 70–71
Lawrence, D H, 119
Le Bon, Gustave, 125
Leckie, Gould Francis, 5, 56, 62–67, 69, 72–77, 79–80, 82–83, 91, 113, 115
Lefebure, Molly, 143, 153
Leigh Hunt, James Henry, 152
Lentini, Jacopo da, 156
*Leopard, The*, 67
*Letters from Malta and Sicily, addressed to a young naturalist*, 16
Lewis, Matthew, 5
*Life and Letters of Washington Allston*, 128
Linnaeus, Carl, 44
Lisbon, 11, 13
Liszt, Franz, 127
Livorno, 134–136
London, 1, 8, 35, 40, 50, 107, 122, 127, 137, 141–142, 144, 146–147, 150–151, 153, 157–158, 162
  Drury Lane theatre, 20, 157
  Highgate, 94, 157–158, 161, 163
  St Michael's Church, Highgate, 163
Loreto, Alessandro, 77
Lowell, Robert, 131
Luque, Alejandro, 56

M'Mahon, Colonel, 75
Macaulay, Alexander, 49
Machiavelli, Niccolò, 95
Mackenzie, Colin, 109, 113
*Madonna and Child with Saint*, 134
*Madrigale*, 156
Málaga, 15
*Malta, Britain, and the European powers, 1793–1815*, 85
Maltese Corps, 89–90
Marettimo, 26
Margate, 147
Martial (Marcus Valerius Martialis), 123

Martin, Captain, 34
Mascalucia, 57
*Massæ, massari e masserie siracusane*, 63
McKee, Christopher, 77
Medway, River, 137
Meli, Giovanni, 72
*Memoir Descriptive of the Resources, Inhabitants, and Hydrography, of Sicily and Its Islands*, 113
*Memoirs of the Opera in Italy, France, Germany, and England*, 76
Mendelssohn, Felix, 127
Messina, 38, 45, 81–82, 87, 109, 113, 116–119
  Gravitelli, Rione, 116
*Messina vista dagli Inglesi*, 116
Metastasio, Pietro, 79, 152
Mill, John Stuart, 163
Minho, River, 11
Misra G ar il-Kbir, 45
Missolonghi, 137
Molloy, Charles, 95
Montagu, Basil, 150
Monte Pellegrino, 4
Monte Rossi, 58–59
Monterosso, Marco, 63–65
Moore, John, 120
Moore, Thomas, 75, 160
Moreno, José, 81
Morgan, John, 146, 151–153, 155, 157–158
Morgan, Mary, 146, 151, 153
Morse, S. F. B., 128
*Most Faithful Attendant, A*, 89
Mottley, James Charles, 9
Mount Etna, 4, 27, 57, 62, 114, 119
Mount Vesuvius, 119–120, 122
Murray, John, 159
*Musica e musicisti a Siracusa nel XIX secolo*, 77

Naples, 13, 34, 38, 53, 56, 73, 109, 117–126, 128, 132
  Church of Santa Maria La Nova, 121
  Monastero di Santa Chiara, 121
  Portici, 123

Naples *(continued)*
  Posillipo, 122–123
  San Carlo, Opera House, 125
  Virgil, Tomb of, 122
Nasolini, Sebastiano, 76
National Archive, Malta, 94
National Archives, UK, 89, 95
Nelson, Vice-Admiral Horatio, 29, 31, 33, 35, 37, 39, 41, 43, 45, 47, 49, 51, 53, 56, 118–119, 124–125, 149–150
Nether Stowey, 90, 145
Nicolosi, 57–60, 62
  Monastery of San Nicolò l'Arena, 58
Noble, George, 126
Norwich, John Julius, 53
*Notes and Journal of Travel in Europe*, 71
Noto, 69

Odessa, 92
Odysseus, 78, 118
Olevano, 130–133, 154
Oliver, Claudia, 89
*Opium and the Romantic Imagination*, 159
*Orizonte della longitudine, L'*, 117
Ossaia, 133
Ottery St Mary, 21

*Paese altro, Il*, 78
Paestum, 123
Palermo, 4, 25, 67, 76, 81, 117
Paley, Morton, 154
Parmigianino (Girolamo Francesco Maria Mazzola), 134
*Parrochie di Regalpetra, Le (Salt in the Wound)*, 114
*Pascal Bruno*, 27
Pascal, Blaise, 41, 48
Pasley, Charles William, 92, 107, 109, 122, 124, 149, 151
Paule, Antoine de, 37
Penrith, 142
Perugia, 133
*Pescatrice, La*, 77

Piccinni, Niccolò, 77
Piccolo, Lucio, 27
Pigot, Major, 34
Piranesi, Giovanni Battista, 159
Pisa, 134–135, 163
  Piazza dei Miracoli, 134
*Poet's Pilgrimage to Waterloo*, 12
Polidori, John, 108, 147
Poole, Tom, 145, 147
Pope, Alexander, 123
Porto, 11
Portsmouth, 8–9
Preble, Commodore Edward, 77, 80
*Provinciales, Les*, 41
Public Secretary (in Maltese adminsitration), 49–50, 97–99, 106–108

Quantocks, The, 31, 114, 145
Quincey, Thomas De, 41, 93–94, 145–146, 149–150, 159

Rabat, 94–95
  Santo Spirito Hospital, 94
Radcliffe, Ann, 5
Ramsgate, 161
Reggio Calabria, 118
*Reminiscences of Samuel Taylor Coleridge and Robert Southey*, 136
*Resolutiones Morales*, 48
Rickman, John, 6
Rodomonte Roero, Fra Giovanni, 33
Rohan-Polduc, Grand Master Emmanuel de, 99
Rome, 126–129, 131–133, 141, 144, 152
  Antico Caffè Greco, 127
  Palazzo Tomati, 129
  Piazza di Spagna, 126, 129
  Sistine Chapel, 132
  St Peter's, 131
  Trinità dei Monti, 126
  Villa Farnasina, 132
Rossetti, Gabriele, 163
Royal Commission Report, 1812, 103
Royal Corsican Rangers, 90
Ruffo, Cardinal Fabrizio, 53

Russell, Thomas, 127, 132–133

'S.T. Coleridge's Colonial Gaze', 40
Sabine Hills, 130
Sale, Gigault de la, 65
Salerno, 123
*Samuel Taylor Coleridge and the Fine Arts*, 154
*Samuel Taylor Coleridge in Malta and Italy*, 21
*Samuel Taylor Coleridge: A Narrative of the Events of his Life*, 58
San Anton Palace, 37–38, 43–44, 46, 69, 90, 103–107, 142, 144
San Pietro, 57, 63
Sanchez, M G, 17, 22
Sardinia, 26, 36, 87, 92
Schiller, Friedrich, 1, 42, 129
Schinkel, Karl Friedrich, 64–65
Schlegel, August Wilhelm, 128
Sciascia, Leonardo, 114
Scott, Walter, 13
Selim Effendi, 41
Shakespeare, William, 129, 146, 157
Shelley, Mary, 8, 78
Shelley, Percy Bysshe, 48, 78, 159
Shropshire, 1
Sierra Nevada, 25
Sintra, 11–12
    Monserrate Botanical Garden, 12
Skiddaw, 120
Skinner, Captain, 82
*Sleepy Hollow*, 127
Sloane, Robert, 131
Smyth, Captain, 113
Sockburn-on-Tees, 7
Somerset, 1, 68, 90, 114, 145, 156
Sotheby, William, 158
Southey, Robert, 6, 11–13, 21, 25, 94, 96, 136, 142, 147, 149, 154, 161
Spada, Lionello, 37
*Speedwell*, 1, 5, 7–11, 13, 15, 17, 19, 21, 23–27
Spinoza, Baruch, 46
St Cyr, General, 81
St Omer, 35

St Paul's Bay, 104
Staël, Madame de, 128
Stendhal (Marie-Henri Beyle), 127
Stirling, John, 163
Stoddart, John, 31, 39, 95, 109, 133
*Storia Generale dell'Etna*, 58
Strozzi, Giovambatista, 156
Stuart, Daniel, 41
Stuart-Wortley, Emmeline, 22
Südtirol, 119
Sultana, Donald, 21, 26, 37, 41, 48, 68, 76, 80, 82, 87, 95, 99–100, 109, 113, 119, 121
*Sweet South: Impressions of Spain, The*, 22
Swinburne, Henry, 58–59, 66, 70, 115
Syracuse, 4–6, 25, 51, 56–57, 62–65, 67–70, 72–73, 76–77, 80–82, 109, 111, 113–114, 116, 119, 152
    Arethusa Fountain, 4, 68
    Castello dei Bonanno, 63–64
    Ciane, River, 68
    Corso Gelone, 70
    Ear of Dionysius, 70
    Grotta dei Cordari, 70–71
    Magnisi, 72, 113
    Neapolis, 63, 70–72
    Opera House, 72, 77–78
    Ortygia, 4, 56–57, 65, 68, 72, 81
    Piazzale Guglielmo Marconi, 70
    Ponte Santa Lucia, 81
    Ponte Umbertino, 81
    Syracuse, Cathedral, 57
    Tremilia, 63–64, 70, 76, 113
    Via Roma, 78
*Syracuse: City of Legends*, 56

Tagliana, Fortunata, 101
Taormina, 114–116, 119
    Roman theatre, 114–115
Tarifa, 14
Taylor, Elizabeth, 127
Téllez, Juan José, 24
Teresa of Avila, Saint, 150
Terni, 133

'The First Documented Case of Drug Addiction in Malta – Samuel Taylor Coleridge', 69
Tieck, Ludwig, 129, 152
'To Delmore Schwartz', 131
Tommasi, Donato, 63
*Travels in Sicily and Malta*, 27
*Travels in the Two Sicilies*, 58
*Treasury of Modern Biography, The*, 41
Treaty of Amiens, 34
Trieste, 119
*Two Foscari, The*, 121

Università (Maltese administration), 98, 103, 108

Valletta, 6, 28–29, 31–34, 36, 43, 47, 50, 83, 85, 87, 90, 95–96, 102, 104, 106, 109, 111
 Caffè Cordina, 99
 Casa di San Poix, 29, 31
 Casino Maltese, 88, 99; *see also The Treasury*
 Cathedral of St John, 37
 Governor's Palace, 35–36, 40, 47, 88; *see also Grand Master's Palace*
 Grand Master's Palace, 35–37, 40, 47, 88
 Guardia della Piazza, 36
 Manoel Island, 29, 85
 Marsamxett Harbour, 29, 31, 33
 Nix-Mangiari Steps, 32–33
 Old Bakery Street, 31
 Old Theatre Street (Triq it-Teatru l-Antik), 102
 Palazzo Carneiro, 33
 Palazzo Zamittello, 50
 Republic Square (Misrah Ir-Repubblika), 98–99
 Republic Street, 50, 88, 99
 St George's Square (Misra San Gorg), 36, 98
 Strait Street (Strada Stretta), 33
 Teatru Manoel, 102
 The Treasury, 88, 92, 96, 98, 104, 106–107; *see also Casino Maltese*
 Upper Barakka Gardens, 50
*Vathek, an Arabian Tale*, 12
Velino, River, 133
Veneto, 109
*Venus and Adonis*, 146
*Viaggio in Dalmazia*, 79
Vico, Giambattista, 122
*View of Society and Manners in Italy*, 120
Vila Nova de Gaia, 11
Vilhena, António Manoel de, 29
Villa Diodati, 159
Villettes, General, 89

Wade, Josiah, 153
Wagner, Richard, 127
Wallis, George, 127, 130
Wallis, Trajan, 130
Waring, George, 16
Wedgwood, Josiah, 1
Wedgwood, Tom, 145
Wellek, René, 129
Welles, Orson, 127
Wellesley, Lord, 74
Wilson, Frances, 145, 149
Wiltshire, 154, 157
Wordsworth, John, 37, 96, 104, 135
Wordsworth, Mary, 7, 92, 143, 146
Wordsworth, William, 6, 8–9, 37, 42, 45, 92–93, 104, 129, 142–145, 147–148, 150–151, 154, 156–157, 161
 Works:
 'The Pedlar', 92
 *Peter Bell*, 92–94
 *Prelude, The*, 8, 26, 45, 92
Wordsworth, Dorothy, 7, 45
*Written on the Water*, 73

Zakynthos, 96
Zammit (Zammitello), Giuseppe Nicolo, 50
*Zapolya*, 157–158
Zuccato, Edoardo, 41

www.ingramcontent.com/pod-product-compliance
Lightning Source LLC
Chambersburg PA
CBHW071410300426
44114CB00016B/2250